D1713476

AMERICAN INDIANS
IN THE EARLY WEST

Titles in ABC-CLIO's
CULTURES IN THE
AMERICAN WEST
Series

Scott C. Zeman, Series Editor

AMERICAN INDIANS
IN THE EARLY WEST

Sandra K. Mathews

CULTURES IN THE AMERICAN WEST

Scott C. Zeman, Series Editor

A B C  C L I O

Santa Barbara, California   Denver, Colorado   Oxford, England

Library of Congress Cataloging-in-Publication Data

Mathews, Sandra K., 1963–
  American Indians in the early West / Sandra K. Mathews.
    p. cm. — (Cultures in the American West)
  Includes bibliographical references and index.
  ISBN 978-1-85109-823-1 (hard copy : alk. paper) — ISBN
978-1-85109-824-8 (ebook) 1. Indians of North America—West
(U.S.)—History. I. Title.

  E78.W5M34 2008
  978.004'97—dc22
                                        2007043836

12 11 10 09 08   1 2 3 4 5 6 7 8 9 10

This book is also available on the World Wide Web as an eBook.
Visit www.abc-clio.com for details.

ABC-CLIO, Inc.
130 Cremona Drive, P.O. Box 1911
Santa Barbara, California 93116-1911

Senior Production Editor: Cami Cacciatore
Editorial Assistant: Sara Springer
Production Manager: Don Schmidt
Media Manager: Caroline Price
Senior Media Editor: Julie Dunbar
File Manager: Paula Gerard

This book is printed on acid-free paper.

Manufactured in the United States of America

CONTENTS

CULTURES IN THE AMERICAN WEST

SERIES INTRODUCTION

Scott C. Zeman, Series Editor

In my classes on the history of the American West at the New Mexico Institute of Mining and Technology, we discuss the infamous Rock Springs Massacre of 1885 in which an angry mob killed 28 Chinese workers and forced the rest out of the Wyoming mining town. My students are always a bit surprised when I mention that right here at home in Socorro, New Mexico, at about the same time, nativists denounced Chinese immigrants. The local newspaper declared the "Chinese Must Go!" and in the nearby mining hamlet of Kelly (now a ghost town), an anti-Chinese riot broke out (the mob apparently was enraged by the hiring of a Chinese cook—fortunately, the cook escaped harm and the mob leader was killed by his own men).

During its mining-town heyday in the late 19th century, Socorro boasted a diverse population of Hispanos, Anglos, African Americans, Slavs, as well as Chinese. Today, Socorro is home to New Mexico Tech University, the National Radio Astronomy Observatory, and other affiliated high-tech enterprises. New Mexico Tech's student body includes East Indians, Norwegians, Czechs, Vietnamese, Russians, Kenyans, Colombians, nuevo mexicanos, Native Americans, and Anglos. I use this perhaps self-indulgent example because it highlights the multicultural nature and history of the region. It is impossible to imagine Socorro's history—just as it is with the rest of the West—without this simple fact. ABC-

CLIO's Cultures in the American West Series, of which this volume is part, takes the same point of departure: to understand the West—to make sense of it—we must adopt a view that accounts for the incredible variety of its peoples.

The volumes in this series follow the lead of the New Western History, which brought to the forefront of Western historiography issues of race, ethnicity, and gender. To use the words of one of the school's foremost historians, Richard White, "The American West is a product of conquest and of the mixing of diverse groups of people. The West began when Europeans sought to conquer various areas of the continent and when people of Indian, European, Asian, and African ancestry began to meet within the territories west of the Missouri that would later be part of the United States. The West did not suddenly emerge; rather, it was gradually created" (*"It's Your Misfortune and None of My Own": A New History of the American West*, 4).

The volumes in the series take on the challenging task of demythologizing the most heavily mythologized region in the United States. In *Gunfighter Nation: The Myth of the Frontier in Twentieth-Century America*, Richard Slotkin's monumental study of the myth of the frontier in modern America, Slotkin argues that "according to this [frontier] myth-historiography, the conquest of the wilderness and the subjugation or displacement of the Native Americans who originally inhabited it have been the means to our achievement of a national identity, a democratic polity, an ever-expanding economy, and a phenomenally dynamic and 'progressive' civilization" (10). And, as Slotkin points out especially, "When history is translated into myth, the complexities of social and historical experiences are simplified and compressed into the action of representative individuals or 'heroes.'" The volumes in this series go far in helping deconstruct such a simplistic view of the history of the West.

Each volume in this series, written by experts in their respective fields, focuses on one of the many groups to call the West home. Volumes include discussions of origins, migrations, community development, and historical change, as well as short biographies. The volumes highlight key issues in the history of the groups, identify important historiographical concerns, and provide useful bibliographies.

Steven Danver of ABC-CLIO deserves the lion's share of the credit for this series. I would also like to thank him for being such a delight to work with. And thanks also to each of the authors of the volumes; without them this series would be still only an idea.

PREFACE

When ABC-CLIO issued its call for authors for these volumes on the American West, I immediately contacted the series editor about writing the volume on American Indians in the early West. My training prepared me well for this volume, having completed my PhD with major fields of the American West and Latin American history in 1998 under the direction of renowned Borderlands scholar John L. Kessell, American Indian scholar Margaret Connell-Szasz, Colonial Latin Americanist Robert Himmerich y Valencia, and professional researcher Stanley Hordes. The combination of Western history, American Indian history, Latin American history, and public history under these phenomenal scholars gave me an opportunity to understand the West not from the perspective of most U.S. historians who look at the West from an Eastern bias, but from the perspective of someone who has studied Spanish and Mexican history, as well as American Indian history.

My advisers directed my dissertation on Pueblo Indian land rights between the 1680s and the 1860s, which focused on aboriginal land rights and the attempts to protect them against Spanish, Mexican, and U.S. Territorial legal machinations. In the dissertation, I came closer than any scholar has to uncovering a generations-old fraud that Anglo-Americans and their Mexican American cohorts perpetrated upon the Pueblo Indians in an attempt to either steal their land or limit their legal foundation by manipulating documents and the legal process. Since the dissertation, I have extended this interest in debunking this preponderance of one-sided perspective of U.S. history into my American Indian history class offered at least twice yearly. But my interest in the West stretches long before I studied it professionally.

I grew up in Nebraska with parents who took us camping instead of to resorts and hotels. As a family we stopped at every historical marker as we traveled throughout the West (and we mostly headed west). We stopped at major historical sites and walked the hallowed grounds where Indian warriors and white soldiers died valiantly defending what each personally or corporately believed was right. We spent summers near an Ojibwa reservation in northern Wisconsin, and I began to learn about the Ojibwa; it taught me a respect for native culture, even if I did not fully understand it.

The West, I would argue, helped define me, ingraining in me a love of the outdoors, a great interest in recycling and sustainable development, a respect for people different from me, and an appreciation of the solitude the West offers, which heals me spiritually in so many ways. So when I pursued my graduate career, I included Western and American Indian history in my studies. I continued to read and learn and became fascinated, encouraged, and saddened by the continual struggle of American Indians to survive, to reclaim and speak their language, to have opportunities on and off the reservation, to reclaim the dignity denied them by European colonial (then U.S.) policies, and to find a new place in their ever-changing world.

I have continued to gain knowledge through my own research, as well as by attending conferences like the "American Indian Leaders: Red Power and Tribal Politics Conference" at the University of Kansas in 2000 to commemorate and celebrate the great advances that American Indian leaders had made in the 1960s. I appreciated the importance these great men and women placed on trying to influence a room filled with a new generation of Indian activists, educators, and politicians. I have taught American Indian history to Pueblo Indians in New Mexico and to mostly white students at Nebraska Wesleyan University for more than a dozen years, and I appreciate that the more I learn about tribal histories, the more that I realize I do not know. Even more, I recognize that I can never truly understand history from an Indian perspective. Therefore, the aim of this work is not to present an American Indian perspective or even a complete history of American Indians in the early West, but rather to introduce the readers to some of the major (as well as less sensational) experiences that American Indians experienced from the perspective of a Borderlands and American Indian scholar looking to the north and east.

This volume will look at precontact tribes and development of community, as well as the history of the attempted subjugation by colonial powers and how tribes attempted to survive under the new sovereigns who claimed Indian homelands as their own. Necessarily the work will proceed from traditional cultures to the influence of the Spanish empire in the Southwest, the French west of the Mississippi River, and the Russians in Alaska. Each colonial regime provided a unique dilemma to the American Indians they encountered, but none lasted as long as the Spanish empire, nor did any provide as many legal protections as did Spain.

Understanding Spanish history and colonial policies provides a unique perspective of the Spanish conquistadores and settlers, the American Indians they encountered, and the Spanish cultural and legal system that constructed the stage upon which they were forced to react to and interact with each other—whether willingly (in the case of the Spanish) or not (American Indians). The juxtaposition of two cultural systems in the Southwest is one unique and long-term example of the intermixing of peoples, cultures, lifeways, systems, and engagements that permeated the West long after the arrival of the Spanish.

Overshadowing the Spanish experience is something called the "Black Legend," the idea that the Spanish were uniquely cruel in their conquest of the "New" World. While the Black Legend did grow out of a report published by Bartolomé de las Casas in the early 1500s decrying Spanish mistreatment of Caribbean Indians in the late 1490s and early 1500s, it was actually a call for the king (Fernando II of Aragon until 1516, but Carlos I afterward) to moderate the method of interacting with the Indian people. The king listened and sympathized and, by 1550, actually stopped all exploration and colonization efforts to debate the question of what right the Spanish actually had to subjugate the American Indians. This is the only time in history that a colonial nation stopped to argue that question based on legal and religious principles. Furthermore, the same conclusion was not reached by the United States until the famous Standing Bear decision of 1879. While Las Casas's argument won the approval of the king, Spaniards who lived far from the oversight of the Spanish crown found that the new policy of "pacification" of the Indians seemed more of a suggestion than a rule and continued enslaving Indian people through various means, such as illegal usage of the *encomienda* (grant of Indian tribute) and the *repartimiento* (impressment of labor for a period of time based on a percentage of an indigenous community). Such questions will be explored in the text, as well as various Indian responses to these laws and actions of renegade and sanctioned Spaniards.

The French provide an interesting counterpoint to the Spanish, for their colonization was based on a mutual economic benefit—the fur trade. Instead of a royal policy at the outset of colonization and conversion of the natives, France instead allowed individual trappers and traders to move among Indian communities to gather pelts for the French markets. Therefore, instead of confronting large contingents of Spanish soldiers who, in the words of Borderlands scholar John L. Kessell, looked as if they had marched off a medieval tapestry, they encountered one or two lone Frenchmen who adapted to their lifestyle where they could, learned indigenous languages, and even married into the tribe for the resulting and mutually beneficial economic gains. Not until the late 1600s did the French express much interest in establishing posts in the Mississippi River region, and they never did establish permanent posts west of St. Louis. Individual trappers and traders operated as far west as the Missouri, Platte, and Loup rivers, as the Villasur "Massacre" of 1720 would prove. The juxtaposition of the French and Spanish experiences and the native response to both is a topic explored extensively in my American Indian history courses. Both were oppressive in their own ways, and both demanded that native cultures alter their lifestyles and, to a varying extent, their religion. The Spanish and French were not the only colonial powers to bully their way into indigenous lives, however. The Russians took a great interest in the Aleutian Chain as early as the 1740s and began to expand their dominance over the fur trade in Alaska until they sold out to the United States in 1867.

Over the past eight years, my research interests have taken me north to Alaska, the geographical location for my book entitled *Between Breaths: A Teacher in the Alaskan Bush* (Albuquerque: University of New Mexico Press, 2006), but also to engage with northern indigenous history for inclusion in my American Indian history courses. Much like the Spanish Borderlands have been neglected in most historical texts, so too is Russian Alaska. For that reason, this volume will discuss those regions with as much "gusto" as the more commonly popularized Plains tribes. Their history evolved quite differently, mostly because of their location, the topography, and the climate. Proximity to fur-trading regions of western Siberia made the Alaskan chain of islands a logical stepping-stone for the Russian czar to expand the fur trade, and by the 1740s, the Aleuts suffered tremendously under the dominance of Russian traders. While Russia found itself sharing its claims in the southernmost regions of Russian Alaska with British, U.S., and Spanish interests, perhaps its biggest threats to continuance of dependable trade came from the Tlingit tribe, as well as the Hudson Bay, American, and Northwest Fur Trade companies.

The response I have received teaching American Indian history is very similar, whether I was teaching New Mexico History at the University of New Mexico, American Indian History and Spanish Borderlands History to nontraditional Pueblo Indian students at the Southern Pueblo Agency, or American Indian History to mostly traditional and white students in eastern Nebraska. They are surprised that so many different cultures, linguistic groups, and religious traditions existed in the Americas. Even Pueblo Indian students said that they did not know that so many different Indian tribes existed and with so many varied experiences. And imagine my naive surprise when a large percentage of my New Mexico history class thought Indians spoke "Indian." Dispelling myths, held so long by too many, continues to be a mission in my own teaching. Therefore, this volume will try to uncover some of those myths of the earliest days of American Indian history in the U.S. West. Logically then, this volume will depend on knowledge from many fields, including history, archaeology, anthropology, population studies, art history, musicology, biology, medicine, religious studies, oral history, and much more, to bring together a coherent image of some of the major experiences of American Indians before the early 1800s.

While an increasing number of books about American Indian history have been published since the 19th century, only since the 1960s have authors published books that attempted to provide a more inclusive American Indian perspective. More recently, American Indians have published historical narratives, theoretical works, anthologies, and collections of indigenous knowledge. They have also introduced arguments against Indian history as researched and told by outsiders. Understandably, frustration mounts because of the colonization of their historical past, and therefore what they understandably perceive as the colonization of their own history. Yet I, as well as many others who teach American Indian history and culture, believe the more opportunities people have to learn about American Indian history from as many perspectives as possible, the more likely it is that some of those myths that have so long shaped the illogical view of American Indian history will finally disappear. In the past, Indian history from their own perspective had been overlooked, ignored, and even dismissed by a few as based "merely" on oral history; therefore, it was assumed to be only myth, and not substantiated. The fact remains that American Indians played a key role in the West and in the formation of U.S. policies of westward migration, military action, and intercultural exchange. American Indians had to answer to and function within an atmosphere of U.S.-driven cultural antagonism and a white superiority complex, and it ended up directing their own actions at times. More importantly, American Indian history should not merely be studied for its effect on non-Indian culture, but it should be understood for the role it played in intertribal and intratribal relations. American Indian history should not be defined by how it was influenced by non-Indians alone. Therefore, this volume attempts to engage the reader with American Indian history from many perspectives from the pre-contact period up to the early 1800s, long before the United States had a strong foothold in the westernmost regions of North America. To assist readers in their geographical understanding of where tribes were located, as well as where the non-Indian colonizers lived and established a permanent presence, ten maps appear following this preface. Throughout the text, readers will be directed to the appropriate maps.

Therefore, the goal of this book is to provide readers with a purposeful overview of the American Indian experience leading up to the 19th century by looking at numerous regions and cultures, the subjugation of the native peoples by outsiders, and the responses to that subjugation, but it does not endeavor to cover the entire experience of all populations living in the Trans-Mississippi West. Selective chapter bibliographies, as well as an annotated bibliography, will direct readers to more specific resources on various regions, tribes, eras, and sovereign nations before the early 1800s.

ACKNOWLEDGMENTS

I would like to thank series editors Scott Zeman and Steven Danver for the opportunity to write for this important historical series and for providing me with a style guide to follow for coherence for the entire series, and Alex Mikaberidze for the excellent editorial suggestions offered to me during the process. Also, I would like to thank Julie Dunbar for her excellent assistance with images, Cami Cacciatore for her guidance through the production process, and copyeditor extraordinaire Betsy Crist. Second, I would like to thank my family for their endless support of my projects. I can never repay all that they have done for me. I also thank my wonderful mentors John L. Kessell, Margaret Connell-Szasz, Robert Himmerich y Valencia, Stanley M. Hordes, and Oakah L. Jones, Jr., for teaching me about research and writing and for providing a balanced view of the past. Special thanks are due Ken Jones, whose sense of humor and motivational support, as well as deep appreciation for native cultures, gave me the incentive I so desperately needed at the end of this project. I also thank my longtime friend Dale Benham for his encouragement on this and other projects. I would also like to thank my parents, Jack and Dorothy Mathews, and my siblings, Dan and Diane (and their spouses Annie and Tim), for their endless support. I would be remiss in not thanking my archaeologist-trained sister Janet and her husband Mike for their assistance on the first chapter and their continued encouragement, as well. Finally, I would like to thank Dulcinea, whose endless comic relief has carried me through the most difficult dry spells I have encountered as an author. Her boundless energy infuses with me with vigor to return to my work with all the passion I first had for this subject when I began graduate school. While many have helped me along this process, any errors are mine alone.

Sandra K. Mathews
Lincoln, Nebraska

MAPS

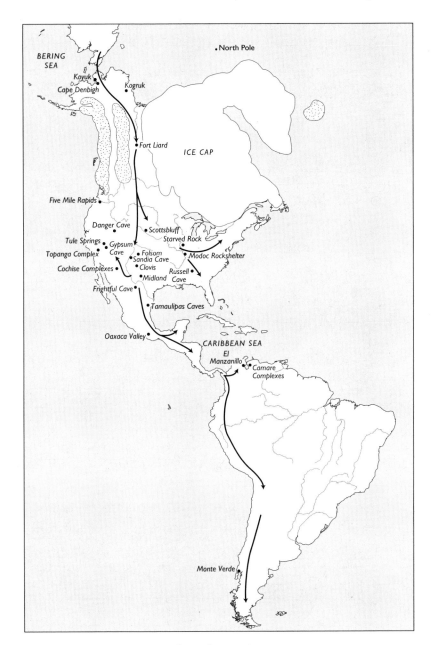

Map 1. Beringia: Migration Routes from Siberia to the Americas

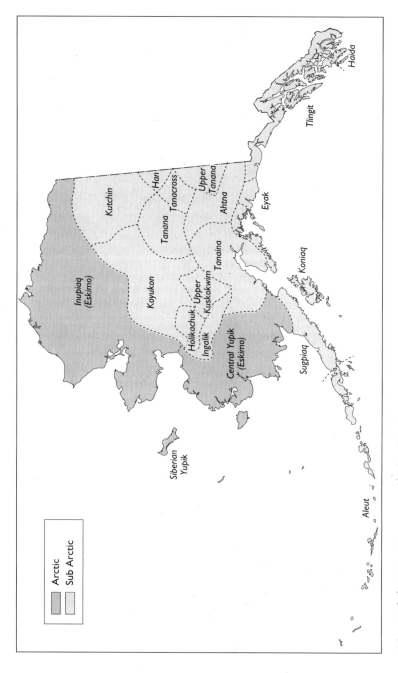

Map 2. Alaska Native Linguistic and Cultural Regions

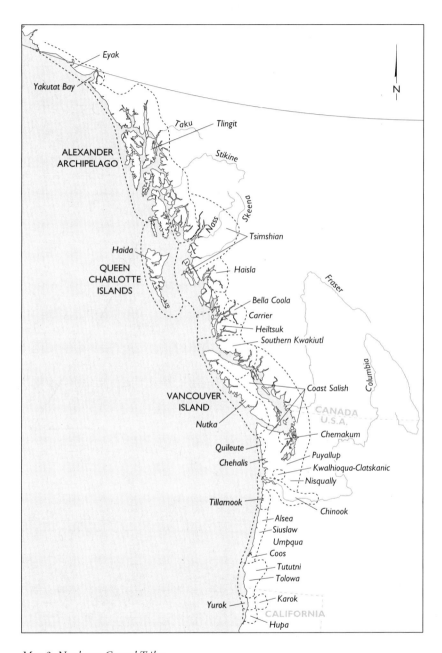

Map 3. Northwest Coastal Tribes

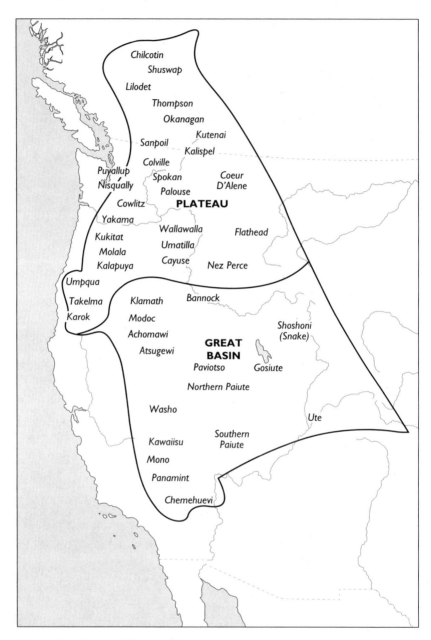

Map 4. Great Basin and Plateau Tribes

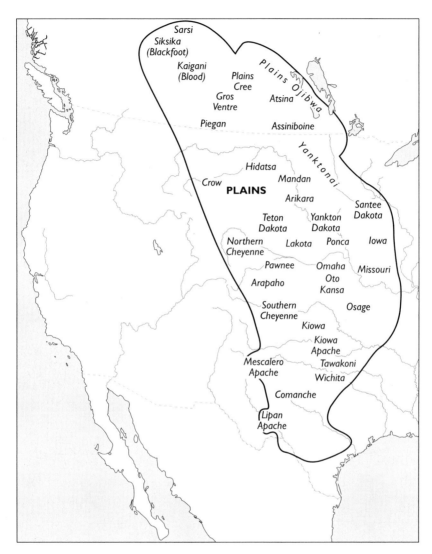

Sarsi
Siksika
(Blackfoot)
Kaigani
(Blood)
Plains
Cree
Gros
Ventre
Atsina
Piegan
Assiniboine

Plains Ojibwa

Yanktonai

Hidatsa
Crow
Mandan
PLAINS
Arikara
Santee
Dakota
Teton
Dakota
Yankton
Dakota
Northern
Cheyenne
Lakota
Ponca
Iowa
Pawnee
Omaha
Missouri
Oto
Arapaho
Kansa
Southern
Cheyenne
Osage
Kiowa
Kiowa
Apache
Mescalero
Apache
Tawakoni
Wichita
Comanche
Lipan
Apache

Map 5. Plains Tribes

Map 6. Southwest Tribes

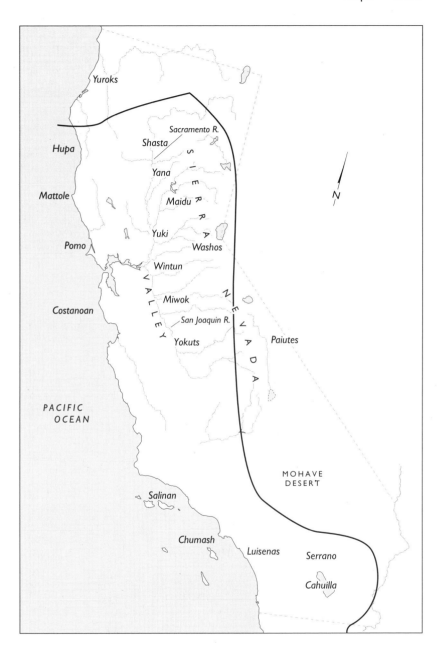

Yuroks

Sacramento R.

Shasta

Hupa

Yana

Mattole

Maidu

Yuki

Pomo

Washos

Wintun

Costanoan

Miwok

San Joaquin R.

Yokuts

Paiutes

PACIFIC
OCEAN

MOHAVE
DESERT

Salinan

Chumash

Luisenas

Serrano

Cahuilla

Map 7. California Tribes

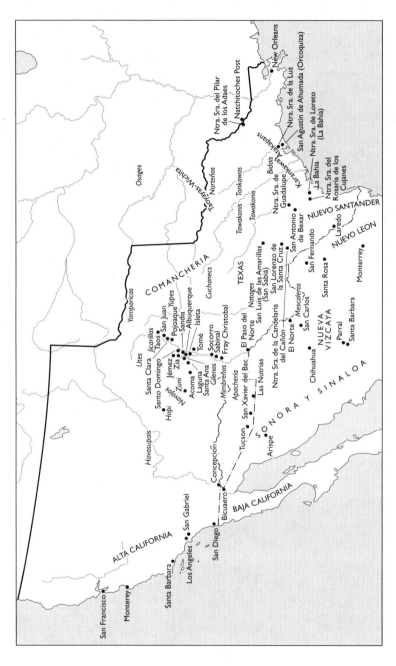

Map 8. New Spain: Tribes, Settlements, Missions, and Presidios

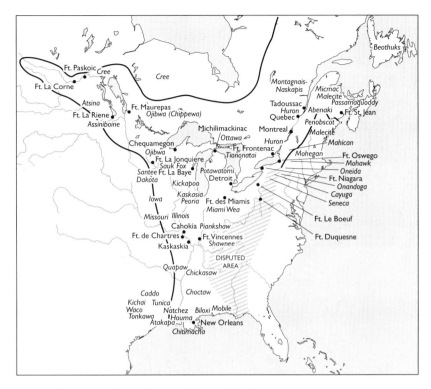

Map 9. New France: Tribes, Outposts, Forts, and Settlements

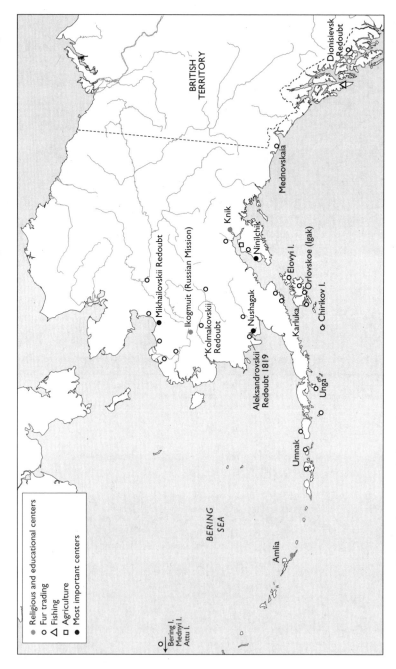

Map 10. Russian Alaska: Settlements, Redoubts, and Areas of Economic Significance

CHAPTER
ONE

ORIGINS AND
MIGRATIONS

After the Atchison, Topeka and Santa Fe Railroad (AT&SF) linked Florence, Kansas, with the Pacific Coast in the early 1880s, the Southwest became a destination for the newly emerging, predominantly Anglo-American, tourist industry. Thanks to the vision of Fred Harvey and the AT&SF, Harvey Houses began springing up every 100 miles along the tracks, beginning in 1876, to provide travelers with a more than hospitable dining experience during their travels west. In these Harvey Houses, as well as in train stations along the East Coast, paintings by Thomas Moran (1837–1926), Albert Bierstadt (1830–1902), and other famous Western artists began to appear, enticing people to travel west along the AT&SF and experience the beauty and grandeur of the ex-panses in the West. By the turn of the century, tourists flocked west along the AT&SF. They stayed in the Harvey House hotels while visiting the Grand Canyon in Arizona, and they stayed in the Montezuma Hotel near Las Vegas, New Mexico, while visiting the New Mexico pueblos for a firsthand look at the awesome formations of the land, the transforming capacity of the climate and hot springs, and the "oddities" of the seem-ingly vanishing Indian cultures. The Southwest became a tourist destina-tion, built on the historical past—one that few people had truly understood or frankly cared about, much less had an interest in saving as independent and for its unique cultures—of those indigenous communi-ties that still survived the onslaught of colonialism and the disruptions it brought.

As tourists streamed into New Mexico, so too did researching authors such as Charles F. Lummis (*A Tramp Across the Continent*, 1892; *The Land of Poco Tiempo*, 1893; *Mesa, Canyon and Pueblo*, 1925), anthropologists such as Adolph Bandelier (*The Delightmakers*, 1890), and archaeologists such as Alfred V. Kidder (*Introduction to the Study of Southwestern Archae-ology,* 1924). Between the sketches they drew with words, and the images painted by E. L. Blumenschein and other members of the Taos Society of Artists (which was formed in 1915 to support the beginnings of artistic discovery in the western United States), the public became very interested in the history of the West. Even as American Indians were declining in population and U.S. Indian policies of containment and reduction on reservations severely limited their ability to sustain their traditional ways, for those who had a bourgeoning fascination with the history of American Indians it became of paramount interest to record their past before their culture purportedly would disappear entirely.

Eastern philanthropists decried the treatment of Indian people by the U.S. government (Helen Hunt Jackson, *A Century of Dishonor,* 1881), and researchers, artists, anthropologists, and archaeologists traveled west to record the last vestiges of the "vanishing Indian." Of course, the Indian was not vanishing; in fact, by the 1930s, many Plains Indian populations had rebounded from earlier declines resulting from U.S. Indian policies, warfare, disease, and lack of nutrition (Lowie, *Indians of the Plains,* 10–11). Nevertheless, this intense interest in Indian history, art, language, culture, music, dress, accoutrements, spiritualism, and much more made its way into Eastern libraries.

An example of these early recorded ethnohistories includes John Wesley Powell's annual reports of the American Bureau of Ethnology, which were compiled for the Smithsonian Institution. From these reports, one can learn about such things as the size, shape, material composition, and color of the Corn Dance accoutrements of a particular pueblo or a detailed description of potlatch ceremonies in the Pacific Northwest. Information found in these reports was gleaned by anthropologists and other researchers who moved and lived among American Indians, asked questions, studied their habits, and then, whether it was acquired willingly or not, published information about the most sensitive and sacred stories, objects, dances, personal lives, living arrangements, political organization, and much more. Although the reports were decried by American Indians at the outset because they had shared sacred and sometimes private knowledge without consenting to publication of that information, generations later some recognized that anthropologists had saved information that tribal people could later use to revive traditional cultural and religious ceremonies. Researchers believed that because of the breakup of tribes by the U.S. government, the information would otherwise likely have been lost.

To learn more about Indian life before the arrival of Europeans, archaeological studies took place across the West, but perhaps one of the most famous and influential was that of Alfred V. Kidder at Pecos Pueblo during the 1930s. He established a method of excavating that set the precedent for all future excavations in the Southwest. For example, he learned that trash heaps, which were often found adjacent to abandoned pueblos, gave researchers a clear picture of what people ate, wore, and used for storage and food as well as how extensive their trade network truly was. Adolph Bandelier's research and archaeological digs near Los Alamos, New Mexico, resulted in a 1890 novel, *The Delight Makers,* based on his work studying the early settlement along the north face of Frijoles Canyon. In the novel, Bandelier described what life must have been like, based on the completed excavations and archaeological evidence at the canyon. Named for him, Bandelier National Monument highlights the story of Pueblo Indian ancestors who moved into the area, known for its long and narrow valleys formed when the Valle Grande volcano exploded and then collapsed in the Jemez Mountains about a million years ago. The thick yet porous volcanic rock of the valleys, created after thousands of years of spring runoff, formed long, deep, and narrow valleys, allowing the ancient ancestors to carve dwellings into the malleable cliffsides with stone tools. Occupied from approximately 800 CE until 1590 CE, the valley saw a variety of clans, including late-arriving Tewa- and Keresan-speaking clans by 1100 CE. Their two- to three-story pueblo, Tyuonyi, included 400 rooms, some of which can be viewed even today from the walking path at the monument. These people lived by a small brook that traversed the valley, eating crops they grew and supplementing their food by hunting local game, such as deer. The petroglyphs and pictographs (i.e., images etched into or painted onto the cliffsides and structures) hint at the clans and their extensive religious systems. Nearly two dozen clans appeared in Frijoles Canyon, but eventually all scattered to the villages of Cochiti and San Felipe, south along the Rio Grande. In large part thanks to Bandelier, who chronicled and collected

A ladder leads to a cliff dwelling in Frijoles Canyon at Bandelier National Monument, New Mexico. (Sandra K. Mathews)

great stores of information, as well as excavated and learned about his Pueblo neighbors, *The Delight Makers* has preserved an understanding of life in Frijoles Canyon; it is one of the only classic works representing the early Southwest written in the 19th century.

Archaeological sites dot the West, and as a result researchers continue to learn more about the past. Although some geographic regions seem to guard their secrets more closely (because of humidity and the breakdown of natural construction materials, such as trees, bark, and fiber), other regions seem to beg archaeologists for more study because their building structures of wood and stone have survived in the dry desert climes. The earth is also a great protector of evidence, and many objects that have been buried for generations, and thus not exposed to oxygen, could stand the test of time. Fibers, grasses, animal skins, tools, trade items, and storage containers excavated from more temperate and dry climates yield a tremendous amount of information about lifestyles across the West.

Besides the American Bureau of Ethnology reports, archaeological discoveries, and information from later anthropologists, American Indians themselves maintained a great wealth of knowledge regarding their traditional past, which they had cautiously guarded for generations. Unfortunately, many of the stories that were hidden from outsiders were lost as the older generations passed on and the younger generations were torn from their families during the reservation period and shipped off to boarding schools, beginning in the last third of the 1800s. These stories and knowledge periodically appeared in works penned by American Indians or works to which they contributed, such as books by Elsie Clews M. Parsons (*Tewa Tales,* 1926; *Taos Tales,* 1940; and *Pueblo Indian Religion,* 2 vols., 1939) and more recently Leslie Marmon Silko's novels (*Ceremony,* 1986, and *Almanac of the Dead,* 1991).

Whether or not non-Indian cultures became fascinated with American Indian traditional ways of life, however, was irrelevant to those who had lived in the West before the arrival of nonindigenous peoples. Outsiders, they argue, could never truly understand what it meant to be a member of a tribe—an American Indian. No single definition of "American Indian" exists. Instead, each tribe looked far back into its own past to understand who they were and how they fit into their world, a past that could never truly be captured completely by written words in books, learned by periodic tourist visits, or even interpreted by museums. But to help others truly understand their experience and correct previous misunderstandings of what it means to be "Indian," all who research should add their understanding to the larger collection of historical knowledge. American Indian culture was, or more accurately *is,* a long and fluid culture and history that stretches back thousands of years to the earliest inhabitants of the American continent. Links to the past can never be broken, which is why U.S. policies of the reservation era, assimilation and termination, would never truly "eliminate" the Indian people.

WHERE DID THEY COME FROM?

Debate has swirled regarding the actual method by which American Indian ancestors arrived on the North American continent, or if they arrived from another place at all. Until as recently as the 1990s, archaeologists have argued that these ancestors traveled from Asia across a nearly 1,000-mile-wide land bridge called Beringia (see Map 1) during the Ice Age (approximately 12,000–15,000 BCE). Glacial formations claimed much of the earth's water and thereby caused the level of the oceans to drop; land masses appeared that have since been submerged in the Bering Sea. Archaeologists argued that during those years prehistoric peoples, flora, and game animals transferred from the Asian continent across Beringia and down into North America. This would have taken many generations—as much as several thousand years—as they likely traveled in small clan groups, following the migration of big game. As they moved farther southward, they developed the necessary skills to survive in each climate, eventually stopping at a permanent (or semipermanent) location.

Yet other theories have also surfaced that suggest prehistoric voyagers from Polynesia, Phoenicia, the Middle East, or Asia arrived in the Americas via sailing vessels. For example, scholars have suggested that early inhabitants of Monte Verde, Chile, and likely other locations along the South American coastline potentially arrived from Japan, Melanesia, and Australia, based on archaeological evidence illustrating that they used boats as many as 25,000 to 40,000 years ago. They could have traveled along the sea routes, which would have provided for food along the way. Because the glacial flow had receded from the shorelines, they could have easily made landfall along the coasts of Canada, the Pacific Northwest, and south to Peru, Ecuador, and Chile as many as 10,000 to 12,000 years ago. Recent cranial and mitochondrial DNA testing from American Indians and what scientists term Mongoloid races (Korean, Japanese, Chinese, Vietnamese, for example) illustrate similarities, although there is a significant indication of uniqueness among American Indian populations. Four mitochondrial DNA lineages, which represent about 95 percent of the entire American Indian population, fall within this characterization, but a fifth line does not have an Asian connection (although it seems to share some similarities to some Europeans who may have emigrated to Eurasia). Further research may need to wait until the entire human genome has been mapped, however.

Some have argued that the American Indians were one of the lost tribes of Israel. Yet others have even credited the appearance of American Indians to the legendary Welsh prince Madoc from the 12th century (Calloway, *First Peoples,* 11). The most likely argument for polygenesis comes from an excavation in Monte Verde, Chile, beginning in 1976. At that location, archaeologists have found precontact materials dating to 12,500 to 15,000 years ago, some 1,000 years before the first recognized permanent habitation in North America near Clovis, New Mexico.

While many theories abound, the most supported seems to be that many of the ancestors of today's American Indians did cross Beringia. Archaeological evidence supports the movement of peoples from East Asia to western Alaska and down to what would become the United States, and even farther south, over thousands of years. The first migrants into the westernmost portions of what became the United States were long vanished by the time the last migrants crossed Beringia and migrated south from the arctic and subarctic climes of Alaska.

Regardless of the scientific discoveries that nonindigenous scholars have studied and analyzed in great depth, Indian oral histories assert that instead their people have always been in the Americas. Tribal histories are replete with stories about their emergence into this world from various locales, whether created by a Great Spirit or by a four-legged creature, or whether they emerged through a series of worlds below or perhaps a sacred lake to the north. For example, Adolf Hungry Wolf tells the story of the creation of the Pitt River tribe. He described how Silver-Fox and Coyote lived together, and one day, Silver-Fox collected sticks from the serviceberry tree. He whittled them down until they had larger sticks and shavings all about them. The shavings became common people, whereas the sticks became warriors and chiefs. The next day, Silver-Fox sent the people off in two different directions. Coyote, however, was jealous and wanted to make people, too. So he mimicked Silver-Fox's actions; but he chased after the women he created, and when he caught them, all of the people he created turned into shavings again. Hungry Wolf also described the creation of the Shasta and many other tribes. In the Pitt River story the creator was Silver-Fox, an animal, yet sometimes the creator was a human character or even a great spirit (Hungry Wolf, *The Good Medicine Book,* 144). Regardless of whether or not they were recorded and published, tribes have their own creation stories that must be respected as the knowledge of their people and the foundation of their tribal heritage.

Besides creation stories, many tribes also embrace stories of migration that illustrate how their people got from the point of emergence or creation to their homeland, and stories were added later about how many were torn from those homelands to reservations hundreds of miles away, like the Navajo Long Walk in 1864 or the Trail of Tears (Choctaw, Chickasaw, Cherokee, Creek, and Seminole in the 1830s). Some historians scoff at oral history because it seems to evolve as each generation retells the stories, and words and sentiment are lost with so many retellings; they do not believe the original stories remain intact. Others argue that oral history's legitimacy is no different from that of new editions of textbooks that also change historical interpretation based on new information. After all, they point out, stories were retold over and over again, word by word, for generations. This debate will rage for years, and new archaeological discoveries will probably continue to be made, like that in Monte Verde, Chile, where a new find puts an Indian community along the coastline at a date far too early for them to have crossed Beringia during the Ice Age and moved down along the coastline to South America. The theory regarding the arrival of seafaring Polynesian cultures, or other Asiatic cultures, in the Americas must also be considered. But such theories should never overshadow the right of Indian people to debate non-Indians' understanding of their own origins with their long-standing cultural knowledge and traditions.

Whenever American Indians' ancestors did appear in the Americas, they did so in smaller groups, based on the availability of game and plant life to sustain them. The most recognized theory of their arrival indicates that when these ancient peoples crossed Beringia, they traveled across Alaska, followed natural trails down the western coast and the Great Basin, and then moved farther east and south through the Great Plains. Some ended up moving beyond North America, settling as far south as the Valley of Mexico and even South America. As they dispersed they developed similar survival skills, which they had adapted from the climate and topography in which they lived, as well as the food sources available to them.

But even the establishment of actual dates of the arrival of humanity on early American soil is debated. Until the late 20th century, historians pointed to the Sandia Man as the first inhabitant of North America, identified by objects found in a cave in the Sandia Mountains near Albuquerque, New Mexico. In 1936, early archaeologists found a "Paleo-Indian cultural profile; that is, successive layers or levels yielding flint knives, scrapers, and points" (Gibson, *The American Indian,* 18). And at a lower level, six-inch-long projectile points were found, which became known as Sandia points because of their distinctive rounded bases. This startling find was dated to 20,000 to 25,000 BCE. Later, however, researchers ascertained that the discovery was fabricated.

One of the best and earliest recognized prehistoric tools, termed America's first technology by some and dated to approximately 11,200 BCE, was the Clovis point, so called after the discovery of the first such spearpoint near Clovis, New Mexico. These carefully crafted points were three to six inches long and were fixed to the end of a lance. During this formative period American Indians also created mauls, knives, and stone scrapers, as well as clothing and sandals made from skins and shredded sagebrush, respectively. Since that discovery in the 1920s, Clovis points have appeared in various archaeological sites across North America. The technology of the bow and arrow arrived much later in the Southeast. The atlatl, a spear-throwing device still manufactured by some Native Alaskans, augmented the ability of hunters on broad, open plains and desert plateaus. Yet spears and atlatls had little use against game in heavily forested regions in the Northwest and the Southeast. Along the coast,

Clovis spearpoints, similar to ones eventually discovered throughout the North American continent, have a distinctive design with six-inch-long, two-inch-wide, fluted points. (Warren Morgan/Corbis)

tribes did not depend as heavily on game because of the availability of proteins in the rivers and along the coastal waters, including five varieties of salmon, as well as cod, halibut, herring, and smelt, for example. Coastal tribes also depended on sea lion, sea otter, porpoise, hair seal, and when they succeeded in the hunt, even whale. They supplemented this food with game animals and plants that yielded edible fruits, stems, leaves, or tubers. This allowed the inhabitants of the region to remain more sedentary, and thus develop a rich cultural tradition more readily than groups that were dependent on following prehistoric mammal herds.

Some of the West's resources that the Indian people used for food, tools, and trade with others varied by region. In the Southwest, corn, salt, turquoise, turkeys, cotton, pottery, cloth, and obsidian (as well as feathers from Mexico and farther south) served important functions in daily life and trade with other tribal groups. Pecos Pueblo, located at the gateway to the Plains in northern New Mexico, was one of the many trade centers in the early world. Here the early southwestern tribes traded for hides and dried meat from the Apache and Kiowa. Along the Pacific Coast, marine shells, slaves, salmon, cedar canoes, and furs provided fodder for intertribal trade. In western Wyoming and the northern Plains, major trade centers were not as prevalent, but a few did exist. Here early inhabitants traded corn and bison hides. They also exchanged items with tribes farther east who had access to pipestone (for example, in the area of Pipestone National Monument in southwestern Minnesota) or with the Ojibwa around the Great Lakes region, who had flint, tobacco, skins, copper, fish, and hides (Calloway, *First Nations*, 23). Exchange occurred for several reasons, not the least of which was to acquire items (foodstuffs, tools, accoutrements, skins, for example) that did not naturally occur in their own area. Other reasons for trade included building relationships and alliances with neighboring communities, which was necessary because of the heightened competition for food resources—the abundance of the land had led to population growth and challenged the ability of its people to harvest its plenty.

Although some tribes did develop a more sedentary and crop-based society, noted Indian historian Colin G. Calloway argued that the adaptation of agriculture did not constitute "progress," rather it was adopted by tribes as an option and not out of necessity. Especially in the Pacific Coast region, wildlife and plant resources provided more than enough nutritional intake for Indian people, without their having to resort to agricultural pursuits—even when they lived in sedentary conditions. Although Calloway believed tribes should not be deemed more "civilized" simply because they adapted agriculture, nevertheless, agriculture caused these communities to adopt new technologies for farming and adapt their worldview to understand the new dependence on a cultivated crop. Agriculture allowed their communities to expand and become more sedentary, and domesticated agriculture allowed for the creation of much more organized social structures, political and religious organization, and structured divisions of labor (Calloway, *One Vast Winter Count,* 16).

As individual cultures emerged, they began to develop languages. They came from numerous basic linguistic families, but each culture developed its own linguistic character based on experiences and evolution of style.

LANGUAGE GROUPS

Language	Tribe
Algonkian	Delaware, Cheyenne, Kickapoo, Blackfeet, Shawnee
Uto-Aztecan	Comanche, Pima, Ute, Hopi, Shoshone,
Shoshonean	Paiute, Chemehuevi, Hopi
Piman	Pima, Quechan
Iroquoian	Wyandot, Oneida, Mohawk, Seneca, Cherokee
Athabascan	Navajo, Tanana, Hupa, Apache: Chiricahua, Mescalero, Jicarilla, Lipan, Western
Hokan-Siouan	Osage, Ponca, Quapaw, Crow, Dakota, Lakota, Nakota, Mojave
Yuman	Cocopah, Havasupai, Hualapai, Pee-Posh
Muskhogean	Choctaw, Chickasaw, Creek, Seminole, Natchez
Caddoan	Wichita, Caddo, Pawnee, Arikari
Kiowa-Tanoan	
Towa	Jemez, Taos
Tiwa	Isleta, Picuris, Sandia
Tewa	Nambé, Pojoaque, San Ildefonso, San Juan, Santa Clara
Keresan	Acoma, Cochiti, Laguna, San Felipe, Santa Ana
Tonkara	

SPIRITUALISM

Most scholars seem to agree that the development of organized spiritualism most often coincided with the appearance of a sedentary lifestyle, which was often an outcropping of agricultural pursuits. An agriculture lifestyle led to the need to store food and seed surpluses, understand natural weather patterns and cycles, and potentially attempt to influence such patterns. Intricate forms of spiritualism may have existed during the earlier hunting and gathering and migration phases, but archaeologically it might be more difficult to demonstrate this possibility with concrete evidence—yet that does not suggest that nomadic and seminomadic spiritualism did not exist.

Spiritualism among the earliest peoples inhabiting North America took many forms, most of which seemed to connect humankind on equal footing with the four-legged creatures, those that swam in the waters, those that flew, the plants, and the earth and sky that surrounded them. Unlike Judeo-Christian tradition, in which the God of the book of Genesis tells humanity that they are the caretakers of the earth and its creatures and have dominion over them, American Indians mostly saw themselves as having a commensurate role in the universe with other elements of creation. In fact, in many American Indian creation stories animals are created first; humans then join the animals and plants on the earth, but only after learning how to respect the other beings and pieces of the natural world as spiritually essential in the balance of that world.

In biology class one learns about homeostasis, the body's ability to regulate itself, for example with the proper amount of oxygen flowing to parts of the brain, muscles, vital organs, and other tissues. Without homeostasis, or a proper balance, the body could potentially become very ill and possibly even die. So it was, in the most simplistic of terms, with American Indians' understanding of the world and their place in it.

To maintain this balance, a series of ceremonies, prayers, and offerings needed to be made if a human being planned to create any sort of imbalance in the world, such as hunting, fishing, digging to plant, or harvesting. Ceremonies also evolved on a much larger scale, and many survived the reservation period and continued into the 20th century (much to the chagrin of the U.S. government and Indian agents at the time), including the Lakota Sun Dance and the Hopi Snake Dance. The painted, sewn, woven, beaded, molded, or carved images of animals and celestial beings found at archaeological sites illustrate that precontact tribes believed the natural world had relevance and influence in their lives.

In particular, the tribes involved in agriculture developed a strong system of knowledge regarding the manner in which the solar system and world around them functioned. As a result of their developing understanding and attempts to influence the natural cycles, their society often evolved into a more stratified system of classes and division of labor. Those who understood the movement of the sun, moon, and stars, as well as seasonal differences (which were typically ascribed to celestial beings), gained particular prominence in agricultural communities. Those who understood and could track changes celestially, by using carvings in rock or other markers, then developed elaborate rituals or ceremonies to mark the changes or perhaps even to attempt to influence the environment (as every aspect of the world was considered to have a living spirit). They attempted to influence the rainfall, sunshine, and other weather patterns (hurricanes, tornados, thunderstorms, drought, floods, and earthquakes, for example).

Besides trying to regulate the natural world and therefore its influence on human life, indigenous people also had to respond to the evil or malevolent spirits that existed in the world. Medicine men, healers, or others well trained in the spiritual balance took an active role in attempting to restore balance. This could be accomplished through various ceremonies, rituals, and dances, or even by reducing spells that had been cast by their enemies or neighboring tribes. These spiritual men, and sometimes women, were revered in their tribes, and on occasion were sought out by other tribes who recognized and respected their great abilities to talk to and influence the other spirits in the world.

Spiritualism among precontract tribes was not universal, nor was it representative across the West. Variations occurred between agricultural and more nomadic tribes, within regions, and within linguistic groups as well. Simply put, American Indian spiritualism varied according to the experiences of each band or tribe. Regardless of the variation across the West, two recognizable forms of spiritualism did develop, sometimes referred to as individual and group spiritualism.

Individual spiritualism consisted of an individual discovery, awareness, or adaptation of spiritualism within the natural world, whether it be having a vision, taking a spiritual journey through ceremony, finding a guardian spirit, partaking in a sweat to have a vision revealed, or following myriad other belief systems. Individual spiritualism occurred to people at different levels and at different times in their development, sometimes based on the level of spiritual guidance within the tribe. Some members became healers, curers, or medicine men after their individual experience, while others might become warriors or headmen. At the same time, not just men partook in the spiritualism of tribes, but women also had an important role—especially in matriarchal and matrilocal tribes where the clan descendants followed the woman's line, not the man's. Regardless of the nature of the individual experience, special powers or knowings were shared with tribal members for the benefit of the whole, inasmuch as possible.

Group spiritualism involved such things as ceremonials, dances, community sweats, or tradition sharing through stories, for example. This spiritualism depended on the totality of the whole in order for the balance to be maintained or achieved (such as the Tlingit potlatch, Pawnee Morning Star Ceremony, Lakota Sun Dance, or Wovoka's Ghost Dance). Therefore, all tribal members had to respect community beliefs, as prescribed by the elders or spiritual leaders, in order for the tribe to continue to be prosperous, survive, feed themselves and their families, or best their adversaries. More detailed descriptions of ceremonies may be found in the sections about specific regions.

It is important to understand that each tribe developed its own worldview; therefore, variations existed from clan to clan, from tribe to tribe, within and between regions, and across the North American West. Sometimes one clan might have the responsibility of keeping the knowledge of healing, others warfare, others spiritualism, and others the maintenance of the natural balance of the earth. In the end, all were affected by decisions made in the tribe, and each determination regarding the spiritual world and restoring balance had a lasting impact on the tribe, the broader community (including the natural world), and their nonhuman relations.

Knowledge of spiritualism was not passed down in a written text but rather through oral tradition, which, as the cultures expanded and

Dance of the Mandan Women *by Swiss painter Karl Bodmer, 1832–1834. (Library of Congress)*

developed, became far more complex. By the time Europeans arrived, children listened in wonderment as their elders recounted their histories from generations past, their knowledge of flora and fauna, and interrelationships among humanity and the plant, animal, and inanimate world around them. Much was memorized word for word from elders, from whom the children had heard the stories sometimes nightly, month after month throughout the winter, year after year from their early childhood until they were adults. This cultural knowledge was unique to each tribe, varying based on their own experiences.

To provide a basic understanding of some of the key differences between regions in precontact North America, the rest of this chapter focuses on regional differences in tribal development.

THE FAR NORTH: ALASKA

Alaska has numerous regional variations, encompasses four time zones, and is more than twice the size of Texas. Measuring 2,400 miles from east to west, and just over half that from north to south, Alaska's diversity cannot be underestimated (see Map 2). "Alaska possesses arctic plains, great forests, swamps, glaciers, ice fields, broad valleys and fjords, the highest mountain of North America, active volcanoes, twelve major river systems, three million lakes, and countless islands," as well as 33,900 miles of seacoast (Naske and Slotnick, *Alaska,* 5). Yet even today it boasts one of the smallest populations of any state in the union. Besides its varied topography and periodically inhospitable living conditions because of its proximity to the arctic circle, the shifting plates just off Alaska's coast can produce earthquakes with deadly results. According to the Alaska Earthquake Information Center, the major fault runs along the southern side of the Aleutian chain all the way toward the panhandle of Alaska, where it then turns south along the Alaska coastline. The Pacific plate is currently moving at a rate of up to three inches per year toward the north, which is causing it to plunge under the North American plate. While today earthquakes are rather common in Alaska, it is believed that they also commonly occurred in precontact periods. Traditional native peoples had to learn how to cope with the earth shaking and, at times, liquefying and developing large crevices near their villages, hunting grounds, or migration routes. Such natural events entered tribal oral histories and affected settlement patterns. The oldest earthquake recorded by non-Indian people occurred in 1788; it caused little damage, but two islands were inundated by a tsunami, killing some people and livestock.

These plates had little impact on the method by which the American Indian ancestors first arrived. The far north includes two distinct geographic regions: the arctic and subarctic. In the subarctic, which was settled first by overland migrants from Asia as long as 12,000 to 15,000 years ago, climatic conditions demanded a much more rigid command of survival in frigid conditions. The subarctic region stretched from Alaska's interior and southern coastlines all the way to the east coast, bordering the North American Plains. Now boasting a preponderance of rivers and coastline, this region is identifiable by its boreal forests of pine, birch, fir, spruce, and tamarack. But even as late as 7,000 years ago, glacial ice covered some areas. For this reason, Alaska was never highly populated by indigenous peoples. Nonetheless, access to caribou and bison provided protein for these subarctic dwellers, and naturally occurring berries (such as salmonberries, raspberries, blueberries, lagoonberries, and blackberries) and other fruits provided sustenance in the summer and early fall

(Pritzker, *A Native American Encyclopedia*, 482–483). Today, Athabascan speakers continue to populate Alaska's interior. The last of their linguistic group finally had to remove themselves from a nomadic lifestyle, settling in a town only as recently as the 1950s (Alaska Report, National Archives Research Administration, Pacific Region, Anchorage, Alaska).

Winters in Alaska can be particularly harsh, as temperatures in Alaska's interior can drop to –50 to –60°F. While the winters are frigid, the annual snowfall in the interior generally averages only around 12 inches of very lightweight snow. Farther north, the Arctic Slope has little timber and is made up mostly of tundra. Today summers see an average July high temperature of 40°F. The southwestern portion of Alaska is influenced by the Japanese current and has more precipitation and wind because of its exposure to the Pacific Ocean. Southeast Alaska, with its dense, tall forests and numerous islands, rarely sees temperatures below 10°F, and summer temperatures average in the 60s and 70s with ample precipitation between 25 to 155 inches per year (Naske and Slotnick, *Alaska*, 4–9). While the conditions were different thousands of years ago, methods of survival required a respect for the arctic and subarctic conditions, and Alaska dwellers made adaptations—some of which continue to be used today.

The arctic consists of the northernmost stretches of Alaska's coastline, the western slope near the Bering Straits, and the Aleutian Islands, which stretch out into the Bering Sea. Scholars have debated whether the inhabitants of these cold reaches migrated directly from Siberia, or whether they migrated instead from the subarctic at a much later time, perhaps as late as 4000 BCE. Either way, the region is populated by Inuits and Yup'iks, as well as those who ventured out on the Aleutian chain. They spoke languages directly related to the Eskimo-Aleut family, including the Inuit-Inupiaq (Inuktitut) and Yup'ik. Anthropologists generally agree that the descendants of the current inhabitants settled in the region long after the Paleo-Indians from 10,000 BCE. In approximately 2500 BCE, the Kodiak culture emerged, and a half century later, the Aleutian culture emerged (Pritzker, *A Native American Encyclopedia*, 519). They continued surviving unencumbered by outside influences until the early 18th century when the Russians burst onto the scene demanding compliance with their brutal fur-trading tactics in the 1740s.

Typical cache utilized by Alaska natives to protect food from scavengers, taken at the Alaska Native Heritage Center in Anchorage. (Sandra K. Mathews)

The difficulty of living in the arctic cannot be overstated. These Paleo-Indians lived in structures made from materials found around them, and in some areas, this consisted of blocks of snow. Men constructed the homes, which measured anywhere from 10 to 15 feet across, and added small entryways, or self-contained porches, that doubled as storage areas for tools, clothing, oils, and other nonfood items. Women helped by filling the gaps between the blocks with more snow. They made beds of snow benches, covered with willow or baleen, and then covered the structure with heavy furs and skins. Seal oil lamps provided light for the homes.

Not all arctic and subarctic people lived in these "igloos," however. Other home styles involved excavating the earth, building wood or whale bone frames, and then covering the structure with sod. Sometimes these homes were accessed through the ceiling and sometimes through a narrow subterranean tunnel. Either way, the entryway had to protect its inhabitants from roaming predators that might smell a storage cache of meat, fats, fish, dried berries, and other foods necessary for survival during the long, hard, and dark winters (Pritzker, *A Native American Encyclopedia*, 520–521). Early dwellers also constructed caches, or small storage units, placed on tall, greased poles to keep nonhuman invaders from raiding their surplus foods.

LIFE ON THE TUNDRA

Alaska Natives before the arrival of the Russians saw little change in their lives. They depended on the plenty of the land, but they also confronted its harshness. They used tools such as knives as well as hatchets fashioned from stones, sinew, and sticks. With small noose traps, they hunted small game on the tundra, capturing birds, squirrels, and rabbits. They also hunted larger game animals, such as moose and caribou. They consumed the meat and used the hides to make mittens, hats, coats, and other articles of clothing to protect them against the windy and subzero temperatures every winter.

Winter in the arctic began early; sometimes snow fell as early as August or September in the northern reaches. Because the winters are long, lasting nine months or so, the Alaska

Natives had much to do to prepare in advance. They fished, dried the meat, and stored it in caches (small wooden storage shelters usually placed on top of four reinforced poles) high above the ground. They used bear or other animals' grease on the poles to keep marauders and would-be thieves out of the caches. They also stored berries and other food items in the caches for the long winters.

By August and September, the days grew shorter and shorter and by the winter solstice, little daylight, if any, peeked just above the southern horizon. Therefore, winters often found the small, tight-knit communities at winter campsites with their caches, walls reinforced by animal skins, grasses, and snow. They would bide their time by repairing clothing items and creating new ones. As late as the 1950s, the last nomadic Athabascan tribe settled into a permanent community in Alaska's interior.

Peoples who lived in the upriver regions of southwestern Alaska (Kuskokwim, Yukon, and Nushagak rivers, for example), typically called Eskimos, spoke the Yup'ik language as opposed to the Inuit of other Eskimo peoples. While their language had a historic tie to Aleut, the two tongues were mutually unintelligible. Because they were not coastal peoples like their Inuit neighbors to the south, the upland Eskimos rarely lived off sea mammals or bears, but instead they depended mostly on anadromous fish, specifically salmon. Besides fishing, they learned to use the expansive tundra for medicinal purposes, food collection (numerous variations of berries, for example), and hunting. Because they were located near inland Athabascan Indians, such as the Tanaina and Ingaliks, they had access to trade and even adapted practices from the other cultural systems to enrich their own. One example of that seems to be their use of wood in constructing fish traps, caches, and structures. In particular, their access to interior forests and shared knowledge from the interior Indians allowed them to build fish traps more than eight feet long using spruce-splint technology. Also, they acquired birchbark canoes and slate for whetstones. Both upriver and downriver Eskimos used wood, birchbark, and willow to construct homes, netting, and bindings (for snowshoes, sleds, or other tools, for example), but the upriver tribes exclusively used the spruce-splint technology for their weirs for blackfish and whitefish runs. Their downriver neighbors, for example in Bethel and farther south on the Kuskokwim River, instead had access to the open ocean and therefore they had contact with other coastal tribes by way of umiak and bidarka. Russians would later build the Kolmakovskiy Redoubt, approximately 170 miles north of Bethel on the Kuskokwim River, which was generally recognized as the boundary between the upriver Eskimos and the interior Indian tribes (Athabascans and Ingaluks). Small communities were scattered along the banks of the interior rivers at safe locations; populations of each reached just over 100. While the upriver Eskimos would periodically split up and move during the summer, they reconvened in the winter and reestablished the strong bond of community during the harsh winter months. The Russians estimated the combined populations of upriver and downriver Eskimos at about 7,000, making them possibly one of the two most populous groups of Alaska Natives in the early colonial period (the other being the Koniag in the area of Kodiak Island).

Generally, in the upriver communities, women and children often lived together, while men lived in *qasgiqs* (living quarters for men, some of which could also double as very large sweat lodges). In the men's quarters, boys were quickly taught their place in society. The greatest symbol of a boy's stage in life was his bench. Young boys occupied the space below the bench, until they had gained the right to be on the bench. The benches were located across from the entryway to the qasgiq. As boys aged, they could have benches along the sides of the qasgiq. At old age, they occupied the locations nearest the entry. A large urine tub and water tub, as well as oil lamps, were the only other accessories in the building. Every morning the male community awoke to an elder speaking on such things as proper behavior, routine lessons about changes in life and emergencies, and other proper aspects of a genial community: no horseplay or fighting, for example.

Even though women and men did not always live together, marriage facilitated their ability to survive. While the men provided the fish and game, women busied themselves in processing the pelts, preparing the meat for eating or storage, and repairing clothing. If the man did not provide for the woman's needs, she could leave him. If the woman hoarded food, the man could leave her. If a woman did not conceive, the community expected a divorce, for children were key to survival in later years. Parents cared well for their children, and they marked various aspects of their son's development, such as his first kill, with a community celebration. When their daughters picked their first berries, they also held a community celebration in which her ability to help with the family's survival was heralded. At the age of nine, a girl participated in all aspects of her mother's tasks. At puberty, she was considered an adult (which meant new taboos and rituals such as the Putting Away the Doll ceremony, for example). Shortly after this point, a girl's family often negotiated a marriage for her. A boy reached adulthood after puberty when he had his first major kill, a large animal. When he acquired his wife, he continued to live in the qasgiq, but all that he killed went directly to the family of his new bride until he had proven that he could provide for her. If not, he could be disregarded by her family as her spouse.

The upriver communities had a very developed religious ceremonial life that involved the use of drums, dances, elaborately decorated clothing, masks, and dance fans. The supernatural and natural worlds were inextricably interwoven, and they played a key role in Eskimo spiritualism. A village shaman would interpret the spiritual world, beings, and forces and would also assist with community life (predicting weather changes, introducing food species, and eliminating diseases, for example). The ceremonies involved elaborately carved and decorated wooden masks, each of which served an important part of the ceremony. Most ceremonies were held between late fall and early winter, such as the Berry Festival, the Bladder Festival, and the Great Feast for the Dead (Oswalt, *Bashful No Longer,* 12–39).

A variety of foodstuffs provided sustenance for these early inhabitants. Besides flora such as roots and berries during the short summer months, arctic inhabitants depended on seal, walrus, and narwhal. Men hunted the ringed and bearded seals by waiting by breathing holes for hours, sitting completely still in the frigid conditions, waiting for their unsuspecting prey to surface for air. Not only did these seals provide fur for warmth, but they also provided meat, blubber, and oil for their seal oil lamps.

Coastal scene with Alaska natives at Port Dick on the Kenai Peninsula, 1794. (National Oceanic and Atmospheric Administration)

Having a source of light in the long dark winter months was essential, and seal oil burned slowly and at a steady pace. Those who lived along the coastline depended on their skill in having the ocean to provide for them. Their umiaks and bidarkas (both often known to outsiders simply as kayaks) provided excellent means of transportation between islands (the Aleutian Islands, as well as the Diomede Islands, Saint Lawrence Island, and others), as well as inter-island communities in the southeast portion of Alaska. The umiaks provided excellent transportation for hunting whale.

Whale hunting was a major undertaking, indeed, requiring cohesion of a sizable workforce for hunting, retrieving the carcass by pulling it onto shore, and finally butchering. People worked as a community to bring in the kill, and they shared the proceeds among the entire tribe. While whale hunting has been drastically curtailed because of the potential extinction of mammals such as the grey whale, traditional whaling occurred as recently as 2007 along the Pacific Coast, although the last tribally sanctioned whale hunt by the Makah tribe occurred in 1999.

Another indigenous group, the Gwich'in, has traditionally followed the caribou herds as their main source of food, using stone and bone tools, including bows and arrows as well as spears. Adapting to the Alaskan interior, perhaps one of the harshest climates in the United States, did not come easily. Speaking Athabascan, like the Navajo and Apache in the Southwest (New Mexico, Arizona, Colorado, Utah, and Texas), these nomadic hunters learned how to subsist in temperatures reaching −50°F at times. They used the fur of rabbits, muskrat, squirrel, caribou, bear, and whatever else they could find to shield themselves from the frigid weather. While traveling, they used skin tents and carried hot embers in specially designed bags so that creating fire each night would not consume their activities. Special care was taken to ensure that the ice that formed on the inside of the tents from the condensation of their breath and body heat would not cause the tent to collapse from its weight.

In winter, the Gwich'in had more formed structures of bent wood, covered with branches, bark, skins, and snow. Caches built off the ground kept unwanted scavengers from stealing their food during the long winter months. During those sunless days, the people consumed the dried fish, berries, and other foods they had stockpiled during the short summer months. In good years, they had enough caloric intake to keep the entire band alive. In a particularly bad year, however, they sometimes found themselves forced to leave their older relatives behind so that the elderly would not slow down the movement of the small tribe on its way to find caribou or moose. Velma Wallis, a member of the Gwich'in tribe and author of three best-selling books on her tribe, wrote about what life was like living off the land (which she did growing up). Her first book, *Two Old Women: An Alaskan Legend of Betrayal, Courage and Survival* (2004), relates the story of two elderly women who no longer did any of their own work, and therefore were left behind to die by their own family members. They remained behind, understanding that if the rest were to survive the long, harsh winter, they stood a better chance without having to slow down, care for, and feed their old and aching bodies.

The Yup'ik (formerly known as Inuit or Eskimo; also known as the Yuit and the Bering Sea Yuit) lived in southwestern Alaska between Bristol Bay and the Norton Sound. Being closer to the shorelines, they had access to the seashore for a variety of food and rivers for salmon. Therefore, their lifestyle did not involve following caribou herds, but rather they had a varied culture that included the use of stone tools and fashioned pottery. The Yup'ik have lived on the mainland at least 4,000 years and have occupied Nunivak Island for at least 2,100 years.

Like many other tribes, the Yup'ik had an established religion based on their understanding of the natural world. They believed all parts of the natural world had spirits that required respect, and from this belief emanated all others (ritualistic taboos and ceremonies, for example). Both men and women could serve as *angakok* (shamans) after acquiring a guardian spirit, and the angakok assisted with the religious leadership of the tribe as a whole. They served as healers, and understood the natural balance of the earth and the importance of ceremony to keeping that natural balance to maintain the health of the whole.

Whaling played an important role in Yup'ik culture, as did sharing the bounty of the whale hunt between neighboring villages. Great honor came to the man who owned the umiak that held the hunters who successfully took the whale. Most ceremonies took place in the spring or winter, as summer and fall would be reserved for salmon fishing, hunting, and gathering berries and other natural fauna for the winter. Some of the tools they used to survive included harpoons, bow and arrow, spears, atlatls, nets, and snares. Caribou, fish, walrus, seal, whale, moose, shellfish, ptarmigan and swan (and their eggs), and other game, as well as tubers, berries, and leafy greens, served as their main sources of food.

To protect themselves from the wet elements characteristic of living along the coastline in southwestern Alaska, they fashioned raingear out of seal gut that they masterfully sewed together, leaving not even a minuscule hole for a dewdrop to penetrate. The bidarkae and the larger umiak, which served as their main method of transportation on the open waters, were fashioned with wood frames, covered with seal gut or seal skins, and also masterfully sewn together and waterproofed. These had to be rebuilt each year, other than the frames, which they stored over the winter.

Among the Yup'ik, gender roles clearly delineated position in family and society, whether in relation to religious ceremony, division of labor, or housing. When a couple wanted to get married, they simply announced their intentions. Sometimes men had more than one partner, and sometimes female partnerships existed. While infanticide was rare, it occurred mostly in relation to female children. Adoption occurred, and it was yet another illustration of the importance and value of children to the community. Young girls engaged in gathering berries and grasses, while young boys engaged in the seal hunt. Not all was work, however, as many games and songs broke up the monotony of surviving on the tundra. Inappropriate behavior such as physical violence or murder, however, could result in ostracism, or even death. Therefore, order seemed to always exist in early communities.

The tribes found throughout the arctic and subarctic zones in what became the United States included many groups besides the Koyukon, Tanaina, Ahtena, Ingalik, Hare, Gwich'in (also known as Kutchin), Tahltan, Alutiiq, Inupiat, and Unangan (also known as Aleut).

THE NORTHWEST COAST

Generally recognized as reaching from Yakutat Bay in Alaska to the border between California and Oregon, the Northwest Coastal tribes stretched about 1,500 miles, but they only ranged about 100 miles inland (see Map 3). The dominant geographic feature in the region is obviously the ocean, but other geographic features include many river systems, islands, and forested mountain regions that reach down to the coast. Even though the area has a moderate climate, the region is known for its high annual precipitation, relentless fog, and strong winter storms. Nevertheless, the numerous tribes that dotted the landscape learned how to adapt and flourish in the coastal region, creating highly skilled artistic designs in carvings, paintings, and textiles.

Unlike the desert Southwest, where archaeological evidence survived for thousands of years, partly because the tribes used stone or rock implements but also because of the dry climate, the likelihood of finding archaeological remains of entire communities in the Pacific Northwest complete with houses, ceremonial garb, food storage, and other pieces of tribal material culture is much lower because of the types of materials available for building and making implements as well as the moist climate. Lack of pottery remnants, coupled with the tribes' use of wood for tools, armor, and houses, has made it difficult to ascertain much about the early culture of these groups. Nevertheless, archaeologists have learned that they shared aspects of material culture, such as the central role of tools for use in fishing and boating, as skills in these areas were essential for the survival of their family and tribes. Therefore fish, and in particular salmon, served as the main staple for most coastal Indians. Stylized salmon images appear in their artwork with great regularity, as do images of ravens and whales.

It is generally recognized that the first humans entered the region as many as 10,000 years ago. Simple tools, such as chipped and flaked stone points, have been found by archaeologists, but little else is known about the earliest people. By approximately 3,000 years ago, archaeologists have determined that they consumed shellfish and other sea mammals. More cultural items also appeared, including stone adzes, beads, and pierced lip ornaments (labrets). Around 1000 BCE, evidence suggests that the people fished extensively, used harpoons for hunting sea mammals, and instituted the use of bark mats and seasonal variations in materials for homes.

Beginning approximately 700 years ago, acquiring wealth appears to have become a primary motivation for activity beyond finding food and shelter. The farther north, the greater the importance of the potlatch ceremony, wherein acquired wealth was distributed by one person, thereby reinforcing the social hierarchy of the group (or reorganizing it, in the case of the Tlingit after the arrival of white traders). Wealth consisted of many things, including plank houses, beautifully woven blankets, massive red cedar canoes, large copper plates, decorated hides, bowls, heraldic poles, and artistically carved bent wood storage boxes.

Perhaps one of the most recognized images associated with the Northwest Coastal people were the beautiful ornamental masks created by gifted woodworkers and other craftspeople of the tribe. Also, the right to claim a particular name, guardian spirit, or crest, even a song, was owned and carefully guarded. Also distinctive of the northern tribes were the truly beautiful representations of animals, such as the whale, raven, and salmon, intricately woven into elaborately decorated robes of mostly red and black. Weaving was an important craft, and a variety of raw materials went into the finished product, including woody materials (bark, root, cattail) and more pliable materials, such as fur from mountain goat, dog, or bird down. Such wonderful materials, decorated elaborately with images of ravens, whales, or other creatures, indicated wealth and status in the community. But these items were then circulated within and outside the community in elaborate ceremonies called potlatches.

Among some Pacific Coast tribes, potlatches were held for a variety of reasons, including to celebrate a wedding, to name heirs, or even to compensate for having suffered public humiliation. Hosts acquired or reinforced existing status by giving away their wealth in a pretentious show in front of family and tribal community members. On some occasions after the Russians appeared in the 1700s, the Tlingits sometimes destroyed items that normally would have been given away during a potlatch to illustrate to the Russians their economic superiority (which will be discussed further in subsequent chapters). The more one gave away, the greater one's prestige among the community. The host of a potlatch expected in turn to be invited to potlatches hosted by his guests at a later time, in which he expected to receive items equivalent to what he had previously given. Reciprocal giving was important for continuing the potlatches and maintaining the social hierarchy. During the ceremony, songs heralded a person's wealth and hurled insults at any potential competitor for his newly acquired and perceivably exalted status. Because the property was distributed to all who attended a potlatch, oftentimes that same property or property of equivalent value would be given away at succeeding potlatches. Thus, wealth was redistributed throughout and sometimes even outside the community or *kwa'an* (a kwa'an was a community based on familial clans, shared experiences, and resource and boundary protection).

Potlatches could not have occurred without the development of a community mentality among the Northwest Coastal tribes, whereby they supported the acquisition of wealth by their *toion,* a local leader who oversaw the well-being of the kwa'an, protected the kwa'an's boundaries and resources from competitors (oftentimes Tlingits from other kwa'ans), and saw to the preservation of the culture and rules of the community. This localization of wealth in their leader itself indicated a stratified social hierarchy. In the Tlingit society, potlatches were particularly important and would be hosted by a toion. The toion demanded goods and services from the members of the community, which included other members of his family, nuclear and extended, who lived in his plank house with their servants (slaves, in essence), as well as other members of the kwa'an, who were considered commoners (upper-class or lower-class free people), or even slaves. The community gained in status as the toion gained status and expected to share with their toion. Punishment could be meted out on those who withheld wealth or goods from the toion.

Before the arrival of the Russians, Tlingit held potlatches for three primary purposes. First, a family would hold a potlatch to honor a recently diseased member of their family. Guests threw items they received into the fire, called out the name of the deceased, and by so doing, the deceased would receive the spiritual equivalent of those gifts. When a funerary potlatch ceremony was complete, the soul of the deceased could finally join the congregation of ancestral souls. Second, a potlatch would be held in honor of the children, and the ceremony might include tattooing the chest and arms or piercing the ears of the child honored. Third, a potlatch would be held on the occasion of the construction or reconstruction of a house. Such an occasion involved sacrificing more than two slaves. The head of the home would give away everything, sometimes even his wife's property (a wife normally retained her own wealth). In fact, after the Russians arrived, the Russians protested what they considered the needless slayings and bartered for the slaves instead. Either way, the slaves would be "dead" to the community, so the end result would be nearly identical to the community.

The potlatch is one of the best indicators of the significance of wealth accumulation among the Tlingit and other Northwest Coastal tribes, for Indian people celebrated potlatches as far south as the Washington and Oregon coasts. Moreover, the entire community would help their toion accumulate wealth. This provided prestige to the entire kwa'an, not just to the leader. Such items as copper plates crafted by community members, beautifully dressed deer skins, slaves, food, shawls, and other items found their way into potlatches. Besides increasing the prestige of the toion and kwa'an, a potlatch also served the purpose of bringing the living more closely connected to those who had moved into the ancestral world.

Along with sharing gifts, potlatches provided an opportunity for sharing ethnocultural and spiritual knowledge among generations and between communities, thereby reiterating the importance and relevance of knowledge, status, kinship, and rank within the community. The distribution process confirmed a person's status within the community or clan hierarchy, as gifts were distributed according to rank.

Wealth accumulation reinforced social positions within tribes, as did periodic raids and warfare conducted against those they considered enemies, some of whom the Tlingit would eventually overcome and incorporate into their tribe, such as the Eyaks who lived to the north at Yakutat Bay. With wooden helmets and armor made from slats of wood, the Tlingit augmented their defenses with offensive weapons available to them: clubs, bow and arrows, daggers, and spears fashioned from stone and wood. Perhaps the tribe best known for their ability at warfare was the Tlingit of Alaska's Panhandle. They engaged in raids to acquire slaves from other tribes and any material goods to which they had no ready access that could enhance their status within the community. Some researchers have estimated that perhaps one third of the entire tribe was made up of persons who had been taken from other tribes and forced into servitude in the community.

Because they traveled between their island communities via water on bidarkas, the Tlingits became excellent boat makers, although they truly appreciated the great workmanship of the exceptionally large canoes made by tribes farther south that could carry up to 100 rowers. The abundance of trees, in particular red cedar, gave the Tlingit a ready source of material for their canoes. Their cedar canoes, sometimes large enough to accommodate as many as 40 or more oarsmen, stretched up to 60 feet in length. With strategic use of fire and the adze, boat makers hollowed out and then decorated these massive canoes, using them not just for raiding but also for trading and for hunting sea mammals and whales in the inlets and oceans. While the Tlingits in particular were largely associated with warfare by non-Indian observers in the 1700s and 1800s, generally, conflict was not common.

Northwest Coastal people had a rich spiritual heritage, complete with extensive rituals and ceremonies, all based on the ideal of a guardian spirit, which might be an eagle, whale, beaver, raven, bear, and so on. A guardian spirit came through extensive spiritual quests, usually in remote areas. Spirits often did not reveal themselves immediately; sometimes people had to wait as many as 20 years to acquire their spiritual helper.

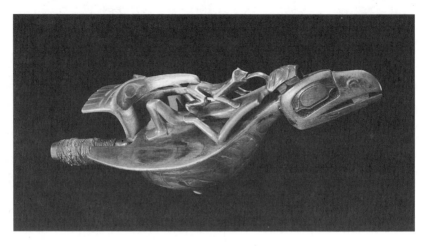

Tlingit rattle, carved in the form of Raven, an important figure in Tlingit spiritualism. (Christie's Images/Corbis)

The spirit was typically associated with a song and dance and instilled in its individual wisdom, luck, or some useful skill. The dances and songs were often performed throughout the winter at various ceremonies and other occasions.

Farther south, tribes did not acquire the extensive wealth of their northern neighbors, but like their northern neighbors, they also depended on fish, sea mammals, and other wild game to sustain them. They wore few clothes because of the temperate climate; clothes were mostly made of shredded cedar bark, plant fibers woven together, or, in the colder seasons, animal skins. Men adorned themselves with nose ornamentation, and both genders practiced tattooing. Similar to some of the tribes to their east, they also used cradleboards to help flatten the heads of infants, for in their cultural tradition flattened heads represented beauty and prestige within the tribe. Their slaves could be singled out easily because they often came from other tribes, and therefore their heads were shaped naturally.

In the Pacific Coastal region of today's United States, tribes prized the albino deer skins, obsidian blades, and small, tusk-shaped dentalia (shells) that were used as currency by some tribes father south and in California. Because the shells were so highly prized by tribes to their east, the more southerly located Northwest Coastal tribes, like the Yupas, Yuroks, and Chinookan speakers, traded them at the great trading site at the Dalles. The Dalles had served as a gateway between the Plateau and Great Basin, as well as the tribes in California and the Northwest Coastal regions, for generations when Meriwether Lewis and William Clark encountered the region in 1805 on their way to the Pacific Ocean.

Some of the more recognized tribes in the region included the Tlingits and Haidas; the Salishan-speaking Klallams, Lummis, Muckleshoots, Nisquallys, Puyallups, Snohomish, Snoqualmis, Tillamook, and Taulalips; and the Makahs, Quinalts, Chinooks, Coos, Tsimshian, Bella Coola, Kwakiutl, Nootka, Hupas, and Karoks (the latter two found in northern California as well).

WHALE HUNTING

Because of the increase in whaling and fishing in the Pacific Ocean, particularly by the Japanese, the population of gray whales has experienced a precipitous decline. As a result, the international community has instituted a ban on whaling. But to those who have traditionally depended on this form of sustenance, the ruling seemed unjust, for they had long fought for the right to hunt a whale traditionally to survive. In 1999, the Makah tribe of northwest Washington won a temporary victory. They were permitted to organize a whale hunt; and animal rights activists were there to protest their traditional hunt.

According the Makah tribe, "More than anything else, whaling represents the spiritual and technological preparedness of the Makah people and the wealth of culture" (Makah tribe, "Whaling: A Gift from the Sea," www.makah.com/whaling.htm). Whales provided everything from oil and meat, to bones, sinew and gut for storage purposes.

Before any hunt, whalers had to prepare themselves spiritually by praying, fasting, and bathing alone. Preparation could take months. By springtime, men watched for good weather conditions, then paddled eight to a canoe to meet the whales at daybreak. Paddlers canoed to the left of the whale, matching its speed. When the whale surfaced, the harpooner shot the whale and the canoers paddled backward ferociously to avoid the thrashing animal. Inflated sealskins attached to the harpoon line would later guide the men to the animal, tired from fighting the harpoon and swimming hard from the paddlers, where it could be fatally lanced. Once a diver tied the mouth shut, the men began the long process of paddling the whale to the beach. Songs made paddling less burdensome, and the power of their purification ceremonies gave the men strength.

When the Makah tribe took part in their last hunt in 1999, few in the tribe even remembered the taste of whale meat. It had been 70 years since the last hunt because of the international ban on whaling.

THE GREAT BASIN

In the Great Basin, which stretches from the Rocky Mountains to the Sierra Nevadas across Utah and Nevada, including small portions of Idaho, Oregon, California, Arizona, and Wyoming, the lack of dependable precipitation continues to make this region the driest climate zone in the United States (see Map 4). The region mostly comprises deserts, vast salt flats, and lakes, and is ostensibly barren of vegetation to sustain populations. This region provides few resources for those who try to eke a living out of its unyielding harshness, and as a result of the continued movement of the people who did live there, as well as their scattered presence, little is known about this region's earliest inhabitants. But bands of Indians did survive, owing to their ingenuity and skills in finding food where it seemed impossible to those who did not call the region their home.

As a result of the land's apparently harsh and unforgiving landscape, large populations of American Indians did not emerge in the Great Basin region. Those communities that did remain and survive lived in small bands that moved often in search of food, their main preoccupation. As a result, these Shoshonean-speaking tribes did not have the leisure time to develop extensive religious systems with elaborate and extensive ceremonies (like the Sun Dance among the Lakota), impressive community sites (like Pueblo Bonito at Chaco Canyon), extensive designs in textile

Mano and Metate, with ancient village of Tyuonyi and cliff dwellings in background, Frijoles Canyon, Bandelier National Monument, New Mexico. (Sandra K. Mathews)

weaving or on pottery (like the Northwest Coastal tribes, such as the Tlingit), or agricultural techniques (like the massive irrigation systems that the Tohono O'odhom constructed) because of the lack of rainfall. (Interestingly, however, from the Great Basin and Plateau region many years later perhaps one of the best-known ceremonies of the 19th century emerged, the Ghost Dance religion.) The tribes of the Great Basin did, however, continue to develop at the pace set by the earth and their ability to live within it.

For more than 10,000 years, Hokaltecan-speaking peoples have lived in arid climate of the Great Basin. The little evidence that exists suggests that sporadic hunting of Pleistocene mammals took place, and by 9,000 years ago, the region represented something archaeologists termed the "Desert Culture." These people likely used caves and rock shelters as homes and bark, and woven grass for beds. They likely had such tools as the manos and metates (grinding stones for milling), atlatls, digging sticks, wooden clubs, and manufactured woven baskets. One of the oldest known baskets in the United States, dating to approximately 9,000–10,000 years ago, was found in this region at Danger Cave. Along with the basketry, archaeologists also found netting, sandals, furs, and tumplines (straps attached to baskets and stretched across a person's forehead for load bearing). They harvested small seeds, as well as every other form of edible foods in the region, which allowed them to survive in the region for thousands of years.

By about 6,000 years ago, Utaztecan speakers began to infiltrate the region and apparently drove the Hokaltecan speakers to California or the Colorado River region (some scholars believe this happened as many as 3,000 years later). Approximately 5,000 years ago, some agricultural techniques appeared in the Colorado Plateau region, and by approximately 4,000 years ago, peoples living in the region developed the ability to use regional lakes as a food source. They fashioned nets and fishhooks, and by 2,000 years ago, they even used duck decoys. They grew dependent on salmon, mussels, and other riverine food sources. As the years passed, instead of depending on small seeds, people grew dependent on acorn seeds and piñon nuts, grinding them with mortars and pestles instead of the mano and metate, into a powder that they either ate as a paste, cooked as a mush, or fried as a paperlike bread called tiki bread (so called by Pueblo Indians of New Mexico). Their housing style changed to a form representative of the wickiup. By approximately 400 to 1200 CE, Shoshonean speakers began to move into the area and continued to survive fairly unchanged throughout the turn of the millennium.

Because of their dependence on such a sparse landscape, these early Great Basin dwellers found themselves moving often, following a seasonal migration to food sources that they had learned to find during different times of the year. To collect their food, they used deep baskets held on their backs and digging sticks—which led to outsiders calling them "Digger Indians," a rather derogatory term by today's standards. They not only collected roots, berries, nuts, and grasses, but they also supplemented their caloric intake with game hunted with bow and arrow, such as deer, antelope, and mountain sheep. They made good use of the bounty of the land, eating roasted grasshoppers, lizards, prairie dogs, mice, birds, and rabbits. To expedite their hunting, they used fire to drive the animals into trenches; others they trapped with nets. Periodically, they gathered for communal rabbit drives; and in the spring, they joined forces to drive antelope toward corrals made of brush where they killed the animals and shared the felled game with each other. Farther to the north, along the Snake River in southern Idaho, salmon, beaver, and other riverine animals supplemented diets. Because the land could be harsh, people dried the surplus salmon to eat at a later time.

Because the carrying capacity of the land could not sustain large numbers of people in limited geographical areas, family groups consisting of no more than two or three dozen likely lived and traveled together. While most have argued that no formal tribal organization existed, the Great Basin dwellers did have sweat lodges, which also served other functions, such as lodging for single men and gathering places to build a sense of community. Within that community, no permanent leaders existed as recognized by the tribe; however, they did recognize the wisdom of elders, whom they called "talkers." They also had deep respect for those whose strong "medicine" dreams separated them from the rest, allowing them to become healers and recognized as important to the well-being of the group. Organization within bands was loose; sometimes families would return to the same band yearly to live in the eastern portion, and at other times they resided instead with bands in the western portions. Therefore, the composition of these smaller groups oftentimes changed throughout the year and their lifetimes. As a result, small band variation occurred because of the constant and continuous contributions of the shifting membership of each band. While there was little tribal identification based on a unified clan or family system, a form of community kinship was rekindled each time the bands rejoined for rabbit or antelope hunts, the harvest, or various ceremonies. Besides singing, sharing oral histories and spiritual stories, and gambling, the men also joined together in sweat lodges.

Because of the climate's heat during most of the year, those living in the region wore little clothing. They fashioned sandals from fiber and used leggings to protect their legs from the devil's claw, yucca, and various other desert scrub and cacti. During more inclement weather, they used robes made of rabbit to repel the elements. The people adapted to the variables of the desert environment to make their lives more sustainable and comfortable where they could. Women wore basketry hats to protect them from the sun. They used woven baskets to transport goods, food, and even water as well as to boil their food (by immersing rocks heated in fires into baskets sealed with pitch and filled with water). Their lives would not always involve adapting to the environment without externally available tools. Even before the arrival of white men, other tribes introduced them to a strange new creature previously unknown to the Americas (other than its distant ancestor, the eohippus, which had been extinct for thousands of years): the horse.

By the early to mid-1700s, eastern Great Basin tribes acquired horses and, as a result, could create a lifestyle more approximating abundance than austere subsistence. It should be pointed out, however, that subsistence living was not a detriment to the existence or cultural development of any tribe. Rather, it should be recognized as a time-honored respect of the plenty of the land into which they believed their Creator placed them, an interwoven existence with and respect for the environment in which they lived. When they acquired horses, those tribes began traveling east to the Plains to periodically hunt buffalo. Through their growing knowledge of animal husbandry, tribes such as the Shoshone increased the size of their horse herds to the point that their surplus allowed them to trade

A winter count represented by a Shoshone buffalo skin robe, stretched and painted with figures that record tribal history and horses used for trade, warfare, and hunting. (Angel Wynn/Nativestock Pictures/Corbis)

away horses when Meriwether Lewis and William Clark arrived generations later. The Shoshone became particularly adept at managing their horses and their hunts, to the extent that they began to use ceremonial accoutrements, such as headdresses and other types of regalia (whether ceremonial or otherwise). They began raiding other bands for horses, partly in retaliation, but also to compensate for their suffering losses at the hands of tribes such as the Blackfeet, who had acquired guns from white men by the 1700s.

Competition for resources, the continued drying of the region due to further climatic changes, and the influx of tribes from the east caused more pressure on the Great Basin tribes, resulting in a need to "regroup"; some even intermarried with other tribes for political and economic reasons and to allow for continuity of their own tribes.

Those living in the Great Basin included such tribes as the Achomawi, Atsugewi, Bannock, Chemehuevi, Gosiute, Kawaiisu, Klamath, Modoc, Mono, Paiute (Northern, Southern, and Owens Valley), Panaminut, Paviotso, Shoshone or Snake (Wind River, Northern, Western), Ute, and Washoe.

THE PLATEAU

Between the Cascade and Rocky mountains is the Plateau region, where a variety of resources provided an abundance of food for its inhabitants (see Map 4). Such disparate geographical features as mountains; streams and rivers running through canyons and valleys; and desolate, volcanically created badlands forced its residents to survive by incorporating the wide variety of foodstuffs that the environment yielded, although perhaps grudgingly at times. While along the rivers fishing provided an abundance of food, gathering and hunting provided more of a challenge farther east. Permanent habitation came slowly, beginning approximately 9,000 years ago. These inhabitants began to adapt to the Desert Culture's way of life, through basketmaking and the use of such tools as manos and metates, which indicated a society primarily dependent on gathering. But as the climate became cooler after approximately 4500 BCE, regional variations began to appear. Those closer to dependable river systems began depending primarily on fishing, establishing permanent communities along waterways. In the next 1500 years, to 3000 BCE, new settlers from more wooded regions moved into the riverine area, bringing polished stone tools, pipes, copper, and various effigies and carvings of stone, and introducing the use of burial mounds. It would appear that the newcomers and those indigenous to the area melded their two cultures into one that is now recognized as the Plateau Culture.

Most of these people then developed more "deliberately," adopting aspects of the new cultures they encountered, including those with whom they traded on the Pacific Coast. By the time whites arrived, little distinctive tribal identity existed. Most communities operated as autonomous units with their own headmen, who were chosen based on their wisdom, courage, or accomplishments. These headmen served more as cultural guides and counselors than as "chiefs" of the entire tribe or linguistic group. They would oversee the community, which, in the winter, lived in round earthen structures, similar to pit houses in that they were submerged partially underground to guard against the cold winter winds. Sometimes the winter housing resembled long houses, analogous to the Iroquois tradition, where several families shared the dwellings, and family fires were placed in a row down the middle of the long structure. In the summer, however, *jacals* were used; these were branch-framed structures covered by fibrous materials woven together, or perhaps even by bark, which allowed the summer winds to penetrate the walls. These structures provided excellent air circulation while still keeping out unwanted scavengers or guests. Along the Columbia River, housing was distinctive to the Plateau—as they had access to tall trees that provided long planks for their plank houses, which were found more commonly in the coastal region of the Northwest.

Because they shared common linguistic and cultural bonds, and resources abounded, Plateau dwellers did not appear to be aggressive or prone to warfare. Periodically, several villages gathered to trade, harvest the bounty of the land, hunt wild game, or even join forces to raid an interloping adversary in retaliation. A major source of food, whether they gathered together or not, was the salmon that swam upriver from the Pacific Ocean each summer. Besides salmon, these precontact fishers took other types of fish as well.

FISHING TECHNIQUES

Precontact fishers used nets, traps, and spears, and sometimes caught fish literally by hand. Fish nets in rivers caught all sizes of fish, large and small, as well as anything else coming up or down the river. Set nets, used along the coastlines, were laid out and buoyed from the beach. When the tide came in, fish swimming along the shoreline would get caught in the nets. Fishers with boats would paddle along the submerged net and collect the fish caught in the net. Or they could wait until the tide went out and walk along the exposed and visible nets lying on or near the beaches and gather what had been collected during high tide when the nets were submerged. This indicated a very sophisticated knowledge of lunar and tide schedules and a social hierarchy, at least one of knowledge.

Another practical method of fishing involved the use of fish traps. These consisted of six- to nine-foot-long sticks tied together, with as little as an inch separating them at the bottom, and as much as six inches at the top, to form a basketlike chute. At the bottom, sticks would be positioned

Fish trap used to catch salmon in streams. (Angel Wynn/Nativestock Pictures/Corbis)

on the inside pointing up and blocking the exit hole where smaller fish could escape but larger ones became entrapped by the current and the small opening at the bottom. The basket chute was placed on its side with the small end pointing downriver. Periodically, the basket was raised and the fish removed. Fish traps were banned in 1959 after Alaska became a state to avoid further depleting the fish population.

Beyond fish, the Plateau dwellers also depended on the locally abundant roots, berries, tubers, and other vegetation, which provided necessary sustenance. They did not depend on domesticated agricultural produce, and therefore had no need for long-lasting and waterproof pottery for the long-term storage of seeds. Rather, they wove beautiful baskets like the Great Basin peoples and, through trial and error, also figured out how to make them waterproof. They also constructed baskets sealed with pitch that could contain liquids, including boiling water heated from stones warmed to piping hot in the campfires and then dropped in the baskets to cook their food. They did not take food, from whatever its source, for granted. They believed all things came from their Creator and that even though they might take from the natural world to feed themselves and their families, they could not do so without giving proper credit and thanks.

Therefore, spiritualism played an important role in their lives. Young men would seek at least one guardian spirit to guide them throughout life. Those whose guardian spirits were particularly strong transformed themselves into healers, and then they took care to cure their village members. A major religious festival, the Winter Spirit Dance, was held annually and, like many spiritual festivals, was accompanied by great feasts, dancing, socializing, and singing.

The Plateau people were not completely isolated, as river travel took them to the coast to trade with coastal tribes. Their dugout canoes provided them with safe and secure passage, not just along the Columbia and other inland rivers, but also as far away as the Puget Sound. They also traveled by foot, trading with tribes from the surrounding regions. Because of their location, tribes who established their homes near what is known as the Dalles, a key site along the Columbia River that linked the western coast with the Plains to the east, became trade brokers for the region. Their home was the site of major trade fairs that hosted tribes from as far away as the Shoshone to the east and the coastal tribes to the west.

By the time of the Lewis and Clark expedition, the Nez Percé were one of the most powerful and populous tribes in the Northwest, probably having as many as 6,000 members. They lived in small communities, during the summer along rivers for the salmon run. They also used the surrounding areas, which ranged for hundreds of square miles, for gathering such things as roots and berries to sustain their populations. They likely derived from those that spoke the Penutian language, arriving from Alaska as early as 10,000 years ago (potentially even earlier), following the migration. Certainly they had begun living along the Snake River by 6,000–8,000 years ago.

According to archaeological finds, they do not appear to have had a warlike tradition, although they likely developed periodic coalitions with neighboring tribes for such things as defense, trade of goods and foods, and unions between tribes. Nonetheless, the Nez Percé were a distinct tribe with their own homeland. They lived in a rugged location, with large rivers and rugged hills. To protect themselves against the elements, for clothing they used bark, fur, breechclouts, and even leg wrappings when it became cold. The women learned how to weave hats from available plants, and they decorated their clothing with beads, shells, elk teeth, and other ornaments traded from coastal tribes.

Their homes consisted of pit houses, with reed mats to protect against the cold, damp ground. As they developed, the homes became larger as extended families began to cohabitate. Soon, shelters reached up to 100 feet long. People slept along the inner walls of the buildings, and fires down the center aisle of the lodge kept them warm.

The Nez Percé did not practice agriculture, but instead they depended on the bounty of the land. Besides salmon, they also ate a root called kouse, which they boiled, beat into a mush, cooked, and stored. They also ate other wild plants, such as berries, nuts, carrots, bitterroots, serviceberries, blackberries, and strawberries. They pressed these and saved them for winter use. The men hunted by use of the bow and arrow, becoming so adept at its use that they could put an arrow completely through an animal. Both men's and women's roles in food collection proved essential, for if they could not store enough for the long winters, they could easily starve.

Although the Nez Percé did not appear to be warlike, they did have to contend with others who challenged their right to hunt and gather. The Nez Percé frequently challenged the Shoshone, Bannocks, and Paiutes in battles. However, in the early summer a general truce was always declared so that trade could take place between the numerous tribes that occupied the region. As soon as the trade fairs were over, however, the fighting resumed. To their west, the Nez Percé found more amicable relations with tribes as far as the coast, such as the Sahaptins, Salish, and Chinook speakers, as well as those who lived near that all-important region along the Columbia River, the Dalles. At the Dalles, the Wishram, Waso, and Wyampam Indians built permanent fishing communities, and their location provided ample opportunity for a consistent flow of fish, as well as trader traffic from the coastal regions and the Plateau. To this trading community, the Nez Percé brought many things (elk teeth, animal hides and furs, various roots, bear claws, dried meats). In return, they received items indigenous to points farther west (shells, fish oil, dried clams, baskets, and wooden instruments, for example). At the Dalles, cultures intermixed, and various pieces of native cultural knowledge became shared, including the story of Nez Percé creation and cultural heroes (such as the coyote). They also learned new skills from each other, adapted new styles of dress and adornment, and acquired new decorative designs and weaving techniques. Cultural interchange was indeed dynamic (Josephy, *The Nez Perce Indians,* 15–24).

One trade item that the Nez Percé had acquired from other tribes by the early 1700s was the horse. Traded from farther south, the Plateau tribes, particularly the Nez Percé, became quite adept at animal husbandry. In fact, even though they did not acquire horses until the late 1700s, the Nez Percé are generally credited with the "creation" of the Appaloosa, a breed famous for its sure-footedness on difficult mountain trails. The Cayuse and Yakama also became horse tribes as a result of the arrival of the Spanish horses. This allowed them to travel much farther and more extensively. In fact, some tribes left for hunting grounds of Montana and Wyoming for as long as a year or two at a time. They even adopted many of the Plains tribes' customary housing styles, the tipi, for example, skin clothing, feather headdresses, and other animal hide items. The river tribes of the Plateau continued to rely primarily on the bounty of the river and traveled upon it, while the eastern tribes instead adopted the horse into their culture, leaving their old riverine culture behind. Perhaps it was a portent of things to come.

Tribes located historically in this Plateau region include the Cayuse, Chilcotin, Coeur d'Alene, Colville, Cowlitz, Flathead, Kalapuya, Kalispel, Klamath, Klikitat, Kootenai, Lillooet, Molola Okanagon, Nez Percé, Palouse, Sanpoil, Shuswap, Sinkiuse, Spokan, Thompson, Umatilla, Walla Walla, Wishram, and Yakama.

THE PLAINS

The Plains region, stretching east of the Rocky Mountain range to the 100th meridian (or for some, to the Mississippi River), is perhaps forever linked by popular culture with the warriors on horseback, the "marauding" Indians that threatened overland migration in the 19th century. Hollywood often portrayed all American Indians as either Plains Indians or Apaches, riding horseback with beautiful headdresses and ominous war paint with drums beating out a warning to all who neared their homelands. These images, however, take away from their rich historical heritage, the variation between tribes, and the complexities of Plains cultures (see Map 5). After all, less than 1 percent of all those who died on the overland migration to the West died at the hands of Indians they encountered. Rather disease and accidents caused the majority of those deaths.

Archaeological evidence points to habitation on the Plains up to 10,000 years ago. These early Plains people hunted mammoth and prehistoric bison with fluted spearpoints. By 7,000 to 10,000 years ago, archaeological finds indicate the presence of nomadic bands, probably small family groups, traversing nearly all of the Plains. As the years passed, however, the climate became hotter and less precipitation fell, likely causing larger game to move north out of the area. Therefore, until approximately 2500 BCE, their survival shifted toward hunting smaller game and gathering food from the naturally occurring plant life.

Between 500 BCE and 1000 CE, a recognizable cultural grouping had emerged, the Plains Woodland cultures. Characterized by their pottery style and mound building, their villages and agricultural fields popped up along various rivers, including the Mississippi and Missouri rivers, in eastern Kansas as well as Oklahoma. Their cultivation of crops such as corn (acquired from the tribes to their southwest in modern New Mexico and Arizona) and beans indicated a shift from hunting and gathering to a more permanent community with semipermanent structures and storage facilities for surplus crops. Other Woodland period sites have been found farther north in Nebraska and even into Colorado.

The Mississippian group appeared as the next major cultural group on the Plains. Far more sedentary, their widely dispersed communities extended as far north as Minnesota and as far south as Texas. Extending into the Plains from three fronts, the Mississippian group included Siouan and Caddoan speakers. They depended on agricultural more intentionally, settling along river valleys, mostly along the eastern Plains, where they also had access to woodlands. To sustain their communities, the women cultivated corn, beans, sunflowers, and squash with digging sticks and animal bone implements, while the men supplemented their family's caloric intake by hunting bison and various other forms of large game. They lived in rectangular homes, usually either earthen or mud-plastered structures. The structures were surrounded by earthen pits or ditches, complete with stockades of sharpened sticks to keep out marauders and other unwelcome guests.

Even more people would move into the Plains from points farther east or north by about 1500 CE, however, and a new tradition emerged, the Coalescent tradition. Agricultural development continued, as did the growth of the communities along the Missouri River and the central plains. Their homes became circular in shape, while the southern Plains saw the development of grass-covered lodges. Such tribes as the Mandan, Hidatsa, and Arikara appeared as distinctive cultural groups and controlled the vast trade network on the northern Plains. These Plains tribes developed cultural traditions that had become more distinct, whereas in the western Plains, newcomers did not have as great an impact, and those more indigenous to the region continued their dependence on hunting and gathering, supplemented with some rudimentary planting as the environment would allow. As a result, semipermanent year-round settlements, which based their survival on an understanding of the natural cycles of the moon, rain, sun, and snow, found the role of men who had knowledge of the natural world even more imperative to their survival. Tribes had developed a clear understanding of the passage of time and of seasons. To begin to understand and transfer their knowledge of important events, they created "winter counts," or yearly calendars that recorded key events in tribal or community history.

WINTER COUNT

During the winter on the Plains, American Indians took special note of the occurrences of the year past and recorded what the elders decided was the single most memorable event (not necessarily the most important) during that year. Most often drawn in a circular pattern on a buffalo (or deer) hide, the winter count recorded the history of a tribe from the oldest recorded count to the most previous.

The winter count provided the tribe with a visual memory to go with the extensive storytelling that would explain the history of the event that the image illustrated. These stories would be told every winter; thus, years later, when the winter count keepers no longer recorded the history, tribal members

Detail of a winter count, a pictographic calendar of Plains Indian history, drawn by a Yanktonai Sioux called Blue Thunder. It records events that took place between 1792–1793 and 1902–1903. (Werner Forman/Art Resource, NY)

could explain to interested parties what each of the images related to in their past.

Generated in a spiral design, the winter count normally began in the middle of the hide and worked its way out. The drawings depicted everything from a successful buffalo hunt or horse raid, to an important trade agreement or peace treaty, and even to a record of how many were killed in a raid or by smallpox. These winter counts have been deciphered with the assistance of American Indians who had them in their possession at reservation forts, recording this knowledge for posterity.

Such traceable events as the Leonid meteor storm of November 1833 clearly recorded by the tribes, could be used to provide dates for surrounding events. These winter counts were often copied when the old counts wore out, or when a new winter count keeper took over, causing some variation in the images represented. To view a collection of winter counts, go to wintercounts.si.edu/html_version/html/thewintercounts .html.

Regardless of their levels of perceived "development" (as termed by outsiders), the Plains Indians that lived in the drier regions of the Plains evolved into diverse and strongly differentiated cultural groups. In the upper Missouri River region, the Blackfoot Confederacy emerged, consisting of the Piegans, the Bloods, and the Siksikas (Blackfeet). Farther west and north lived the Crow (both River and Mountain Crow, two bands of the same cultural group), and in the Dakotas, Nebraska, Wyoming, and even into Colorado were the 13 subdivisions of the Sioux tribe who spoke Lakota, Nakota, and Dakota. Together, they referred to themselves as the Seven Council Fires (political divisions), including the Teton in the West, the Eastern group (Sisseton, Wahpeton, Wahpekute, and Mdewakanton), and the Central (Yankton and Yanktonai) (Priztker, *A Native American Encyclopedia,* 316).

The Lakota, perhaps the most recognized northern Plains tribe, had not always lived on the Plains. Like the other Siouan groups, they emerged from farther east, where the Ojibwa pushed them out of the region east of the Red River (in Minnesota) after acquiring guns from the French beginning as early as the 1680s. Up until that point, however, the Sioux were like many of the other tribes, depending on traditional food sources, including fish, wild rice and berries, and game animals. One of the symbols of the Lakota, well known to and often misrepresented by Hollywood, was the sacred pipe. Given to them by the White Buffalo Calf woman, it gave them their connection to the universe and was only taken from its pouch during very special occasions (establishing peace or during some calamity such as famine that befell the community). After their forced removal from Wisconsin and Minnesota, the Sioux likely inhabited more than 100 million acres of land, from Minnesota and parts of Wisconsin to Iowa and the Dakotas.

To the west of the Lakota and Sioux, and sharing the Siouan root linguistically, in southwestern Montana and northern Wyoming lived the Crow Indians. Known by their own name, the Absaroke, they had previously lived south of Lake Winnepeg. They also had found the pressure of the Ojibwa and Cree unbearable, moving from their traditional homeland and ending up near the Yellowstone, Powder, and Musselshell rivers. After their move from farther north, they split into two branches, the Mountain and River Crow. Each year they regrouped, which gave them an opportunity to recount their oral traditions, participate in ceremonies, and engage in various other activities. They depended on each other for survival, and so like most Plains tribes, generosity was valued. For example, if one warrior led a successful raid against another tribe, he could keep all the booty, but under the weight of social obligation, he usually gave it away to other community members. This sharing allowed the tribe to maintain economic equality, but yet gave honor for and celebrated great feats of bravery and ability. .

The Crow also honored their dead by dressing them in their finest, painting their faces and fixing their hair, then placing them on a scaffold. Later, their bones would be hidden among rocks, sometimes in a cave. People sometimes mourned the dead by cutting off their fingers or hair and giving away their property. Pretty-shield, medicine woman of the Crow, described a time in her life where she lost a child and mourned for a long period. During this time, she found her helpers, the Ant People. She had grown up a River Crow, but when her aunt's child died, Pretty-shield's mother gave her to the aunt to ease her sorrow and sadness.

Besides having two divisions of the tribe, the Crow also organized by matrilineal clan. One could never marry inside the clan, and oftentimes girls were acquired by purchase before they reached puberty. Men could also acquire wives during raids or by inheriting them from a male family member who had died. Families consisted of a loose configuration of clan relations, and no child would be parentless. Both parents spent an inordinate amount of time teaching their children how to behave, what taboos to avoid, where to find food, where lodges could be set up, how to respect the "helpers" (animals or insects that serve as spiritual guides for individual Crow Indians), and much more.

Growing up on the plains was never easy. Few histories of life as a child were ever recorded by historians or anthropologists, but at least one did survive of growing up a Crow girl.

CHILDHOOD AS A CROW INDIAN

Just as in any society, parents of Crow children set boundaries that the children had to follow to preserve the best interests and survival of the people as a whole, but mainly to protect the children against harm. Unlike that of today's children, however, Crow life seemed far more lenient. Pretty-shield, who later became a medicine woman, recounted her life to Frank B. Linderman at the end of her life. Some of the stories she told about her early childhood exemplified the freedom children had, but also the danger of not following established rules.

The nomadic Crow moved often to follow the bison herds on the northern Plains; as a result, children had responsibilities to gather up their things and pack them for the journeys. Pretty-shield loved moving because it meant she could pack up, move, and then set up her own miniature lodge for her doll. The lodge was large enough that she actually stayed in it on occasion, keeping it well into her adult life.

At five years old, she remembered that she was in charge of herself during these moves. She rode her horse during these journeys to the next campsite and periodically offered to watch after the babies of other Crow mothers. In one incident, she had a baby's cradleboard secured behind her on the horse, but forgot about it and took off in a race across the plains with her friends. Only later did she realize that the baby was no longer there. The punishment of losing another woman's child was unbearable and she raced back, finding the baby unharmed. She learned from the experience and never borrowed any more babies as a child, and certainly never lent out her own babies to anybody when she grew older.

Pretty-shield also learned a valuable lesson about not harming the guardian spirits. After seeing someone throwing things at the chickadees, which served as one woman's "helpers," she learned that the action would come back to

haunt that person unless he or she restored the balance by
asking for forgiveness. Pretty-shield also learned the
importance of cultural traditions regarding establishing camp.
When she was young, she watched a woman hurry and put up
her lodge in the wrong place before Pretty-shield's mother
could assemble her lodge, which went against the respecting
of order and spacial organization expected of all tribal
members. That woman was later mauled and killed by a bear.
    Lessons were indeed harsh, but they were necessary for
survival and for the good of the tribe.

The Cheyenne and Arapaho, also nomadic hunters, occupied the
central Plains. They provided an important trade link to the western and
northern Plains. They developed trade networks and a distinct culture as
well as beautiful, elaborate, and important cultural traditions shared
orally through generations. According to George Bird Grinnell, like many
Plains Indian tribes, the Cheyenne believed the world was once covered
by a large flood (*The Cheyenne*, 1924). One person who floated about the
water asked the waterbirds to dive down and find the earth below, but
only a small duck succeeded in bringing up some mud on his bill. From
this mud, the earth was created. From this mud also, a man and woman
were created who represented the winter and the summer. But they had
no offspring, so more people were created, multiplying and overspread-
ing the earth. Unlike the origin stories archaeologists have identified for
other tribes, the Cheyenne have no stories of migrating to the American
continent. Instead, they believed their ancestors lived underground and
arrived at this level of the earth long ago when one of their ancestors followed a light to the surface.

    As a people, they learned how to use the land for sustenance; for ex-
ample, they used the rabbit for food and clothing during the winter.
Their homes consisted of lodges built from lodge poles, covered not in
buffalo skins but grass bundles, which were then covered in mud plaster.
Later, after they were forced onto the Plains, their sustenance and lodging depended on the bounty of the land. They depended more heavily on
the buffalo for sustenance, and no longer covered their lodges in grass
bundles. Their ancestors had originally lived near the Mississippi River,
but by the 1680s they had moved to the Red River region in west central

Minnesota as a result of René Robert Cavelier, Sieur de La Salle trading guns to the Ojibwa, who turned on the Cheyenne. This began more than 100 years of slow migration west and then south, and by the 1700s, to southern North Dakota. In North Dakota, their principle village consisted of approximately 70 lodges, each having a rather substantial diameter of more than 40 feet. For a while they lived along the Cheyenne River where they acquired European trade goods for the first time. Horses, glass beads, and metal knives were found at some of these early archaeological sites, but there were no visible signs that guns had been acquired. With horses, they could travel farther in search of buffalo, which, together with corn, beans, and squash, formed the basis for their diet. Around the 1800s, the Cheyenne moved farther onto the plains where they acquired horses, gave up farming, and became nomadic buffalo hunters on the plains of Wyoming, Colorado, and western Nebraska and Kansas.

The Cheyenne lived in smaller bands during the winter so they could have successful hunts without having to organize a mass migration of peoples. During the summer, however, they came together for a traditional communal hunt and to participate in sacred ceremonies. Spatial organization of the community, similar to that of most tribes, was key to respecting status within and among bands. Bands carefully followed the positions designated for their lodges. Rarely did tribal members disrespect communal traditions. For example, they considered murder dishonorable and would ostracize or exile the guilty party for life. Honor played a key role in society, and bravery in battle or in the hunt was paramount to gaining status and honor in the society. One thing that likely confounded (and delighted) Europeans that they would later encounter involved counting coup on their enemy, accomplished by tapping the enemy with a coup stick and getting away during battle, gave a man more prestige than actually killing his enemy. For women, chastity was very important, and because the process of winning one's future wife was overseen by both families and generally took a long time, she would be watched by both her family and his. To pass the time, the Cheyenne enjoyed gambling, lacrosse, and various other games.

The Cheyenne built alliances with the Arapaho, and later, the Lakota. They even ventured as far south as Santa Fe in 1695, drawn in by the annual trade fairs in which the Spanish and their Pueblo allies traded agricultural goods and Spanish products acquired from New Spain.

To the south of the Crow homeland lived the Comanche, the Kiowa, and the Kiowa-Apache. Each of these tribes developed a strong horse culture after the arrival of Spanish horses in New Mexico and Texas by the 1600s. Long associated with buffalo hunting, they also gathered roots and berries to supplement their diet. They too engaged in the extensive trade network that existed on the Plains, some of whom traded as far as away as the annual trade fair at Pecos and later Taos, New Mexico, for agricultural produce of the Pueblo Indians, and as far north as southern Minnesota for pipestone. They also exchanged food with the agricultural Mandan, Hidatsa, and Arikara to supplement their diets. The Comanche were perhaps best known for their rapid and expert adaptation to the horse culture in the 1600s.

Originally part of the Shoshone tribe, the first Comanche homeland fell along the Gila River in Arizona between 3000 BCE and 500 BCE. They grew corn and migrated to the north when the drought hit the Southwest in the 13th century. They passed Salt Lake and lived by hunting and gathering throughout the Great Basin. By the end of the 1600s when the Comanche acquired Spanish horses, they had finally separated from the Shoshone as a distinctly separate tribe and eventually moved out onto the Plains near the Arkansas River. On the Plains, they began to challenge Apache homelands, eventually forcing out the Apaches who had previously forced the Jumanos from the Plains. The Jicarilla Apache (located now in north central New Mexico) practiced agriculture like the Navajo to their west. They quickly learned that the Comanche saw them as sitting targets for raids, and as the droughts came by the early 1700s, they began to suffer. Spaniards even reported a "general collapse" of the Apache throughout the area. The Comanche were emboldened by the retreat of the Apache and became the most feared horsemen of the southern Plains.

Comanche spirituality was not as elaborate as the spirituality of the Pueblo Indians, but they did have reverence for the sun and moon, for example. The Beaver Ceremony and Eagle Dance served as an important part of their ceremonial life. Vision quests by the young men, who went alone to remote locations and fasted, were meant to help them find a helper that would guide them spiritually throughout their lives. Known by many as the horsemen of the Plains, the Comanche eventually acquired large bands of horses and lived off the buffalo hunt and raiding, developing a warrior tradition that caused the Spanish great consternation until the 1780s.

To their west lay the Apache and Navajo nations, the part-time agriculturalists and semisedentary tribes who benefited from their location on the trading trails north of the valley of Mexico where corn had first been cultivated by the Nahuatl-speaking tribes, then traded north to the Mogollón, Pima, and Papago, and beyond. As the Spanish moved into New Mexico and established a permanent settlement by 1598, the Apache and Navajo saw the value of these new four-legged creatures, stealing them first for food, and then for transportation. When the Ute and Comanche arrived in the area by the early 1700s, they would also find the horse to be a valuable commodity. These tribes would trade surplus horses to other tribes for various items or to gain status, and thus the horse trade began and spread slowly from New Mexico's Rio Grande Valley to the north and east. The western Plains were among the many tribes to acquire horses, and much like the other tribes, began to improve their ability to follow and hunt migrating bison herds. No longer would they have to use the old methods of hunting buffalo. As a result, their presence was felt on a much grander scale throughout the Plains.

JUMP KILL

Archaeologists use the term "jump-kill site" to refer to specific ravines or cliffsides where prehistoric cultures used to run animals, particularly prehistoric bison, toward and over the cliffside. A jump-kill site could not occur without numerous tribal members cooperating to surround and scare the animals toward the cliff's edge. More importantly, they had to act in concert, which often indicated a stratification of labor, or organization. After they surrounded the animals, they would begin to make noises and gradually close in on them. The frightened animals would run, directed by the hunters, toward the cliff's edge. Unable to stop, they would plummet either to their death or to a serious enough injury that they could not get up and run or defend themselves.

Plains tribes driving buffalo to death over chosen sharp drops in the prairies, thereby creating a massive meat supply at the bottom, as painted by Alfred Miller, 1867. Before acquisition of the horse, tribes performed the hunting maneuver on foot. (Library and Archives Canada/Bibliothèque et Archives Canada)

· Besides taking the meat, these early hunters also took bones for tools and hides for shelter and clothing.

Sometimes communal, sometimes noncommunal, these jump-kill sites often allowed the people to acquire numbers of bison in excess of what would satisfy the people. Archaeologists have identified more than 40 jump-kill sites across the Plains, some of which are located along the route of the Lewis and Clark trail in Montana.

Incidentally, other methods of hunting bison included running the animals into frozen rivers at the beginning of the winter where the ice would give way under their nearly 2,000-pound bodies. They would fall through the ice and drown. Farther down the river, the Indians would find places to recover the carcasses and process the animals for food, shelter, clothing, and tools.

Tribes such as the Comanche extended their horse herds to several thousand horses, placing great stress on the ecological balance and, as some have argued, perhaps even undermining the ability of the bison herds to survive as they had in the past. In fact, historian Thomas Kavanagh argued that the Comanche were the first of the Plains Indians to have and adapt to horses, even as the Cheyenne still lived in their permanent earth lodges. The Comanche, like many of the Plains tribes, did not function as one monolith, but rather as a collection of smaller units called bands. They were organized by rank, in response to honor and respect. Honor itself created the authority that existed within the tribes. Honor could be gained through either "medicine power," generosity (accumulation and then redistribution of wealth), or warfare for men. In the first method, through medicine power, they achieved their medicine by searching for a particular power (not by a random vision quest where power found the individual, as on the northern Plains) (Kavanagh, *The Comanches*, 28–30).

When the Europeans arrived, they had a difficult time discerning kinship relations within the various Comanche bands, because their terminology for familial relations (mother, father, sister, and brother, for example) was used by the Comanche to indicate a broader relationship. For example, because of kinship ties, sometimes more distant relatives would be called sisters or brothers, for example. Several bands existed, often with little contact throughout the year with the other Comanche bands. The physical separation of the several Comanche bands allowed them to accomplish many important things. For example, the Comanche had acquired horses relatively early owing to their close proximity to the Spaniards in New Mexico and later Texas (permanently by the early 1700s). As a result, their horse herds grew, and it was not uncommon for one band of Comanche to have a few thousand horses. The environmental impact of this adaptation had a ripple effect throughout the natural world, as the more horses the Comanche introduced onto the arid Plains, the less forage was available for traditional Plains grazers, including the buffalo. The population of the Comanche grew as well, partly because of the abundance of the buffalo and their increased ability at the hunt with the acquisition of horses from the Spanish and, later, guns from the French. Their population also expanded because of the practice of capturing young women and adopting and marrying them into the tribe.

By the 1860s when the United States established a firm presence in the West, the Comanches still did not operate as a unified or single tribe (as did most Plains tribes), but rather they occupied a broad range expanding from western Oklahoma and central Texas and nearly to the Rio

Grande valley. While they rarely ventured north of the Arkansas River, their reputation as the "Lords of the Southern Plains" was recognized by central Plains tribes. Instead of a single tribe, they organized themselves by bands, as many as 13 in prehistoric days, but by the 1800s, only 5 could be identified. The Penetethka, or "Honey Eaters," were well known in Texas history because of their traditional culture and the importance placed on their warrior culture. To their north, and sometimes venturing into the mountains of New Mexico, lay the Nokonis ("the Wanderers" or "Those Who Turn Back"). The Nokonis shared their range with two small bands, the Tanima, or "Liver-Eaters," and the Tenawa, or "Those Who Stay Downstream." Together, these three bands have been referred to as the Middle Comanche. In western Oklahoma, along the Canadian River, were the Cochetethkas or "Buffalo Eaters." The most northerly band, the Yamparikas or "Root Eaters," extended as far north as the Arkansas River. Finally, the Quahada, or "Antelopes," ranged along the Llano Estacado in western Texas and eastern New Mexico ("Comanche Indians," Handbook of Texas Online www.tsha.utexas.edu/handbook /online/articles/CC/bmc72.html). Several hundred band members lived together, traveling the southern Plains and sustaining their families through hunting, gathering, trading, and even raiding. Some have estimated their numbers as anywhere from just under 2,000 to more than 20,000, but a more likely figure approximates 3,000 or so. The difficulty in counting lies in the Comanche's loose band structure, their shifting populations within those band communities, captivity and trading, and periodic movement.

The Plains tribes who adapted to the horse culture through trading— or, if they were too impatient because of shifting power structures on the broader Plains, through raiding—began to adapt their traditions as well. Warriors continued their long-standing practice of raiding to illustrate their bravery in battle, but now they could do so more quickly and effectively on horseback. Instead of having to count coup on foot, warriors could do so on horseback. This also meant that adversarial tribes likely also had horses and might attempt to steal theirs, so they had to devise new methods to watch over and protect their families and their homes, as well as increase their herd size so as to remain the most formidable on the

Plains. But if a warrior returned from a raid having counted coup and returned with more horses, tribal respect for him grew, and the tribe recognized him as a man of great courage and prowess. Such acts of exceptional heroism could potentially lead the warrior to positions of authority within the tribe. Therefore, the horse actually did not change Plains culture on the whole, rather it enhanced it. Horses became a favored gift demanded by fathers of prospective brides, and they became important bargaining chips when trying to negotiate with other tribes or trade with outsiders. They were also used as payment for services rendered within the tribe, such as a healing ceremony or the services of a midwife.

With the advent of the horse culture, Plains tribes had the capability of transporting larger lodges as they followed bison herds. Traditionally drawn by their domesticated dogs, lodge poles were fashioned into *travois* (trah voy), but only so much as the dogs could pull. With horses, lodge poles could reach upwards of 20 feet, and the heavy buffalo hides that served as the walls could be dragged in the travois by horses much more easily than dogs. Horses facilitated a larger and more extensive hunt, and they helped increase the size of the lodges, which improved the status of individuals within the tribe, and the ability of men to illustrate their prowess and courage and strength as warriors. As a result, the size of the herds grew; thus, causing more stress on the land and reducing the forage for native animals like deer, antelope, bison, and elk. By the time European outsiders arrived from the east, Plains tribes had significantly changed their modes of production, but not necessarily their culture. Horses enhanced their capabilities and allowed them to venture onto the edges of more materialistic cultures (although one must be careful using such terminology). At least one well-known tribe, however, did shift from a primarily semisedentary gathering and agricultural tribe into a more nomadic group dependent on following herds: the Pawnee.

By the time the Europeans arrived, the Plains cultures consisted of Piegan, Crow, Pawnee, Dakota (Santee, Yankton, and Teton), Lakota, Nakota, Northern and Southern Cheyenne, Arapaho, Kiowa, Kiowa-Apache, Comanche, Wichita, Tawakoni, Osage, Kansa, Oto, Omaha, Missouria, Ponca, Iowa, and of course the Mandan, Hidatsa, and Arikara (and farther north into Canada, the Assiniboine, Cree, Atsina, Blackfoot, and Blood).

An Indian village on the move. Artwork by Charles M. Russell, 1905. (National Archives)

THE SOUTHWEST

Perhaps the most studied of precontact tribes, the Anasazi, are from the Four Corners region of the U.S. Southwest (where New Mexico, Arizona, Colorado, and Utah meet). Other well-known precontact groups in the region are the Mogollón, of southern New Mexico and Arizona and perhaps into west Texas; the Hohokam and Sinagua of Arizona; and the Patayán of the Colorado River basin at the California-Arizona border and farther north (see Map 6). Some of the famous sites that draw tourists include Crow Canyon in south-central Colorado, Mesa Verde National Monument in southwest Colorado, Chaco Canyon and Frijoles Canyon national monuments in northwest New Mexico, Montezuma's Castle National Monument in central Arizona, and Casas Grandes National Monument in southern Arizona. But many more sites are scattered throughout the Southwest that have not been excavated and are protected by federal law (the Native American Graves Protection and Repatriation Act of 1990).

PUBLIC LAW 101-601: THE NATIVE AMERICAN GRAVES PROTECTION AND REPATRIATION ACT OF 1990

The Native American Graves Protection and Repatriation Act (NAGPRA), passed by Congress in 1990, calls first for any federal agency or museum that receives federal monies to inventory its collections (human remains and associated funerary objects) and write summaries of unassociated funerary objects, sacred objects, and objects of cultural patrimony that they own or control. Based on those inventories, federally recognized Indian tribes or Native Hawaiian organizations request repatriation of those remains or objects.

Second, NAGPRA calls for the protection of Native American graves and associated cultural items. Archaeologists are to avoid archaeological sites containing graves, as well as abstain from "making intensive surveys to identify such sites." Before conducting archaeological research (or other such investigations that could potentially disrupt such sites) on federal or tribal lands, archaeologists have to consult with American Indians affiliated with that site. Federal permits and consultation with affected tribes or groups have to be obtained before investigations of grave sites on said land as well.

Finally, NAGPRA specifically prohibits trafficking in human remains and related cultural items. It also provides grants to help researchers comply with the Act and establishes a review committee to mitigate disputed cases.

The Mogollón are widely recognized as the first to adapt to the corn culture in what would become the United States. This occurred primarily because of their proximity to trade corridors emanating from the Valley of Mexico where maize or corn originated. From Mexico, they traded their corn, traveling up the trade corridor from the Aztecs all the way to the inhabitants of the Mogollón Rim, who in turn traded such things as dentalia (shells) from the Pacific Ocean and turquoise mined in what is now Arizona and New Mexico. The Mogollón hybridized the corn to increase production of kernel per ear and to ensure that the corn would survive in the more arid desert regions and shorter growing season. To improve the yield as they came to depend more on corn, they also developed floodwater irrigation techniques. Sites in the Mogollón region illustrate the presence of squash and maize as early as 2000 BCE, as well as various tools for preparing produce (manos, metates, mortars, and pestles, for example).

After the Mogollón had grown enough surplus, they traded it along well-established trade corridors farther north, west, and east for items not naturally occurring in their area, such as jerked buffalo meat and buffalo hides. Their pit houses date to 500 BCE just south of the Arizona border in Mexico, and 200 CE farther north. Between 2000 BCE and 500 CE, analyses of remains show a movement away from domesticated agriculture, but by 700 CE, agriculture again took firm hold and wild foods declined in usage. During this period, hybridization of corn became apparent, as the number of kernel rows dropped from 16 to only 8.

Housing also shifted, adapting to an agriculturally based culture. Previously, Mogollón had lived in caves adapted as home sites, but by the turn of the millennium they built villages of compact block homes around a central plaza. Their homes were multiroomed pueblo structures using masonry. They had domesticated turkey for mostly ceremonial and personal uses, such as interweaving turkey feathers into their clothing and blankets for added warmth during the cold winters in the mountainous regions. They also used the turkey feathers for decoration and for religious fetishes. A more sedentary lifestyle emerged because of the agricultural surplus. The increased need for storage vessels led to the creation of simple and functional pottery. Later, partially as more leisure time came about because of their improved ability at agriculture, they created white pottery elaborately decorated by designs in black paint drawn by yucca fiber brushes, which they adapted from their northern neighbors, the Anasazi, between 900 CE and 1200 CE. By the 1240s, they began to develop more structured apartment-style communities with buildings several stories high with up to 335 rooms. Their kivas, subterranean ceremonial chambers, signified a much more structured religious community as well. Trade items found at Mogollón sites indicate an established and widespread trade network, stretching as far as the Gulf of

California (such as shell trade bracelets found at the Mogollón sites), for example. But by the 1450s, their communities had been abandoned as they searched for better farmland elsewhere.

Similar to the Mogollón, the Anasazi appeared throughout the San Juan Basin as hunters and gatherers, but then they began to supplement their gathering with agricultural products such as corn, beans, and squash. Divided into two groups by ethnologists, the Eastern and Western Anasazi developed similarly, but some distinctions occur (related to architecture, kivas, pottery, burial mode, and other artifacts). The Western, known for rectangular kivas and more plaza-centered room blocks, lived in the westernmost segments of New Mexico, southwestern Colorado, southeastern Utah, and northeastern and north-central Arizona at such sites as Canyon de Chelly, Hawikuh, Chevelon Ruin, Oraibi, Awatovi, Kayenta, Betatatkin, and Kiet Siel.

Incidentally, the terminology "Anasazi" was designated by Albert V. Kidder, an early archaeologist in New Mexico who first used the archaeological method of stratigraphy at Pecos. He based this word on a Navajo term that he thought meant "old people." Unfortunately, he mistook the meaning; for Anasazi actually comes from a Navajo term meaning "enemy ancestor" (Plog, "Prehistory: Western Anasazi," 108).

According to some archaeologists, the Western Anasazi region demonstrated the existence of human habitation as early as 10,000 BCE; although if they did exist that long ago, it certainly was not in large numbers. Certainly after 3000 BCE organized local traditions evolved. The Anasazi developed pottery as early as 300 CE, later decorating it with a black-on-white design, similar to the Mogollón. Their housing style originally consisted of pit houses, shifting to cliffside structures between 700 CE and 900 CE. The most famous site at Chaco Canyon was not inhabited until after 900 CE, and by 1100 CE, some 5,000 Anasazi occupied the apartment-style structures with kivas, built around central plazas. The famous D-shaped Pueblo Bonito occupied the largest surface area and housed more than two dozen kivas, one being of enormous size. The Anasazi complemented the Chaco site with an impressive and necessary water system of dams, acequias, and reservoirs to collect and distribute water to their crops.

Pueblo Bonito at Chaco Canyon National Historic Park in northwestern New Mexico.
(iStockPhoto.com)

The Anasazi had more than a dozen towns scattered throughout the northern New Mexico region, but they extended far beyond that with more than 70 communities spanning more than 25,000 square miles across the Four Corners region. Their communities were held together with the assistance of more than 400 miles of roads emanating from Chaco Canyon, complete with roadbeds, curbs, ramps, and stairways. Some have argued that the roads also had ceremonial purposes, such as indicating the directions from which clans came or pointing to spiritual sites or shrines. The roads served as an avenue for the extensive trade and exchange networks that, with the connection through ritual, helped maintain a cohesive culture that revolved around a developing complex religious and spiritual system.

The era known by some as the "golden age of prehistory," a term applied to development by scholars in their attempt to understand the evolution of communities, occurred throughout the Americas when indigenous communities developed recognizable linguistic and culturally distinctive groups and developed cultural objects with decorations that typified their particular group, for example. Most often, the culturally unique adaptations of the material world (artwork, pottery, architecture, weaving, stitching, beadwork, for example) that was unique to their tribe or clan came on the heels of agricultural developments; although it must be noted that the dependence on sedentary agricultural systems was not the only method by which these advances would develop.

Other western tribes located in the Southwest included the Patayán, who lived along the southern portion of the Colorado River, just above the confluence of the Gila River; the Hohokam, who resided along the Gila River to their east; and the Sinagua, who lived just north of the Hohokam.

One of the more difficult of climates, this region sees only 6 to 10 inches of rainfall annually, and those inches often came during the summer "monsoon" season. As a result, the Hohokam learned to depend heavily on the existing river systems (including the Gila, Salt, Santa Cruz, and San Pedro rivers). They utilized the rivers well, connecting them to hundreds of miles of irrigation canals, or acequias, as the Spanish would later call them. Of all Hohokam communities, Snaketown continues to be the most famous because it was continually inhabited from approximately 350 CE to 1100 CE.

The early Southwestern people used food gathering and hunting, the latter improved by the adoption of the bow and arrow by around 900 CE to 1000 CE from tribes farther east. They placed an increased emphasis on agriculture and domestication of animals, such as turkeys and dogs. They all used the turkey, as did the Mogollón. Dogs served as protection for their homes and assisted in the hunt. While they continued basket-making, they learned the process of pottery from tribes farther south and with surplus crops and leisure time, had the capacity to begin to decorate the storage vessels increasingly as the years passed. Just as other tribes had, these Southwestern groups attempted to understand the natural world and their place in it, and spiritualism connected to the land evolved into a rich tapestry of understanding, in which they attempted not only to regard nature as a partner in their survival but also to influence it.

Often ignored by historians, the nomadic tribes also had an important role in prehistoric development in the region. While recognized as latecomers (compared with the Anasazi, Hohokam, and others), the

Athabascan-speaking Navajo and Apache tribes filtered into the Four Corners region, perhaps as early as 1000 CE, and perhaps as late as 1525 CE (depending on which archaeological text one adheres to). Because they were relatively late comers, they could not live along the Rio Grande Valley, which was already occupied by the Pueblo Indians. Moreover, they had recently experienced a long migration that likely brought them from either the Rocky Mountains or the Great Basin more than 1,000 years ago. Both the Apache and Navajo depended on hunting, gathering, and fishing, using a variety of spear and arrow projectile points, bows, harpoons, and decorating their clothing with porcupine quills. They used baskets and dogs for transporting goods and had a loosely organized band system built on kinship. Several bands, based on extended family groups, could comprise a tribe. They ranged in size from several dozen to several hundred people. They often acted independently from the whole as autonomous units, yet often respected one band as the most powerful and would adhere to their political decisions in the region. They had no single chief, but rather organized labor based on short-term "task forces" that would disband once a task was complete. They had a religious system built on shamanism and used various types of rattles with their music (Brugge, "Navajo Prehistory and History to 1850," 489–490). Some argue that as they moved southward during their migration, they split into two distinguishable groups, the Apache and the Navajo—referred to by the Spaniards as the *Apaches de Navajó*. But they were not all one cohesive unit, and in fact developed very different traditions.

The Apache and Navajo had filled in the areas around the Rio Grande pueblo villages to the east, south, north, and northwest by the time the Spaniards arrived in the region in the late 1590s and early 1600s. The Hopi occupied three mesas in Arizona, and the Zuni and Laguna occupied some portions of western New Mexico, so the newly arrived nomadic tribes filtered in, settling around their villages. One of those tribes, the "Apache," has a distinct name that is actually derived from a Zuni word meaning "enemy." Perhaps they earned that name from the Zuni based on their reputation as able raiders, taking goods from the sedentary pueblo people—something the Pueblos purportedly had not experienced to that extent before the arrival of the Apache. Matrilocal in nature, kinship formed the basis for the Apache home sites.

While they shared a common language, even among the Apache much variety existed. As many as six large divisions of Apaches existed: the Kiowa and Lipan Apache in the east (Texas, Kansas, Oklahoma), the Jicarilla of northern New Mexico, the Mescalero of southern New Mexico, the Western Apache (Tonto, White Mountain, and Warm Springs, for example), and the Chiricahua who often straddled the borders between New Mexico, Arizona, and Mexico. Technically, those borders did not exist until after the Mexican-U.S. War in 1848 with the signing of the Treaty of Guadalupe Hidalgo (and the subsequent Gadsden Purchase in 1853), making borders irrelevant during this precontact period. Leadership roles and respect among most bands of Apache were gained by their ability in warfare, strength of character and wisdom, generous spirit, or great oratorical skills.

Traditionally, historians have relied on colonial, military, and other official reports to describe interaction with the Apache people, which often results in inaccurate and shallow portrayals of the Apache as purely raiders, with little regard to the lives and property of other non-Apache (and certainly non-Indian) peoples. But the Apache people had a very deep sense of spiritualism and a clear understanding of their place within the earth and the universe.

Even though they were often labeled renegades or warlike, the Apache had distinct religious beliefs that allowed for men and sometimes women to intercede with the spiritual world to accomplish tasks, such as healing, seeing into the future, protecting people against evil and illness, and guaranteeing success in hunts or raids. Because of their late arrival in the Southwest, the influences of other tribes are apparent in their ceremonies. For example, one Jicarilla ritual included elements of Athabascan, Pueblo, Great Basin, and Navajo ceremonialism or cultural accoutrements, such as enclosures, masks, dances, and sand paintings.

They also believed in spirits that dwelled within certain mountains. These Gans, or mountain spirits, possessed incredible power (both good and evil) to influence the people. During ceremonies, dancers would dress in black masks and headdresses made of tall slats, to represent the mountain spirits. While outsiders have misunderstood these representations as evil or depictions of the devil, the Apache understood their full meaning and the power behind them.

Fear of and respect for the dead required Apache Indians not to speak of their departed by name or recreate images of them, as they believed ghosts could visit the living. Therefore, possessions and homes of the dead were oftentimes burned. They also feared witches and witchcraft. Puberty ceremonies, still a very important part of Apache life, were celebrated with great pageantry and, like many important ceremonies, were closed to outsiders.

Navajos, also Athabascan speakers, moved into the Four Corners region at approximately the same time as did the Apache. They also continued a relatively nomadic lifestyle, and periodically raided Pueblo communities for foodstores during difficult times. Unlike the Apache, however, some have argued that the Navajo adopted some of their rituals and spiritualism from the Pueblo Indians, adapting them to their own religious understandings. Stated simplistically, they believed in the Holy People, or supernatural beings, and the Earth Surface People (humans). The former held great powers that could hurt or help mortals. Only through careful balance with ceremonies and rituals, very meticulously carried out, could harmony be maintained in the universe. When that harmony was altered, illnesses would manifest themselves among the people. Through healing ceremonies, illnesses could be eliminated and balance restored once again. Therefore, healers played a tremendously important role in the community.

While the Najavo were traditionally nomadic, they also depended on agriculture, which they adopted from the Pueblo Indians. They grew such foods as corn, beans, squash, fruit trees, and, after the Spaniards arrived, oats and wheat. From the Spaniards, they also adopted sheep, horses, goats, and cattle (acquired through trade or otherwise).

West of the Pueblos, the Navajo, and the Apache, in south-central and southwest Arizona, lived the Pima and Papago. Speaking the Uto-Aztecan language, their historical arrival in the Southwest is far less certain. By the time the Spaniards arrived, however, the upper Pimas had a well-established tradition of being river dwellers, living along the Santa Cruz, San Pedro, and Gila rivers. They called themselves the Akimel O'odham, or river people. This differed from the Papago, who lived mostly in more desert regions to the south, who called themselves the Tohono O'odham, or desert people.

The western regions of the Sonoran Desert, homeland to the Pima and Papago, yield the most extreme and dry conditions of the United States, where temperature hit highs of 115 to 120°F in the summers and as low as 17°F in the winters. Because of the natural environment, these precontact people found themselves traveling significant distances across desert and mountainous regions to search for water. They followed the harvest of various wild plant species, including cholla buds (a type of cactus) and saguaro fruit, mesquite, cat's claw, prickly pears, and desert agave, for example. They also hunted game, such as bighorn sheep, two types of fox, bobcats, bats, javelina, deer, and antelope, as well as smaller animals, such as hares, rodents, cottontails, and ringtails. They were also known to eat various types of snakes and lizards as well as fowl. As Bernard Fontana explained, environmental conditions forced them to follow a nomadic life, marked by camping, bartering, and learning how to make the desert provide for them with unique tools for such tasks as harvesting (Fontana, "Pima and Papago: Introduction," 125–136). Fontana also argues that little can truly be known about the precontact period of this region because archaeologists have found little evidence that establishes without a doubt a coherent history of precontact Pima cultures.

Another group located in the Southwest, one encountered by many travelers to Grand Canyon National Park, is the Havasupai tribe. Only in the past 30 years have they regained access to tribal lands taken from them by the United States. Traditionally, they argued, they had occupied lands stretching nearly to Flagstaff, Arizona, in the southeast, the Little Colorado River on the northeast, and the Colorado River in the northwest. A Yuman-speaking tribe, they have close affiliation with the Walapai and Yavapai, who are also located in northwestern Arizona. Likely direct descendants of the Cohonina, they first arrived on the northwestern plateau around 600–700 CE. Rather small in number, they tripled in 200 years, and doubled in the next 100. Arguably this expansion resulted from dependence on sedentary agricultural production, which caused them to require more farmland. They began to farm on the canyon floor by 1050 CE, and this led to a seasonal shift in population from the canyon bottom during the summer for agricultural production to hunting on the mesa tops during the winter. The Havasupai raised corn, beans, and squash, with the assistance of hoes, digging sticks, and irrigated fields. Between 1050 and 1200 CE, interlopers caused the Havasupai to build more defensive cliffside home sites. By the time they returned to the Coconino Plateau in 1300 CE, the region had undergone a climatic change, causing the Havasupai to depend less on domesticated agriculture and return to hunting and gathering during the winter. They stored their surpluses and never again returned to permanent habitation of the plateau. After the arrival of the Spaniards, the Havasupai began to cultivate sunflowers, peaches, figs, and apricots as well as raise horses by the 19th century. They exchanged the surplus and manufactured items (baskets, food, and buckskin) that they could acquire with neighboring tribes that had access to their own trade circles. Through this trade network, the Havasupai acquired horses, hides, pottery, cotton, and many other items.

The central organizing body of the Havasupai was the family, both nuclear and extended. Gender divisions of labor were more fluid than in some cultures. For example, almost all assisted in agricultural and home-building pursuits, and likely hide tanning. Some manufacture seemed to fall to a particular gender: men made clothing, while women made items associated with home (sleeping mats, cradleboards for children, baskets and pottery for storage).

Spiritualism held a minor place in the Havasupai culture. They believed each person possessed a soul, which at death would travel to the place where the dead resided in the sky. If a soul returned to earth and was seen by a human, that person would die. Therefore, the Havasupai had fear of going out after dark. One major ceremony, affiliated with the harvest, occurred each year: the Round Dance. Several other neighboring tribes would be invited, and during the three-day ceremony, the Round Dance was held. It was also a time to trade, barter, and share food and conversation. Four types of shaman played a role in Havasupai tradition: a general curing shaman (to deal with illnesses or countering imbalances, for example), a weather shaman, a hunt shaman, and a healing shaman (who dealt specifically with injuries and bites).

Of the tribes in the Southwest, perhaps the Pueblo Indians, Navajos, and Apaches are best known, but other tribes existed in the difficult desert and mountain climes. Numerous tribes lived in Arizona: Walapai,

Havasupai, Yavapai, Mohave, Halchidhoma, Queeham, Cocopa, Pima, Maricopa, Jocome and Jano, Ute, Navajo, and Apache (Western, Chiricahua, Mescalero, Jicarilla). Living in New Mexico were the Pueblo Indians, which consisted at one time of more than 100 separate pueblos speaking more than seven languages. Now only 20 pueblos exist: the Hopi, Zuni, Acoma, Laguna, Taos, Picuris, San Juan, Santa Clara, San Ildefonso, Nambé, Pojoaque, Tesuque, Sandia, Isleta, Cochiti, Santo Domingo, San Felipe, Santa Ana, Zia, Jemez, Tigua, and Pecos (and these latter two are no longer inhabited). New Mexico also saw periodic visits by the Comanche.

MESA VERDE NATIONAL PARK

Perhaps one of the most famous of all Paleo-Indian sites in North America is Mesa Verde National Park, located in southwest Colorado on what used to be the Ute Mountain Ute Indian Reservation. Typical of how the U.S. government authorized the secretary of the interior to negotiate for the acquisition of national parks, monuments, and forests, the interior secretary was to negotiate for the "relinquishment of the Mesa Verde tract from the Utes and an appropriation for the survey of the area" between 1901 and 1903.

By 1906, Congress had passed the Mesa Verde National Park Act, which President Theodore Roosevelt, a champion of the outdoors, signed. Another key step toward saving the historic and Paleo-Indian past for the future was the passage of the Act for the Preservation of American Antiquities (Antiquities Act of June 8, 1906). From this point, it would be a federal crime "to collect or destroy any historic or prehistoric object or building on federally owned land." Mesa Verde is the only cultural national park in the United States, and it was designated a World Cultural Heritage Site on September 8, 1978.

Inhabitants of Mesa Verde, called the Basketmakers, lived in the various caves in the region from approximately 1 to 450 CE. They wove beautiful baskets, sandals, bags, and blankets, and even intertwined domesticated dog hair into their weaving. They used the atlatl, spear, and digging sticks. Their trade network was extensive, as jewelry made from seashells would attest. Between 450 and 750 CE, the "modified" Basketmaker

View of Cliff Palace, an Anasazi settlement at Mesa Verde National Park, Colorado. This large structure, accessible to its residents only by climbing up the rocks, housed between 100 and 150 people. (Corel)

period, they used pit houses and incorporated the bow and arrow as well as pottery. Their continued use of baskets decreased as they developed clay jars, bowls, and pots. As leisure time increased after they adapted beans, an excellent source of protein, they began to decorate the pots.

From 750 to 1000 CE, the "developmental Pueblo period," the Pueblo people began to build attached structures in a curved row fashion. They also developed kiva, or underground ceremonial chambers and stone masonry and adobe mortar homes with vertical walls. From 1100 to 1300 CE, the Great Pueblo period flourished with apartment-style structures in compact communities of more than 100 people, at first on mesa tops, then in cliffsides. The people farmed on the mesa tops and valleys, carrying the harvest of corn, beans, and squash to their well-protected homes. Kivas and tall towers typified this period. But by the late 1200s CE, a severe drought, overutilization of natural resources, and the migration of more nomadic peoples like the Navajo and Apache into the region are credited with the disappearance of these cliff dwellers (Mesa Verde Web site, www.nps.gov/meve/home .htm; "Mesa Verde National Park," National Park Service Web site, www.nps.gov/meve/).

CALIFORNIA

By far the most diverse and populated region north of Mexico, California's temperate climate hosted a population of between 300,000 and 350,000 by the 1700s (see Map 7). Precontact numbers were likely higher though because periodic contact with European sailing vessels as early as the 1540s brought disease. Juan Rodríguez Cabrillo visited California in the 1540s, Francis Drake in the 1570s, and in 1769 the Spanish established the first permanent foothold in California. Through their extensive trade network with Mexico, the Spaniards unwittingly unleashed smallpox, the common cold, influenza, and many other European diseases, which resulted in devastating population losses; and these devastating diseases soon traveled north (Josephy, *Indian Heritage of America,* 138; and Pritzer, *A Native American Encyclopedia,* 112). The early people of California spoke as many as 300 dialects of perhaps as many as 100 languages, but as extensive as these differences were, the people shared a few cultural characteristics. They lived in small groups of anywhere from 50 to 500 people, overseen by a headman who controlled the economic destiny of the band. Mostly patrilineal, these bands of California Indians were not as cohesive or well recognized as separate entities by outsiders who arrived in the 1700s.

Archaeological records clearly support human habitation of California for at least the past 4,000 years. Earlier records exist, but they are less reliable in establishing a pattern of behavior and land use. While archaeologists have located Clovis-type points in California that date to 10,000 or 11,000 years ago, some have claimed that human habitation dates back to 26,000 to 48,000 years ago. Most are reserving opinions, to avoid another fiasco like the Sandia Cave find in New Mexico during the 1930s. Because California's environment differs between coastal and inland as well as between the south and north, making generalizations about all California tribes would be a disservice. Therefore, a complete overview will not appear in this chapter. Instead, a general overview will be provided as well as a look at a few particular examples in California.

According to archaeological evidence, hunting and gathering gave way to seed collecting as a major source of caloric intake between approximately 9000 and 2000 BCE. Up until the shift, big game was hunted through the use of a small dartlike projectile point. While no "smoking gun" of a dart tip embedded in a large animal's remains has been found, most archaeologists agree that early humans hunted by this method. They also hunted smaller mammals and waterfowl and collected shellfish and wild plants. Because their shelters were temporary, they left few traces for archaeologists to find thousands of years later. Sometimes they used caves or rocky overhangs, but the lack of refuse deposits either obviates that supposition or, perhaps, their transitory lifestyle caused them to use these shelters for only short periods at a time. Clovis-styled projectile points, found at various locations (including Borax Lake), indicated habitation of at least 12,000 years ago.

By 6000 to 3000 BCE, a shift to seed collection and gathering is indicated by the appearance of large numbers of milling or grinding stones that are dated to this period, especially in the southern portion of California. Other areas of California, however, likely adapted to seed collection as a result of immigration of peoples from other regions. Even though they lived close to the oceans, they did not develop a dependence on marine life until later, as evidenced in the absence of remains from shellfish, fish, and marine mammals. During this period, burials occurred, but little accompanied the dead. Farther north, little evidence of seed collection exists except near Sacramento.

By 3000 BCE, regional variations appeared, likely a result of distinctive and local environmental conditions, which led to different types of food collection; in other words, tribal adaptations to the regional conditions. Artistry and crafts became more prevalent as surpluses allowed for the leisure time to create beautiful pottery, baskets, and items made from stone, shells, and bone. Trade provided the inland tribes with access to coastal food and other trade items, such as shells. They became immersed in trade networks farther east when they learned that dentalium and conch shells were highly prized by non-coastal tribes as far east as New Mexico. Besides trading shells, these locally harvested items became important as accoutrements for burying the dead. During this period, increased rainfall seems to have made the more deserted regions of California more habitable, and as a result, populations of plants, animals, and humans reclaimed those previously poorly occupied regions. As the environments became more conducive to supporting populations, which in turn became more diverse in their food sources, some communities even demonstrated the development of wealth acquisition.

With a deeper comprehension of their world, they also developed an understanding of what happened to family members at death. Shells, as well as other decorations, were used in the burials of the dead, who were laid prone and face down, facing the west. The dead were accompanied by various items to assist them on their journey to the next world. Religion had obviously expanded to the point that the afterlife had become an important consideration during their lifetimes.

By 2000 BCE, the people had integrated numerous subsistence patterns. They used early spears to hunt everything from ancient species of horse (eohippus) to camel to bison. They also ate small mammals, fish, birds, shellfish, and native flora. Their diet had great variety in years of plenty. Individual linguistic distinctions occurred; for example, in the Great Central Valley, most of the occupants spoke Penutian languages, replacing the original Hokan speakers. By 500 CE, cultural differences had advanced so much that distinguishable tribal groups evolved as illustrated by the cultural patterns and customs witnessed in the early contact period. Populations grew and became more complex as they learned how to more expertly use the resources in their regions with newly developed or adapted tools.

At this time, most California Indians depended on acorns as a main staple. They collected acorns in the fall during specially designed excursions. Once shelled, they then let the sun bake the kernels, after which they pounded the nuts into flour. Women removed the acidity by pouring heated water over the flour, which was then turned into a soup, turned into mush, or baked into bread. Sometimes, however, the acorn crop would fail because of a lack of precipitation and they would have to depend entirely on other food sources, such as buckeye (a type of nut that they roasted, peeled, and mashed), sage seed, wild cherries, and epos root. They incorporated datura, a plant that had hallucinogenic properties, in particular rite-of-passage ceremonies. Other common foods the land provided included fish, deer, elk, and antelope. To store their surplus and carry things, they manufactured beautiful basketry. While they were not primarily an agricultural people, they did grow tobacco.

By 1000 CE, they began to create rock art, such as petroglyphs (carvings) or pictographs (paintings) to record their experiences or spiritual understandings. Much of the artwork was for ceremonial purposes (hunting, puberty rituals). Some of the designs included crosses, wheels, dots, and other geometric designs, as well as representations of people and animals. These designs would be later found by Spaniards when they traveled some of the traditional Indian trails hundreds of years later. The California Indians continued trading with neighboring tribes, following long-established trails across California. Coastal Indians traded dentalia (shells), clamshell disks, magnesite beads, salt, acorns, fish, baskets, hides, pelts, obsidian, and bows with other tribes.

Because of similarities between California tribes, albeit scattered from north to south, little warfare occurred, and they could focus on their primary task of food collection and survival. When warfare did occur, however, rarely did it follow traditional European-style protracted war. In fact, most preferred short and surprise attacks where few casualties occurred. Fights might break out for numerous reasons, including retaliation for murder, rape, sorcery, or simply hurling an insult on another. Regardless, after a short fight, the headmen of each community would come together and resolve the details of the dispute; therefore, most conflicts were limited to a minimum of deaths. Moreover, compensation for murder or property loss played an important role in resolving disputes.

Mild coastal climates allowed California peoples to adopt simplistic forms of housing and attire. Men often went without clothing or wore simple loincloths, while women wore skirts and basketry hats to protect their skin from the intense and continuous sun. Although they were usually barefoot, the people also made fine moccasins to wear on nut or other food-gathering expeditions or in cooler climates. Their homes consisted of a dome-shaped pole structures, covered in earth, rush mats, bark, or wood slabs. Farther north, the Yuroks built wood plank houses, like their neighbors in the Pacific Northwest. Although building materials varied from region to region, they mostly seemed to build conical-shaped dwellings.

The Yuroks, whose traditional homeland lay on the Pacific Coast on the lower 45 miles of the Klamath River, lived a sedentary life because of the abundance of (and their knowledge of gathering) various types of fish,

Petroglyph at Lava Beds National Monument in California. (iStockPhoto.com)

shellfish, sea lion, deer and elk, and acorns. They had a recognizable form of social stratification, using spatial location (homes atop hills) and accoutrements (attendants, clothing), and leaders were chosen from those of higher social standing. The Yuroks also traveled widely.

As religious understanding began to form, tribes recognized their own creation stories, some of which were recorded many generations later. The Shasta creation story is an example of how religion was used to understand and create order in the natural world. According to the story, many years ago, the earth was new and flat. Chareya (Old Man Above) could not see it, nor could he step down onto it because it was so far away. He used a stone to push a hole in the sky, where he threw down snow and ice. All of the snow and ice formed into a pyramid, down to which he stepped by way of cloud stepping-stones. Once on the earth, the hole in the sky began to melt the pyramid of snow, causing it to have holes. When the earth warmed up, Chareya poked his finger in the ground and planted trees, and the melting snow from the pyramid watered them. When the leaves fell from the trees, he scooped them up in his hands, blew them into the air, and they became birds. He found a stick, which he broke into many pieces. The small pieces became fish and animals, and the large pieces became the grizzly bear, who became master of earth. The bear walked upright with a club, and so intimidated Chareya that he bore a hole into the pyramid of ice and snow and turned it into a tipi. The people knew he still lived there because they could see the smoke coming from the top of the tipi. When the whites came, Chareya went away because no more smoke came from the hole (Hungry Wolf, *The Good Medicine Book,* 144–145). Mount Shasta, as it is known today, still holds great reverence for the Shasta Indians and others. Understanding origin was important, as was establishing order in the tribe, which could be done through social controls in the family unit and inside the tribal unit.

Rites of passage provided one method in which social controls could provide order. One of those benchmarks in the community involved marriage, which occurred after puberty. In some societies, marriage was highly regulated and based on a rather rigid class structure, which consisted of rich, commoners, and the poor. Headmen or healers could take more than one wife, but only if they could support them. And slavery existed within some tribes, like tribes in the Pacific Northwest, just a few days' trip to the north. Some tribes had healers who, after communing with spirits, would gain their great powers. Some healers used blood-letting (through sucking from the mouth) to eliminate evil spirits or diseases, while others used datura to obtain visions to give them a connection to the spiritual world. Such visions helped them acquire influence or potentially restore the balance with the natural world. Other California tribes had ceremonies that centered on the salmon, which gave them another opportunity to share their rich oral history and mythology with the younger generations, as well as to display accumulated wealth (something not typically associated with prehistoric tribal cultures). Music and dance played a key role in most of their rituals, as did tobacco. All major events in one's life were honored in ceremonies, making ceremony likely a common and certainly important occurrence in village life.

Cultural accoutrements varied across California. In the north, for example, tribes tended to follow the more opulent demonstrations of the Northwest Coastal tribes. At ceremonies, such as the Deer Dance, they proudly displayed their valuable white deerskins and dentalia (shells), among other prized items, illustrating the importance of wealth acquisition. Farther south in the Santa Barbara region, the Chumash carved effigies of birds and fish in stone, revered the California condor, and built plank canoes (the only ones in North America). In the southernmost regions, "ground paintings," similar to Southwestern sand paintings, were part of initiation rites.

In whichever region they lived, the people had a rich heritage of oral history, songs, and stories. Not all in life was serious, though, as the prevalence of games illustrated. Children played hoop-and-pole games to improve their speed, prowess, and dexterity, all important skills in hunts. They also played hand games, cat's cradle, a form of lacrosse, and dice, and they held athletic contests to demonstrate their strength and abilities.

Tribes located throughout California are numerous, but the commonly recognized ones include the Athabascan-speaking Hupas, the Ritwan-speaking Yuroks, the Hokan-speaking Shastas, Pomos, Chumashes, and Pitt River Indians. The Miwoks, Yokuts, Cahuillas, Luiseños, and Fernandeños lived in central California, while the Yuman Diegeños lived in southern California. Contact with the Spanish, who arrived in 1769, would ravage the indigenous populations, sending their populations spiraling downward into the 19th century when U.S. Indian policies (official and otherwise) would attempt to eliminate tribe after tribe.

FINAL NOTE

For all of the tribes in the West, perhaps the greatest and most demanding changes occurred with the arrival of the Europeans and Russians in their homelands. These outsiders brought tools, animals, goods, and even European germs that would either enhance Indian lifestyles or be detrimental to their very existence. The Indian people adopted tools such as metal pots, knives, traps, and guns, so it was no longer necessary to make tools in the traditional way. As a result, formerly important skills were lost or not passed down through the generations, such as creation of war materiel (bows, arrows, spears, wood or animal skin shields, and helmets) and daily tools (such as flint knives, napping tools, manos and metates, pottery, and gut sacks) among tribal members. Therefore, with less need to use the natural products of the land to create the tools they needed to survive on a daily basis, their production shifted into other areas. Some of that energy was shifted into creating even more beautiful artistic designs on pottery, woven into basketry and shawls, painted onto lodges or hides, and in creating more surplus that could be traded for other items not readily available in their home region, for example. Therefore, the already existing trade network expanded to include items acquired from white trappers and traders, like black powder, guns, lead for shot, metal implements, and novelties such as beads, bells, jingles, mirrors, and buttons.

Of perhaps a greater impact regionally, those tribes that had access to European trade goods (especially guns, lead shot, black powder, and alcohol) gained power in the region and therefore tipped the precarious balance of power that had existed and been negotiated between peoples with the same access to tools and resources for generations. Access to European trade goods also allowed those who had "partnerships" with the newcomers to become key trade partners and powerful trade brokers in the region—*if* they survived the diseases brought by the interlopers. These issues will be discussed more fully in subsequent chapters.

What scholars do know based on documentary evidence is that the first Europeans to establish a continuous presence in the Americas were the Spanish in the 1490s, then the French in the 1530s, the Dutch by 1609 officially (albeit shortlived), the English in the early 1600s, and finally the Russians in the 1740s. Only the Spanish, French, Russians, and a few Englishmen appeared in the American West before the 1800s; therefore, it is mainly American Indian responses to those sovereign nations that will be explored in the rest of the book. When those outsiders *did* begin to arrive in the Americas, they encountered a land occupied by Indians who had existed for centuries; who had hunted, gathered, cultivated crops, built intricate and extensive irrigation systems, traded, fought, developed religion, evolved into stratified societies, and created major centers of civilization complete with five- to six-story apartment complexes (the likes of which would not be seen among the European immigrants in the U.S. cities until the late 1800s). The tribes had long histories that tied them to their homes and sacred places, some of which they had lost to rival tribes, forcing them to move to another homeland (such as the Lakota and Comanche), thereby causing a major shift in their own religious worldview shaped by geospacial issues as much as an understanding of the environment by the time the European invaders arrived on the Plains. But they adapted and survived, and this ability to adapt and survive would serve them well as these invaders sought to force their cultural understanding, religion, language, customs, and more upon what they termed Godless, uncivilized heathens.

BIBLIOGRAPHIC ESSAY

The wonderful, albeit dated, reference used for a broad segment on the regional variations of early American Indian history was Alvin M. Josephy, Jr.'s, colossal work *The Indian Heritage of America* (New York: Alfred A. Knopf, 1968). Another more recent (although also now dated) resource, which divides Indian history into regions controlled or claimed by European powers by chapter, is Arrell Morgan Gibson's *The American Indian: Prehistory to the Present* (Lexington, MA: Houghton Mifflin, 1980). Even with its periodic flaws, Gibson's book still gives a good introduction to early American Indian issues and provides one of the broadest historical treatments of all of the non-Indian influences from the 1400s to the end of colonialism. Also used for this chapter was Barry M. Pritzker's more recent *A Native American Encyclopedia: History, Culture, and Peoples* (New York:

Oxford University Press, 2000), which provided an excellent overview of each region. Unlike Josephy's work, Pritzker looks at every single tribal grouping individually and presents updated information for each tribe about location, population, history, religion, government, customs, dwellings, diet, key technology, trade, notable arts, transportation, dress, war, and weapons. He also includes more current information about government and reservations, economy, legal status, and daily life. The volume is a magnificent reference for very detailed information about specific individual tribes, affiliated tribes, broader regional history, and current tribal status. For precontact history, see James E. Dixon, *Bones, Boats, and Bison: Archaeology and the First Colonization of Western North America* (Albuquerque: University of New Mexico Press, 1999), and Shepard Krech III, *The Ecological Indian: Myth and History* (New York: W. W. Norton, 1999). Most recently, Colin G. Calloway's magnum opus, *One Vast Winter Count: The Native American West before Lewis and Clark* (Lincoln: University of Nebraska Press, 2003), is a phenomenal study of early American Indian history that will likely become the standard text; in addition, Calloway's study *First Peoples: A Documentary Survey of American Indian History* (Boston: Bedford/St.Martin's, 1999) serves as a wonderful combination of primary sources and interpretation. See also Wendell H. Oswalt, *This Land Was Theirs: A Study of North American Indians,* 5th ed. (Mountain View, CA: Mayfield Publishing Company, 1995). For more general anthropological, cultural, spiritual, and traditional knowledge, see Adolf Hungry Wolf's *The Good Medicine Book* (New York: Warner Paperback Library Edition, 1973). An interesting study of the transition from Paleo-Indian to Archaic is T. Douglas Price and Anne Birgette Gebauer, eds., *Last Hunters, First Farmers: New Perspectives on the Prehistoric Transition to Agriculture* (Santa Fe, NM: School of American Research Press, 1995). For a discussion about mitochondrial DNA sequencing, see S. L. Bonatto and F. M. Salzano, "A Single and Early Origin for the Peopling of the Americas Supported by Mitochondrial DNA Sequence Data," *Proceedings of the National Academy of Sciences USA,* 94 (1997): 1866–1871; Robson Bonnichsen, *Method and Theory for Investigating the Peopling of the Americas* (College Station, TX: Center for the Study of the First Americans, 1994); Dean R. Snow, *The Archaeology of North America* (New York: Chelsea House, 1989); and the authoritative work by Jesse David Jennings, *Prehistory of North America,* 3rd ed. (Mountain View, CA: Mayfield Publishers, 1989). For information about the impact of interest in Native remains and funerary sites, consult Roxana Adams, ed., *Implementing the Native American Graves Protection and Repatriation Act* (Washington, D.C.: American Association of Museums, 2001) and the following Web sites: www.cr.nps.gov/nagpra/ MANDATES/25USC3001etseq.htm and cita.chattanooga.org/fedlaws.html. For information about early site dating, see Peter I. Kuniholm, "Dendrochronology," *American Journal of Archaeology,* vol. 99, no. 1 (January 1995): 99–102; Patricia C. Rice, *Doing Archaeology—A Hands on Laboratory Manual* (Mountain

View, CA: Mayfield Publishing Company, 1998); and Marvin A Stokes and Terah L. Smiley, *An Introduction to Tree Ring Dating* (Chicago: University of Chicago Press, 1968). And for a history of the early buffalo and the interaction between the buffalo and humankind, see Francis Haines, *The Buffalo: The Story of American Bison and Their Hunters from Prehistoric Times to the Present* (Norman: University of Oklahoma Press, 1995). Finally, for an excellent online source related to origins (and history in general), see the Encyclopedia Smithsonian at www.si.edu/Encyclopedia _SI/nmnh/origin.htm.

For the northernmost region of the West, see Velma Wallis, *Two Old Women: An Alaskan Legend of Betrayal, Courage and Survival* (New York: Perennial, 2004); *Bird Girl and the Man Who Followed the Sun: An Athabaskan Indian Legend from Alaska* (New York: HarperCollins, 1997); and *Raising Ourselves: A Gwich'in Coming of Age Story from the Yukon River* (Kenmore, WA: Epicenter Press, 2003). For an overview of Alaska, see Claus-M. Naske and Herman E. Slotnick, *Alaska: A History of the 49th State,* 2nd ed. (Norman: University of Oklahoma, 1987); Dorothy Savage Joseph, *Fishcamp* (Bend, OR: Maverick Publications, 1997); Steve J. Langdon, *The Native People of Alaska* (Anchorage: Greatland Graphics, 1993); Jan Halliday with Patricia J. Petrivelli and the Alaska Native Heritage Center, *Native Peoples of Alaska* (Seattle: Sasquatch Books, 1998); Ann Fienup-Riordan, *The Living Tradition of Yup'ik Masks: Agayuliyararput, Our Way of Making Prayer* (Seattle: University of Washington Press, 1996); Ann Fienup-Riordan and Alice Reardon, *Wise Words of the Yup'ik People: We Talk to You Because We Love You* (Lincoln, NE: Bison Books, 2005); and Ann Fienup-Riordan, *Boundaries and Passages: Rule and Ritual in Yup'Ik Eskimo Oral Tradition* (Norman: University of Oklahoma Press,1995). Excellent resources on Alaska Natives include books by Wendell H. Oswalt, *Eskimos and Explorers* (Lincoln: University of Nebraska Press, 1999); Wendell H. Oswalt, *Kolmakovskiy Redoubt: The Ethnoarchaeology of a Russian Fort in Alaska* (Los Angeles: Institute of Archaeology, 1980); and Wendell H. Oswalt, *Bashful No Longer: An Alaskan Eskimo Ethnohistory, 1778–1988* (Norman: University of Oklahoma Press, 1990). And, of course, one must consult the series edited by the late Peter Sturdevant, including David Damas, ed., *Arctic,* vol. 5 of the *Handbook of North American Indians* (Washington, D.C.: Smithsonian Institution, 1984). See also Andrei Val'Terovich Grinev, *The Tlingit Indians in Russian America, 1741–1867,* translated by Richard L. Bland and Katerina G. Solovjova (Lincoln: University of Nebraska Press, 2005). For more information about whale hunting, see Robert Sullivan, *A Whale Hunt: How a Native-American Village Did What No One Thought It Could* (New York: Scribner, 2002). See also Makah Tribe, "Whaling: A Gift from the Sea," ww.makah.com/whaling.htm; and "A Makah Elder Denounces Her Tribe's Whale Hunt," www.hsus.org/marine_mammals/what _are_the_issues/whaling/makah_the_tribe_who_would_be_whalers/a_makah _elder_denounces _her_tribes_whale_hunt.html.

For the Plateau region, see Robert Thomas Boyd, *People of the Dalles: The Indians of Wascopam Mission: A Historical Ethnography Based on the Papers of the Methodist Missionaries* (Lincoln: University of Nebraska Press in cooperation with the American Indian Studies Research Institute, Indiana University, Bloomington, 1996); Alvin M. Josephy, Jr., *The Nez Perce Indians and the Opening of the Northwest* (New Haven, CT: Yale University Press, 1965); Alexander Gunkel, "Culture in Conflict: A Study of Contrasted Interrelations and Reactions between Euroamericans and the Wallawalla Indians of Washington State" (Thesis, Southern Illinois University, Carbondale, 1980). See also the following by Robert H. Ruby and John A. Brown: *The Cayuse Indians* (Norman: University of Oklahoma Press, 1972), *The Chinook Indians: Traders of the Lower Columbia River* (Norman: University of Oklahoma Press, 1976), and *Indian Slavery in the Pacific Northwest* (Spokane, WA: Arthur H. Clark, 1993). See also Donald M. Hines, *Ghost Voices: Yakima Indian Myths, Legends, Humor and Hunting Stories* (Issaqua, WA: Great Eagle Publishing, 1992); Stephen Dow Beckham, *The Indians of Western Oregon: This Land Was Theirs* (Coos Bay, OR: Arago Books, 1977); Robert Bigart and Clarence Woodcock, *In the Name of the Salish and Kootenai Nation: The 1855 Hell Gate Treaty and the Origin of the Flathead Indian Reservation* (Pablo, MT: Salish Kootenai College Press, 1996); Joseph Cone, *A Common Fate: Endangered Salmon and the People of the Pacific Northwest* (Corvallis: Oregon State University Press, 1995); William Dietrich, *Northwest Passage: The Great Columbia River* (Seattle: University of Washington Press, 1995); Ivan Donaldson and Frederick Cramer, *Fishwheels of the Columbia* (Portland, OR: Binfords and Mort, 1971); Donald Hines, *The Forgotten Tribes: Oral Tales of the Teninos and Adjacent Mid-Columbia River Indian Nations* (Issaquah, WA: Great Eagle Publishing, 1991); Dan Landeen and Allen Pickham, *Salmon and His People: Fish and Fishing in Nez Perce Culture* (Lewiston, ID: Confluence Press, 1999); Robert Ruby and John Brown, *Indians of the Pacific Northwest* (Norman: University of Oklahoma Press, 1981); Courtland Smith, *Salmon Fishers of the Columbia* (Corvallis: Oregon State University Press, 1979); Emory Strong, *Stone Age on the Columbia River* (Portland, OR: Binfords and Mort, 1959); and, of course, Deward Walker, ed., *Handbook of North American Indians: Plateau*, vol. 12 (Washington, D.C.: Smithsonian Institution, 1998).

For the Great Basin, see Donald K. Grayson, *The Desert's Past: A Natural Prehistory of the Great Basin* (Washington, D.C.: Smithsonian Institution Press, 1993); Grace Dangberg, *Washo Tales: Three Original Washo Indian Legends* (Carson City: Nevada State Museum, 1968); Warren L. d'Azevedo, *Straight with the Medicine: Narratives of Washoe Followers of the Tipi Way* (Berkeley, CA: Heyday Books, 1985); Emory Strong, *Stone Age in the Great Basin* (Portland, OR: Binford and Mort Publishing, 1969); Emory Strong, *Stone Age on the Columbia River* (Portland, OR: Binford and Mort Publishing, 1959); Ruth Underhill, *The Northern Paiute Indians of California and Nevada* (Washington, D.C.: U.S. Office of Indian Affairs, 1941); Margaret M. Wheat, *Survival Arts of the Primitive Paiutes* (Las Vegas: University of Nevada Press, 1967); Larry Dalrymple, *Indian Basketmakers of California and the Great Basin and Indian Basketmakers of the Southwest* (Santa Fe: Museum of New Mexico Press, 2000); Virginia McConnell Simmons, *The Ute Indians of Utah, Colorado, and New Mexico* (Niwot: University Press of Colorado, 2001); Omer C. Stewart, *The Northern Paiute Bands* (Berkeley: University of California Press, 1939); Julian H. Steward and Erminie Wheeler-Voegelin, *The Northern Paiute Indians* (New York: Garland Publishing, 1974); Ruth Murray Underhill, *The Northern Paiute Indians of California and Nevada,* William W. Beatty, ed. (Washington, D.C.: Education Division, U.S. Office of Indian Affairs, 1941); Catherine S. Fowler, *In the Shadow of Fox Peak: An Ethnography of the Cattail-eater Northern Paiute People of Stillwater Marsh* (Fallon: Nevada Humanities Committee, 1992); Forrest S. Cuch, ed., *A History of Utah's American Indians* (Salt Lake City: Utah State Division of Indian Affairs, Utah State Division of History, 2000); Thomas E. Sheridan and Nancy J. Parezo, *Paths of Life: American Indians of the Southwest and Northern Mexico* (Tucson: University of Arizona Press, 1996); and, of course, Warren L. d'Azevedo, ed., *Handbook of North American Indians: Great Basin,* vol. 11 (Washington, D.C.: Smithsonian Institution, 1986).

For the Southwest, perhaps the best source for the earliest years are the two volumes edited by Alfonso Ortiz, *Southwest,* vols. 9 and 10, of the *Handbook of North American Indians* (Washington, D.C.: Smithsonian Institution, 1979 and 1983). In particular, for specific detailed discussion about the difference between Eastern and Western Anasazi, see Fred Plog, "Prehistory: Western Anasazi," and Linda S. Cordell, "Prehistory: Eastern Anasazi," in volume 9; for a description of the Navajo, see David M. Brugge, "Navajo Prehistory and History to 1850," in Alfonso Ortiz, ed., *Southwest,* vol. 10 of the *Handbook of North American Indians* (Washington, D.C.: Smithsonian Institution, 1983); Bunny Fontana, "Pima and Papago: Introduction," *Handbook of North American Indians,* vol. 10 (Washington, D.C.: Smithsonian Institution, 1983); Douglas W. Schwartz, "Havasupai," in Alfonso Ortiz, ed., *Southwest,* vol. 10 of the *Handbook of North American Indians* (Washington, D.C.: Smithsonian Institution, 1983): 13–24. See also Robert H. Lister, *Those Who Came Before: Southwestern Archaeology in the National Park System,* 2nd rev. ed (Tucson, AZ: Southwest Parks & Monuments Association, 1993); Adolph Francis Alphonse Bandelier, *The Delight Makers: A Novel of Prehistoric Pueblo Peoples* (New York: Harvest/HBJ Book, 1971); Linda S. Cordell and George J. Gumerman, *Dynamics of Southwestern Prehistory* (Washington, D.C.: School of American Research, 1989); Alfred V. Kidder, *Introduction to the Study of Southwestern Archaeology, with a Preliminary Account of the Excavations at Pecos* (Andover, MA: Department of Archaeology, Phillips Academy, 1924); Patricia L. Crown and W. James Judge, eds., *Chaco and Hohokam: Prehistoric Regional Systems in the American Southwest* (Santa Fe, NM:

School of American Research Press, 1991); Charles C. DiPeso, *Casas Grandes: A Fallen Trading Center of the Gran Chichimeca,* Amerind Foundation, Series 9 (Flagstaff, AZ: Amerind Foundation Inc.; Northland Press, 1974); Anne I. Woosley and John C. Ravesloot, eds., *Culture and Contact: Charles C. DiPeso's Gran Chichimeca* (Albuquerque: University of New Mexico Press, 1993); Jonathon Ericson and Timothy G. Baugh, *The American Southwest and Mesoamerica: Systems of Prehistoric Exchange* (New York: Plenum Press, 1993); David Kayser and Charles Carroll, *Archaeological Investigations in West Central New Mexico,* vol. 3, Report of the Final Field Season, Cultural Resource Series No. 5, (Santa Fe: New Mexico Bureau of Land Management, 1988); Carroll Riley, *Sixteenth Century Trade in the Greater Southwest* (Carbondale: Southern Illinois University Press, 1986); David Wilcox and W. Bruce Masse, eds., *The Protohistoric Period in the American Southwest AD 1450–1700,* Anthropological Research Papers, No. 24 (Flagstaff: Arizona State University, 1981); Steadman Upham, *Polities and Power: An Economic and Political History of the Western Pueblo* (New York: Academic Press, 1982); and Timothy K. Earle and Jonathon E. Ericson, *Exchange Systems in Prehistory* (New York: Academic Press, 1977). For a discussion about the false claims of renowned Southwest archaeologist Frank Hibben of Sandia Cave, see Douglas Preston, "The Mystery of Sandia Cave," *New Yorker* vol. 71, no. 16 (June 12, 1995): 66–83; and Tony Baker, "The Elephant in the Parlor: Another Story of Sandia Cave" (May 1, 2005) as found on www.ele.net/sandia_cave /elephant.htm.

For a general overview of the Southwest, see John L. Kessell, *Spain in the Southwest: A Narrative History of Colonial New Mexico, Arizona, Texas, and California* (Norman: University of Oklahoma Press, 2002), and David J. Weber, *The Spanish Frontier in North America* (New Haven, CT: Yale University Press, 1994). See also the books by the "father" of the Spanish Borderlands, Herbert Eugene Bolton: *Anza's California Expeditions* (Berkeley: University of California Press, 1930); *Coronado, Knight of Pueblos and Plains* (Albuquerque: University of New Mexico Press, 1990) with an introduction by John L. Kessell; *Fray Juan Crespí, Missionary Explorer on the Pacific Coast, 1769–1774* (New York: AMS Press, 1971); *The Hasinais, Southern Caddoans as Seen by the Earliest Europeans,* edited and with an introduction by Russell M. Magnaghi (Norman: University of Oklahoma Press, 1987); *An Outpost of Empire: The Story of the Founding of San Francisco* (New York: Knopf, 1931); *The Padre on Horseback: A Sketch of Eusebio Francisco Kino, S.J., Apostle to the Pimas* (San Francisco: Sonora Press, 1932); *Pageant in the Wilderness: The Story of the Escalante Expedition to the Interior Basin, 1776, Including the Diary and Itinerary of Father Escalante,* translated and annotated by Herbert E. Bolton (Salt Lake City: Utah State Historical Society, 1950); *Kino's Historical Memoir of Pimería Alta; A Contemporary Account of the Beginnings of California, Sonora, and Arizona, by Father Eusebio Francisco Kino, S. J., Pioneer Missionary Explorer, Cartographer, and Ranchman,*

1683–1711, edited and annotated by Herbert E. Bolton (Cleveland: The Arthur H. Clark Company, 1919). Other resources from Bolton include Herbert E. Bolton and Ephraim D. Adams, *California's Story* (Boston: Allyn and Bacon, 1922), and Herbert Eugene Bolton and Thomas Maitland Marshall, *The Colonization of North America, 1492–1783* (New York: Macmillan, 1920). For a look into the spirituality, cosmology, and history of the Navajo, see Paul G. Zolbrod, trans., *Diné Bahané: The Navajo Creation Story* (Albuquerque: University of New Mexico Press, 1988); Marcia Keegan, *Mother Earth, Father Sky: Pueblo and Navajo Indians of the Southwest* (Santa Fe, NM: Clear Light Books, 1989); John Adair, *The Navajo and Pueblo Silversmiths,* Civilization of the American Indian Series (Norman: University of Oklahoma Press, 1989); Peter J. Iverson, *Dine: A History of the Navajos* (Albuquerque: University of New Mexico Press, 2002); Jennifer Nez Denetdale, *The Navajos* (New York: Chelsea House Publications, 2005). For information on religion, society, and culture of Pueblo Indians, a variety of sources are available: Leslie Marmon Silko, *Ceremony* (New York: Penguin Press, 1986) and *Yellow Woman and a Beauty of the Spirit* (New York: Simon and Schuster Adult Publishing Group, 1997); Elsie Clews M. Parsons, *Pueblo Indian Religion,* vols. I and II (Chicago: University of Chicago Press, 1939); Elsie Clews M. Parsons, *Tewa Tales* (New York: American Folk-Lore Society, 1926); Elsie Clews M. Parsons, *Taos Tales* (New York: American Folk-Lore Society, 1940); Alfonso Ortiz, *Tewa World: Space, Time, Being, and Becoming in a Pueblo Society* (Chicago: University of Chicago Press, 1972); Edward P. Dozier, *Pueblo Indians of North America* (Long Grove, IL: Waveland Press, 1983); Joe S. Sando, *Pueblo Nations: Eight Centuries of Pueblo Indian History* (Santa Fe, NM: Clear Light Books, 1992); Kathryn Kamp, *Life in the Pueblo: Understanding the Past through Archaeology* (Long Grove, IL: Waveland Press, 1997); Virginia More Roediger, *Ceremonial Costumes of the Pueblo Indians: Their Evolution, Fabrication, and Significance in the Prayer Drama* (Berkeley: University of California Press, 1991); Thomas Mails, *Dancing in the Paths of the Ancestors: The Culture, Crafts, and Ceremonies of the Hopi, Zuni, Acoma, Laguna, and Rio Grande Pueblo Indians of Yesterday and Today* (New York: Marlowe & Company, 1993) and *The Pueblo Children of the Earth Mother* (New York: Marlow & Company, 1983); Frank Waters, *The Book of the Hopi* (New York: Penguin, 1977).

For the Apache, see the following works by H. Henrietta Stockel: *Chiricahua Apache Women and Children: Safekeepers of the Heritage,* Elma Dill Russell Spencer Series in the West and Southwest, No. 21 (College Station: Texas A&M University Press, 2000); *Women of the Apache Nation: Voices of Truth* (Las Vegas: University of Nevada Press, 1991); *The Lightning Stick: Arrows, Wounds, and Indian Legends* (Las Vegas: University of Nevada Press, 1995); and *On the Bloody Road to Jesus: Christianity and the Chiricahua Apaches* (Albuquerque: University of New Mexico Press, 2004). See also Frank Cummins Lockwood, *The Apache Indians* (Lincoln: University of Nebraska Press, 1938); James L. Haley, *Apaches:*

A History and Culture Portrait (Norman: University of Oklahoma Press, 1997); Donald Emmet Worcester, *The Apaches: Eagles of the Southwest* (Norman: University of Oklahoma Press, 1979); Keith H. Basso, *Wisdom Sits in Places: Landscape and Language among the Western Apache* (Albuquerque: University of New Mexico Press, 1996); and Albert H. Schroeder, *A Study of the Apache Indians* (New York: Garland Publishing, 1974).

For the Southern Plains, see Thomas W. Kavanagh, *The Comanches: A History, 1706–1875* (Lincoln: University of Nebraska Press, 1996) and *Comanche Political History: An Ethnohistorical Perspective, 1706–1875* (Lincoln: University of Nebraska Press, 1995); Gerald Betty, *Comanche Society before the Reservation* (College Station: Texas A&M Press, 2002); Charles L. Kenner, *The Comanchero Frontier: A History of New Mexican-Plains Indian Relations* (1969, reprint, Norman: University of Oklahoma Press, 1994); Stanley Noyes, *Los Comanches: The Horse People, 1751–1845* (Albuquerque: University of New Mexico Press, 1993); Morris W. Foster, *Being Comanche: A Social History of an American Indian Community* (Tucson: University of Arizona Press, 1991); William T. Hagan, *United States-Comanche Relations: The Reservation Years* (Norman: University of Oklahoma Press, 1990); Rupert N. Richardson, *The Comanche Barrier to South Plains Settlement* (1933, reprint, Millwood, NY: Kraus, 1973); Ernest Wallace and E. Adamson Hoebel, *The Comanches* (Norman: University of Oklahoma Press, 1952); Vynola Beaver Newkumet and Howard L. Meredith, *Hasinai: A Traditional History of the Caddo Confederacy* (College Station: Texas A&M University Press, 1988); and Timothy K. Perttula, *The Caddo Nation: Archaeological and Ethnohistoric Perspective* (Austin: University of Texas Press, 1992).

For the Northern Plains, see Karl H. Schlesier, ed., *Plains Indians, CE 500–1500: The Archaeological Past of Historical Groups* (Norman: University of Oklahoma Press, 1994); Frank R. Secoy, *Changing Military Patterns of the Great Plains Indians* (Lincoln: University of Nebraska Press, 1992); David J. Wishart, ed., *Encyclopedia of the Great Plains Indians* (Lincoln: Bison Books, 2007); and David J. Wishart, *An Unspeakable Sadness: The Dispossession of the Nebraska Indians* (Lincoln: University of Nebraska Press, 1994). See also Kelly F. Himmel, *The Conquest of the Karankawas and the Tonkawas, 1821–1859,* Elma Dill Russell Spencer Series in the West and Southwest, No. 20 (College Station: Texas A&M University Press, 1999); William E. Unrau, *The Kansa Indians: A History of the Wind People, 1673–1873* (Norman: University of Oklahoma Press, 1998); Raymond W. Wood, *Archaeology on the Great Plains* (Lawrence: University Press of Kansas, 1998); Judith A. Boughter, *Betraying the Omaha Nation, 1790–1916* (Norman: University of Oklahoma Press, 1998); George C. Frison, *Prehistoric Hunters of the High Plains,* 2nd ed. (San Diego: Academic Press, 1991); John J. Mathews, *The Osages: Children of the Middle Waters* (Norman: University of Oklahoma Press, 1961); Willard H. Rollings, *The Osage: An Ethnohistorical Study of Hegemony on the Prairie-Plains* (Columbia: University of Missouri Press, 1992);

Howard Meredith, *Dancing on Common Ground: Tribal Cultures and Alliances on the Southern Plains* (Lawrence: University Press of Kansas, 1995); Roy W. Meyer, *The Village Indians of the Upper Missouri* (Lincoln: University of Nebraska Press, 1977); John S. Milloy, *The Plains Cree: Trade, Diplomacy and War, 1790 to 1870* (Winnipeg: University of Manitoba Press, 1988); John H. Moore, *The Cheyenne* (Cambridge, MA: Basil Blackwell, 1996) and *The Cheyenne Nation: A Social and Demographic History* (Lincoln: University of Nebraska Press, 1987); John Miller Morris, *El Llano Estacado: Exploration and Imagination on the High Plains of Texas and New Mexico, 1536–1860* (Austin: Texas State Historical Association, 1997); Alice C. Fletcher and Francis La Flesche, *The Omaha Tribe*, vols. 1 and 2 (Lincoln, NE: Bison Books, 1972); John M. O'Shea and John Ludwickson, *Archaeology and Ethnohistory of the Omaha Indians: The Big Village Site* (Lincoln: University of Nebraska Press, 1992); George Hyde, *The Pawnee Indians* (Norman: University of Oklahoma Press, 1988); George Bird Grinnell, *Pawnee Hero Stories and Folk-Tales* (Honolulu: University Press of the Pacific, 2003); George A. Dorsey, *The Pawnee: Mythology* (Honolulu: University Press of the Pacific, 2003); W. Raymond Wood and Thomas D. Thiessen, eds., *Early Fur Trade on the Northern Plains: Canadian Traders among the Mandan and Hidatsa Indians, 1738–1818, The Narratives of David Thompson, John Macdonell, Charles W. McKenzie, Francois-Antoine Larocque* (Norman: University of Oklahoma Press, 1999); Roy Willard Meyer, *The Village Indians of the Upper Missouri: The Mandans, Hidatsas, and Arikaras* (Lincoln: University of Nebraska Press, 1977); Alfred W. Bowers, *Mandan Social and Ceremonial Organization* (Lincoln, NE: Bison Books, 2004); Tracy Potter, *Sheheke, Mandan Indian Diplomat: The Story of White Coyote, Thomas Jefferson, and Lewis and Clark* (Helena, MT: Farcountry Press, 2003); Virginia Cole Trenholm, *The Arapahoes, Our People* (Norman: University of Oklahoma Press, 1986); George A. Dorsey and A. L. Kroeber, *Traditions of the Arapaho* (Lincoln: University of Nebraska Press, 1997); Virginia Bergman Peters, *Women of the Earth Lodges: Tribal Life on the Plains* (Norman: University of Oklahoma Press, 2000); Frank B. Linderman, *Pretty-Shield, Medicine Woman of the Crow* (Lincoln, NE: Bison Books, 1974) and *Plenty-Coup: Chief of the Crow* (Lincoln, NE: Bison Books, 2002); Robert H. Lowie, *Indians of the Plains* (Lincoln: University of Nebraska Press, 1982); James Earl Sherow, ed., *Sense of the American West: An Environmental History Anthology* (Albuquerque: University of New Mexico Press, 1998); Hugh A. Dempsey, *The Vengeful Wife and Other Blackfoot Stories* (Norman: University of Oklahoma Press, 2006); George Bird Grinnell, "Some Early Cheyenne Tales," *Journal of American Folk-Lore*, vol. 20, no. 78 (July-September 1907); George Bird Grinnell, *The Cheyenne Indians, Their History and Ways of Life* (New Haven, CT: Yale University Press, 1924); and, of course, Raymond DeMallie, ed., *Handbook of North American Indians: Plains*, parts 1 and 2, vol. 13 (Washington, D.C.: Smithsonian Institution, 2001). Finally, for a description of the White Buffalo Calf

Woman of the Plains, see Arvol Looking Horse, *White Buffalo Teachings from Chief Arvol Looking Horse, 19th Generation Keeper of the Sacred White Buffalo Pipe of the Lakota, Dakota & Nakota Great Sioux Nation* (Williamsburg, MA: Dreamkeepers Press, 2001). For an excellent reference on the southern Plains, see "The Handbook of Texas Online" at www.tsha.utexas.edu/handbook/online /articles/CC/bmc72.html).

For California in particular, see Barry M. Pritzker, "California," *A Native American Encyclopedia: History Culture, and People* (Oxford: Oxford University Press, 2000); Robert F. Heizer, ed., *California Handbook of North American Indians*, vol. 8 (Washington, D.C.: Smithsonian Institution, 1978); Barry T. Klein, *Reference Encyclopedia of the American Indian*, 7th ed. (West Nyack, NY: Todd Publications, 1995); Albert L. Hurtado, *Indian Survival on the California Frontier* (New Haven, CT: Yale University Press, 1988); James A. Sandos, *Converting California: Indians and Franciscans in the Missions* (New Haven, CT: Yale University Press, 2004); Fernando Librado, *The Eye of the Flute: Chumash Traditional History and Ritual as Told by Fernando Librado Kitsepawit to John P. Harrington*, edited with notes by Travis Hudson and illustrated by Campbell Grant (Banning, CA: Malki Museum Press, 1981); George Harwood Phillips, *Indians and Intruders in Central California, 1769–1849* (Norman: University of Oklahoma Press, 1993); Sigismundo Taraval, *The Indian Uprising in Lower California, 1734–1737*, translated by Marguerite Eyer Wilbur (Los Angeles: Quivira Society, 1931); Rose Marie Beebe and Robert M. Senkewicz, eds., *Lands of Promise and Despair: Chronicles of Early California, 1535–1846* (Berkeley, CA: Heyday Books, 2001); Doyce B. Nunis, Jr., ed., *The Letters of Jacob Baegert 1749–1761: Jesuit Missionary in Baja California*, translated by Elsbeth Schulz-Bischof (Los Angeles: Dawson's Book Shop, 1982); Robert Fleming Heizer and Albert B. Elsasser, *The Natural World of the California Indians* (Berkeley: University of California Press, 1980); Daniel Fogel, *Junípero Serra, the Vatican & Enslavement Theology* (San Francisco: Ism Press, 1988); James A. Bennyhoff and Richard E. Hughes, *Shell Bead and Ornament Exchange Networks Between California and the Western Great Basin* (New York: American Museum of Natural History, 1987); Byron Nelson, Jr., *Our Home Forever: The Hupa Indians of Northern California*, edited by Laura Bayer (Salt Lake City: Howe Bros., 1988); A. L. Kroeber, *Handbook of the Indians of California* (New York: Dover, 1976); Report of Bulletin 78 of the Bureau of American Ethnology of the Smithsonian Institution, (Washington, D.C.: Government Printing Office, 1925); Sarah Supahan, *A Time of Resistance: California Indians During the Mission Period, 1769–1848* (Hoopa, CA: Klamath-Trinity Joint Unified School District's Indian Education Program, 1997); Bruce Walter Barton, *The Tree at the Center of the World: A Story of the California Missions* (Santa Barbara, CA: Ross-Erikson Publishers, 1980); and Virginia Marie Bouvier, *Women and the Conquest of California, 1542–1840: Codes of Silence* (Tucson: University of Arizona Press, 2001); Phillip L. Walker, Patricia

Lambert, and Michael J. DeNiro, "The Effects of European Contact on the Health of Alta California Indians," as found in David Hurst Thomas, ed., *Columbian Consequences,* vol. 1, *Archaeological and Historical Perspectives on the Spanish Borderlands West* (Washington, D.C.: Smithsonian Institution Press, 1989): 349–364. Finally, see a rather dated but still useful bibliography, Robert F. Heizer, *The Indians of California: A Critical Bibliography* (Bloomington: Indiana University Press, 1976).

Chapter Two

THE RIO
GRANDE VALLEY
AND BEYOND

The Indian world would not continue to survive in a global vacuum. The world across the ocean to America's east had developed into monarchical patterns and embraced a strong expansionist doctrine. Stronger sovereigns began to exert their dominance regionally over weaker sovereigns who could not withstand the emerging powers. It was only a matter of time before the emerging power sought out new worlds to conquer.

In 1492, the Spanish became the first of the Europeans to permanently burst onto the scene in the Americas. In an attempt to find a quicker passage to the Orient by sailing west, Spanish ships happened upon the islands of the Caribbean. Spanish interaction among the Caribbean people became strained when their hopes were dashed of finding a quick trade route to the west and to the wealth of East Asia. They became frustrated. To make matters worse for the local populations, the arrival of the Spanish brought European diseases for which the natives had no immunity, and the decimation of local native populations began. While the Spanish were not *uniquely* cruel in their subjugation of the Indian people as the Black Legend asserted, their attitudes and actions exemplified cultural misunderstandings of astronomical proportions.

Yet Indians throughout regions that would eventually become actively occupied and claimed by the Spanish learned how to adapt. In Spanish-held territories, many native peoples learned the Spanish language and used the Spanish legal system to their benefit with the

Slaves captured at Cumana (present-day Venezuela) on a forced march by the Spaniards. Engraving by Theodor de Bry, 1590s. (Corbis)

BLACK LEGEND

Unwittingly begun by soldier turned religious missionary Bartolomé de las Casas in the 1500s, the Black Legend has had a lasting impact on not only how the world has viewed Spanish conquest in the Americas, but also on how many continue (even today) to view Hispanos throughout the world. In his report to the crown on the subjugation of the indigenous peoples in the Caribbean, Las Casas reported vividly from having witnessed with his own eyes the awful devastation Spanish soldiers brought to Indian communities. When the sailors did not find the gold their captains had promised them when they signed up for the voyage, they took their frustrations out on the local populations. To make matters worse, the Indians refused to convert and periodically rose up against the Spanish invaders, even refusing to become slaves. The frustration of the soldiers manifested itself in many ways: sword blows, attacks by Spanish greyhounds and mastiffs, erection of gallows, and the hanging of a dozen people at a time. Spaniards also lashed the natives to poles and set fires at their feet, causing them to burn alive. They tore babies from the breasts of their mothers and smashed their heads against rocks, and constructed frames and burned the *caciques* (leaders) until they were dead. When Las Casas wrote about these horrors to the king, he respectfully demanded that the king do something to ameliorate the situation. This was not a Christian way of behaving, nor did it bring many new converts to the Catholic faith. By 1550, the king halted all colonization and exploration in the New World and held a trial at Valladolid to determine the status of these new vassals of the Spanish crown. Las Casas's report was translated into many other languages in the 16th century, and the English turned it into a heralding cry that the Spanish were uniquely cruel in their conquest of the New World. While the report indeed was accurate, it described only the first few years of encounters between Indian and Spaniard. It was not indicative of the continued "pacification" of Indian peoples for the next 400 years. But the mentality that all Spanish behaved in this same fashion during the next 250 years of conquest at every encounter with natives stuck. Even today in history classes, students almost always perceive the Spanish as cruel and deadly, where they see the French as kind and the English as interacting benevolently with the Indians (such as at Jamestown—never mind that the English spent the next several years attempting to eradicate the Wampanoags who had helped them survive that first winter).

assistance of Spanish *protectores de indios.* An official position held by Las Casas and many others throughout the Spanish empire, the protector served as a liaison and defender of Indian peoples and communities in the Spanish empire. Even with an advocate, it would take years of interaction and lessons learned the hard way before Indians truly came to understand what these newcomers intended to do with their traditional lands and their people, and even more years to learn how to combat those efforts—even to work within its system to maintain whatever control they could. After all, Spain had come to the Americas with the baggage of the more than 700 years of Muslim occupation of their homelands—the Iberian Peninsula (711–1492)—out of which they united as a people, established an attitude of religious superiority, created ideologies and institutions for conquest and then pacification, and then used that experience to guide their mission of expanding the *Reconquista* into the Americas for 700 years.

The Spanish had learned to live as an occupied people, finding ways of surviving within a system that forced them to convert to a religion that was not their own or pay a "tax" for not converting. They had to learn how to work within the system imposed by a foreign nation, one whose people had a different language and darker skin than their own, to survive as a cohesive and culturally distinct people—as much as they could. Cultural miscegenation and political marriages played a role in that adaptation and survival. Over those 700 years, previously independent individual kingdoms had become frustrated throughout the Iberian Peninsula, insurrections rose, and leaders worked together, albeit with many difficulties, to demand their homeland, their religion, and their own leadership back. Even though they did succeed in evicting the Moors from their lands, the Muslims did have a great influence on the newly created nations of Spain and Portugal. Each nation's leaders actually adapted some of their technology and ideas, and perhaps fortunately or not, their philosophies of conquest and subjugation. While the Muslim invasion of the Iberian Peninsula may have delayed the development of an independent Spain and Portugal, their influence on Spanish and Portuguese culture should not be underestimated. The Moors were great students of the world and excelled at math, literature, science, and architecture. Their architectural accomplishments and designs are still heralded as exquisite, unique, artistic, timeless, and masterful. While the Spanish did adopt aspects of North African culture, architecture, science, and political systems, both the Spanish and Portuguese kingdoms of the Iberian Peninsula negotiated alliances with their neighboring kingdoms to root out the Muslim "menace" on Christian Iberia, starting in northeastern

Spain and eventually moving east and south. They succeeded by the end of the 15th century when the city of Granada finally fell in 1492.

The man who would become Prince Henry of Portugal (1394–1460) fought in the campaign to remove the Moors throughout the evolving Portuguese empire. He later oversaw the expansion of Portuguese influence in the eastern Atlantic Ocean as early as 1418 by sending his ships south along the African coastline. Under Prince Henry the Navigator, as he came to be known, the Portuguese became the most modern seafaring nation in Europe in the 15th century. They studied, understood, and charted the winds and currents off the coast of western Iberia, West Africa, and the Madeiras, Canaries, and Azores islands. After tearing down the forests on the Madeiras, they seized men and women from Africa to work as slaves in the newly established sugar plantations on the recently claimed Portuguese islands. Their wealth grew as they traded in ivory and gold from sub-Saharan Africa. They even brought African slaves to Europe and sold them to supplement their wealth, becoming one of the key players in the international slave trade of Africans and what would later become the largest forced migration in world history.

The Portuguese expanded ocean travel by creating maps of trade winds and currents; designing caravels (smaller ships) with triangular lateen sails, which they had borrowed from the Arab ships; improving navigational instruments, such as the sextant; and introducing navigation by the stars with astronomical instruments. In fact, in 1480 Prince Henry ordered his astronomers to measure latitude and the altitude of the sun, taking into consideration the seasonal declination (location of true north). This was truly a significant improvement in navigation on the high seas, and his methods of navigation proved key to the success of future generations of European explorers.

Perhaps as importantly, the Portuguese opened a new chapter in European subjugation of other peoples determined to be "lesser" than Europeans based on old arguments reaching back as far as St. Thomas Aquinas, and even Aristotle. Certainly, they believed God had designed some of humanity to serve others, and they believed skin color and the inability of native peoples to fight off subjugation and diseases (such as influenza and the common cold) was a testament to that fact. The idea of hereditary slavery was well entrenched in Europe by the time Europeans set foot in the Americas. But Indians in the Americas posed a different problem because they had never been exposed to Christianity, and therefore, they fell into an unknown category. Should one try to convert them, or should they be immediately enslaved because they were non-Christian and therefore heathen? Even though their skin was a darker color, some of the native peoples did seem inclined toward Christianity and, according to Christian doctrine, one could not enslave a fellow Christian. This argument about what status the Indian would have in a European-modeled world would be debated most acutely in the 1550s in Spain after the eradication of Indians on some of the islands in the Caribbean due to disease, warfare, and protracted and oftentimes abusive enslavement.

SPAIN AND THE "NEW WORLD"

Spain's advent in the New World came after its Portuguese rivals succeeded in initiating a sea trade route to India by rounding the tip of the Cape of Good Hope in southern Africa in 1497–1499 and returning with a ship laden with silk and spices from the Far East. In 1492, the Spanish had just conquered the last remaining outpost of Muslims in Granada in the name of the Christian God whom they believed had blessed their armies, making them successful in the reconquest of Spain. The legend of Santiago (St. James, the patron saint of Spain), or Santiago Matamoros (St. James, Moor Slayer), is disputed by historians, but it generally states that Santiago appeared and rallied the troops in 844 in the northeast of Spain to lead Spaniards on to victory against the "infidels." In an attempt to return to Roman Catholicism, King Fernando and Queen Isabel imposed Catholic orthodoxy upon the newly united Kingdom of Spain and forced non-Christians to either convert or leave Spain. Many Muslims left Spain, as did more than 150,000 Jews, while others remained behind as *conversos* (converts to Christianity). That same year, the crown sponsored the voyage of a navigator and, according to historian John L. Kessell, a mystic from Genoa whose goal was to explore a westward route to the Indies (Kessell, *Spain in the Southwest*, 4).

　　Like most navigators, Christopher Columbus (Cristóbal Colón) understood that the world was round, but he significantly underestimated the distance from Europe to Asia by sea. Based on the most current car-

Christopher Columbus bids farewell to the king and queen of Spain in this 17th-century illustration from Nova Typis Transacta Navigatio. *(Library of Congress)*

tographic knowledge, when the first sailors saw land, they assumed it was *Cipangu* (Japan) and the Spice Islands. Making landfall at San Salvador in the Bahamas, Columbus reported that the inhabitants wore golden rings in their noses. While the Black Legend insists that the Spaniards pilfered the New World for any riches they could find, Columbus was more interested in the long-term goal of finding Cipangu and not bothering with the plunder of a few gold trinkets from a nearly naked people. They had their eyes set on something much larger—opening trade with the Orient. Therefore, instead, they continued to search the Caribbean for Cipangu and the Spice Islands. Columbus's encounter with these new lands influenced a major shift of interest and intrigue in the European world.

As a result of Columbus encountering the Americas, it became apparent that land claims and claims "by right of discovery" could become problematic. A direct route overseas would cause Arab merchants, who had traditionally benefited from the overland trade to the Orient, to lose profit. Furthermore, land disputes would no doubt arise between Portugal, which had explored and begun to profit from Africa, and Spain, which had "found" the Americas. When the magnitude of the land mass became more apparent, it became obvious that Europeans could potentially gain significantly, and to guard against potential battles of territorial claims, the pope issued a decree.

CHRISTOPHER COLUMBUS AND DIVINE PURPOSE

Perhaps what drew the Spanish queen Isabel most to Columbus was his strong Catholic faith. Brilliantly red-haired in his youth, his head had now grayed, but his face periodically flushed red through his still reddish beard. A millenarian at heart, Columbus obsessed over trying to figure out exactly when the Second Coming and the Day of Judgment would occur. Like many others in his day, he believed St. Augustine, who argued that Christ would return during the seventh millenium. Therefore, Columbus postulated, Christ would return in the year 1650, and Armageddon would be upon them. He was not alone; this sense of impending doom appeared throughout Europe.

Columbus had a strong faith, firmly rooted in Catholicism, and he believed unwaveringly that God had chosen him as his "instrument of redemption." It would be revealed to Columbus later that God had indeed ordained him to find the New World. On Columbus's fourth voyage, even as his health had begun to fail him in his early to mid-40s (a ripe old age for the day), he described an apparition that appeared to him on board ship late one night. The heavenly spirit told him that his name would be forever remembered, for he had discovered the Indies, lands given entirely to Columbus to be distributed as he chose. The "keys" to the mighty ocean's barriers that had separated the Americas and Europe, likewise, had been given to Columbus.

Columbus believed God had chosen him to bring about the Christian colonization of the New World and to gather the gold it would yield. In fact, after he lost the ship *Santa Maria* in a storm and was driven aground at what he later named La Navidad, he believed God's hand had led him to that spot as an act of divine intervention. The following days gave him more evidence to that claim, for the natives approached him with a great basket filled with various pieces of gold (plates, ornaments, necklaces, masks). God had indeed blessed Columbus for following his bidding. And on Christmas Day 1499, in a letter embedded with mysticism, he wrote that he would not lose hope because God had spoken to Columbus and consoled him with promises that he would find great wealth in gold within seven years and that God would provide for his every desire. Within three years, God granted Columbus his desires: much gold with which he could use for own use and to help take souls to heaven. All that he found he intended to use to bolster the glory and greatness of Spain, sending report after report back to the Catholic monarchs of his grand successes. His unfinished book of prophecies is filled with astrology, mysticism, and an incredibly complex cosmology. The purpose of the book was simple: God had chosen him as a "divine instrument" to save the world for Christianity before the Second Coming, and the gold he was instrumental in bringing back to his Catholic sovereigns would finance the crusades to recapture the Holy Sepulchre from the infidels. God had also endowed Columbus with great skills in navigation, math, astrology, geometry, and the ability to create new communities that would be added to the realm of God.

Upon Columbus's return in 1493, Pope Alexander VI, the most powerful leader in the Christian world, issued a papal bull that essentially divided the world into two parts based on an imaginary line drawn in the Atlantic. The Treaty of Tordesillas, ratified by Portugal and Spain in 1494, agreed to the provisions of the papal bull: that the pope draw a north-south line in the midst of the Atlantic Ocean, 370 leagues (approximately 960 miles) west of the Cabo Verde Islands (held by Portugal, just off West Africa). Any lands or islands to the east of that line would fall within the realm of the king of Portugal, and those holdings would be Portugal's forevermore. Any lands or islands falling to the west of said line would fall to the king and queen of Spain. The world had been divided in half between two Catholic European superpowers, and the majority of the Americas fell to Spain, as well as the fate of all those who lived within its bounds. Thus, the American Indians were party to the very first treaty regulating American soil yet were not even consulted, or frankly even considered. The extent of their population was not even known—certainly a portent of things to come. The main goal of the Christian conquest of these new worlds coincided with growing challenges to Catholic authority. Frustrations about the purchase of absolution and the expansive power of the pope were embodied later in the Reformation, which officially began when Martin Luther posted his 95 theses on the doors of the Castle Church in Wittenburg in 1517—but had been festering throughout Europe for generations. The papal bull *Inter Caetera* of 1493 explicitly stated that the Catholic King Fernando and Queen Isabel would be charged with expanding their sovereign command throughout the newly found lands and islands (of the Americas), and that they should see to the conversion of all of the inhabitants they found therein. Furthermore, as it was their duty to convert, it was also their duty to protect the newly converted peoples from any dangers. Finally, nothing should deter the Spanish sovereigns from seeing to the sacred duty of bringing this new region and these new converts into the fold of the Catholic Church and the Spanish empire.

With approval from Pope Alexander VI and in agreement with Portuguese King João II, the Spanish set about laying claim to the Americas, converting it to Christendom, searching for the wealth Columbus that had promised existed, and extending the reign of their Catholic monarchs and the pope's domain. Their landfall and attempts at colonization and settlement would forever alter the lives of those people Columbus would call "Indians." With the Spaniards came their tools of survival, their beasts of burden, their families, and all of the necessities, luxuries, and attitudes they could bring from Spain. They also brought weapons, beasts of war, and diseases that could potentially destroy all non-Spaniards they encountered or who challenged them. Therefore, after thousands of years of isolation, the numerous tribes scattered across the Americas would encounter a formidable enemy, a suspect ally, and a harbinger of radical change that would decimate their peoples. They could do little but adapt, retreat, or fight, as they had learned to do for generations with other challengers. But the sides were unbalanced this time.

Unfortunately, the Caribbean tribes saw the worst that the Spanish had to offer: the diseases the Spanish brought wiped out entire communities. Such maladies as smallpox, the common cold, measles, malaria, whooping cough, and influenza were unknown in the Americas before 1492, and an illness that would cause a Spaniard a few days or weeks of discomfort could kill an Indian who had no genetically inherited immunities. The Caribbean Indians whom disease did not kill, sometimes the Spaniards would kill in battle (or out of sheer frustration over the lack of easy wealth in the earliest days of the conquest) during the 1490s and early 1500s during the initial contact period.

Spanish soldiers had been recruited by Columbus to come to the Americas with promises of ready wealth and in their minds the hope of acquiring a noble title for their deeds in the New World. A strictly stratified society based on bloodlines and nobility in Spain provided limited opportunities for advancement for non-nobles, and when commanders promised men wealth and prestige if they would travel to the New World as part of an expedition sanctioned by the king and queen, they expected to find gold available for the taking.

Bartolomé de las Casas described the frustration and outright anger of the Spaniards when they realized that the Indians harbored no sizable stores of silver, gold, or precious metals, nor would they find bars of gold in the streets ripe for the taking. He described how the soldiers took their frustration out on the inhabitants of the Caribbean Island: the Caribs, the Arawaks, the Tainos. (see sidebar on the Black Legend) Their frustrations were sorely misplaced, sadly, yet the native people would continue to pay the cost of Spanish anger.

Why these soldiers acted so violently is difficult to understand, but the suffering felt by the Indian people was unbearable. Las Casas was not the only witness who was appalled at these horrors, but it was his eloquent and honest description of those abuses and demands to change policies toward Indians that eventually shocked the world and started the Black Legend. The king, as well as the Council of the Indies, the "governing board" for the New World, heard his cries and in turn issued new *cédulas* or decrees decrying such ill treatment of the Indians.

One such law, the *Requerimiento,* issued by the Spanish courts in about 1512, required the Spanish conqueror to read to the Indians "conditions" of obedience to the Spanish crown and the Roman Catholic pope, in essence giving the Indians a choice between accepting Spanish authority and the religion of its kings or risking a just war and ensuing enslavement if they lost. Upon hearing about the document that would purportedly end all future misunderstandings between Christian and native, Las Casas reportedly did not know whether to laugh or cry. He knew the Indians would not understand the meaning behind the Spanish words: how they must choose to obey and bow down before a monolithic leader of the political realm they would never see, and how they must relinquish their spiritual understandings for a religion they did not know or understand—or need—which was led by a single man who presided over the religion of many nations. The Spaniards told the Indians they encountered that they should obey the laws and directives ordered from these distant leaders or they would be forced to adhere as required by the Spaniards' duty to spread Catholicism.

Las Casas understood that the American Indians would need an advocate and traveled to Europe on several occasions to press the king and pope for more protections against the enslavement of Indians. Las Casas returned from one trip to personally deliver one such law against Indian slavery to Peru. In 1537, Las Casas persuaded Pope Paul III to issue the papal bull that declared American Indians as rational beings with souls and that the Spanish government should protect their lives and property. Indeed a major accomplishment, this papal bull created the foundation that Las Casas had long sought that would purportedly end Indian slavery and the unjust wars waged against indigenous communities. It also challenged the notion that Indians were subhuman and therefore destined only for servitude. Later Las Casas's arguments convinced King Carlos I to pass the New Laws of Burgos in 1542 outlawing Indian slavery and ending the *encomienda* (a grant of Indian tribute, often abused by its holder) by limiting its hereditary status to only one generation, thus causing the encomienda to be phased out officially (John, *Storms Brewed,* 10–11). Renowned Spanish Borderlands historian John Kessell argued that the New Laws directly challenged the ability of Spanish conquistadors to fill their pockets with the wealth of the Americas. In essence, he continued, the law was intended to control the conquerors and end slavery for Indians.

While this seemed a major gain, the fact that Las Casas continued to press for more protection for Indian people indicates that more infrac-

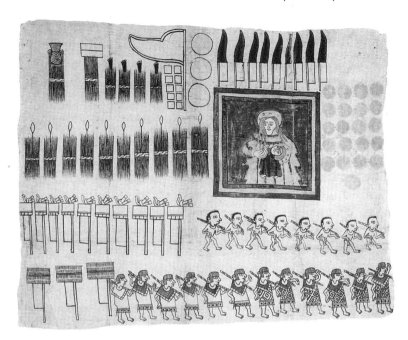

Leaf of Huejotzingo Codex depicting products and services provided as tribute, including a banner of the Madonna and child, 1531. The codex was created by the Nahuatls of Huejotzingo, a town located in the present-day state of Puebla, Mexico. (Library of Congress)

tions continued after the law was put into effect, that individual greed for status (noble title) and wealth was too overwhelming for individual Spanish soldiers, and certainly that the frontier was too remote for the king and the Council of the Indies to control effectively. As a result, the king commissioned the first viceroy to the New World, Antonio de Mendoza, in 1535 to personally and officially represent the interests of the crown. Las Casas wrote a treatise on the history of the Indies and spent 14 years tirelessly defending Indians in Spanish courts in the New World.

By the late 1540s, Las Casas finally had the ear of the king, who in 1550 called for a reprieve to all further colonization and exploration in the colonies to provide time to answer the question Las Casas posed: upon what right did Spain acquire the vassalage of these Indians, forcing them into labor, and giving up their sovereignty and perhaps even their land? Las Casas argued that Indians were human beings, had souls, and possessed the natural rights of liberty and therefore could not be enslaved as the papal bull *Sublimis Deus* stated. In 1550 Las Casas defended Indians in Valladolid, Spain, against the court-appointed opposing view represented by Juan Ginés de Sepúlveda. Sepúlveda argued that while Indians might potentially become Christians, in fact they did not have science, written laws, private property, or any other outward signs of civilized society and that the only way they could be brought to Christianity was through force. , He argued that the Indian was inferior by contrasting the "cultural barbarian" to the "civilized man."

Sepúlveda represented this view to the courts—and it was an interesting position indeed for someone to argue who had never been to the New World and had never seen an Indian in his or her own environment. Even though the crown seemed to side with Las Casas, by the 1520s too many soldiers had become wealthy and gained noble title after splitting the booty of the Inca and Aztec empires; and, as greed is timeless, many Spaniards continued to travel to the Americas primarily for financial gain and noble title. It was impossible to control the individual Spaniard across the ocean in the New World. The king had already had to admonish men such as Hernán Cortés for his illegal and unsanctioned voyage and conquest of the Aztecs. The king feared that nobles, or those aspiring to become nobles, would head to the Americas, ignore the mandates regulating exploration and conquest, and potentially establish their own fiefdoms. Therefore Sepúlveda's philosophy seemed to gain foothold in the Americas even though succeeding kings continued to try to protect Indian rights. Demanding that the laws be enforced was an entirely separate problem.

In an attempt to provide some protection, Las Casas became the protector de indios, whose main task was to defend the Indian people against Spaniards by using the growing body of Spanish law to protect Indian life, liberty, and property. His work had some lasting impact indeed, but it did not protect the Indian people against the growing hubris of Spanish conquerors, soldiers, and settlers. Other men throughout the Spanish empire would follow Las Casas's footsteps, but the damage was done. Eventually, 90 to 100 percent of various Caribbean populations would disappear, mostly because of Spanish diseases, but also at the point of Toledo steel swords.

Spanish conquistadors slaughter Aztecs in this early facsimile of La Historia antigua de la Nueva España, *originally published in 1585. (Library of Congress)*

CABEZA DE VACA'S EXPEDITION AND THE "DISCOVERY" OF NORTHERN NEW SPAIN

Even though the Spanish recognized that they had not discovered a route to Cipangu and the Spice Islands, Spanish expansion throughout the Americas—from north to south—continued into the 1500s. By 1519 the Spanish under the leadership of Cortés had invaded the heartland of the Valley of Mexico, home to the Aztec empire. Two years later he took the Aztec capital in a devastating battle unexpectedly and unintentionally aided by his stealthy yet deadly ally, smallpox, and dominated the region militarily with the ready assistance of the Tlaxcalans (who had previously been conquered by the Aztec empire). The 1520s also saw the expedition of Panfilo de Narváez into Florida; he was charged with seeking a potential location to establish a formal Spanish colony in 1527.

The Narváez expedition set sail from Spain with 600 men and supplies, but the expeditionary forces suffered several calamities before they even arrived at Florida's coastline. After 140 men deserted in Hispaniola and a hurricane nearly wiped out the expedition, they finally made landfall in southern Florida in 1528. The expedition split into two groups, one group of soldiers took horses, armaments, and supplies and began the long trek overland to the north, while a smaller group stayed on board the ships with orders to meet the foot soldiers near what is now Panama City.

Unfortunately the terrain did not lend itself to horses laden with harquebuses, shot, chain mail and coats of armor, shields, swords, and survival gear. Actually the land did not even yield footpaths for the soldiers, but rather bogs, swamps, lakes, alligators, and Calusa Indians who had already had dealings with Spanish slave raiders for the past dozen years and had learned that the Spanish invaders were serious and deadly rivals. The poison-tipped arrows of the Calusa had already claimed the life of Ponce de León at age 47 in 1521 (Kessell, *Spain in the Southwest*, 13). By the time the overland survivors finally reached the beaches of northwestern Florida some six months later, they found themselves besieged by Indians who had grown angry at the hostile infiltration. Every time the ragtag Spanish survivors attempted to go inland from the beach for fresh water, food, or firewood, they met heavy resistance. These wary defenders had already killed more than half of the 400 Spanish soldiers. As the surviving Spaniards camped on the beach to wait for the boats, they found themselves plagued with malaria and dysentery—yet the ships still did not arrive. Becoming desperate, they killed and ate the few horses they had left. They saved the horse hides and, together with the timber they could collect without meeting a hail of arrows, they constructed five barges. They sewed together their shirts and pants for sails and, in their several oddly constructed crafts, headed into the Gulf of Mexico hoping to join up with their fellow countrymen in Veracruz, Mexico. Certainly the Calusa and other Florida tribes had sent yet another message to the Spanish that they would not soon forget. Those tribes whom they would soon encounter along the Gulf Coast, who had no prior knowledge of these white outsiders, would quickly learn about the military (or lack thereof) potential and vulnerabilities of the Spanish.

Álvar Núñez Cabeza de Vaca, the expedition's treasurer, led one of the more fortunate of the five barges and ended up near Galveston, Texas. Cabeza de Vaca reported in his journal the condition in which the local tribes found them on the beach, "And with the great grief and pity they [the Indians] felt on seeing us in such a state, they all began to weep loudly and so sincerely that they could be heard a great distance away"

(Adorno and Pautz, *Álvar Núñez Cabeza de Vaca,* vol. I, 101). The 80 or so Spaniards who had survived the barge voyage to near Galveston diminished to 15 over the course of the first winter in Texas as expedition members died of disease, hunger, cold, drownings, and injuries. Their desperate hunger was so great that some of them even resorted to cannibalism, which shocked the native people—no doubt leading them to see the Spaniards as barbarians (just as the Spanish had perceived the Caribs a generation before). Some Indians, upset either by the intrusion or for some other reason, had killed more of their numbers. By 1534, only three members of the original expedition had survived the harrowing ordeal besides Cabeza de Vaca: Alonso del Castillo Maldonado, Andrés Dorantes de Carranca, and Estevan, Dorante's slave from Azamor, Morocco.

During their hiatus among the Karankawas of the south and south-central Texas coastline, as well as several other tribes of Texas, these Spanish survivors became the first non-Indians to see the American West, buffalo, prairie dogs, and numerous other North American flora and fauna. They also learned key lessons about the healing and nutritional properties of plants in the region that would serve them well. They developed positive interactions with tribes they would encounter in upcoming years. Because they lived with various Texas tribes for a half dozen years, they even learned Indian languages, or portions of them, in order to communicate. Almost as important, they introduced the Texas tribes to Europeans for the first time and taught them the rudiments of Catholicism. No doubt the natives thought that the Spaniards were barbarous, appearing without clothing, starving, and resorting to cannibalism. Yet the Spaniards negotiated their way through their new relationships with these Texas Indians, and at the same time learned a great deal about indigenous survival, culture, healing techniques, tribal spirituality, and intercultural communication.

Cabeza de Vaca marveled at the generosity of the native people and said of them, "These people love their children more and treat them better than any other people in the world" (Adorno and Pautz, *Álvar Núñez Cabeza de Vaca,* vol. I, 109). Cabeza de Vaca learned from them and even became a healer, using a mixture of Christian prayer and native practices. While embracing the cross and repeating chants and prayers, he also used techniques of blowing on the patient, chanting, and dancing that he had copied from the Indians. One day, tribal members called him to the side of an Indian leader who had been shot in the heart with an arrow. Cabeza de Vaca performed surgery and removed the arrow from the man's chest cavity. The tribe delighted in Cabeza de Vaca's ability to tap the power of healing through the spiritual world, and word spread about his ability to work miracles. As the years passed, he gained status in the tribe as a result of his healing capabilities and adaptation to their culture. The tribe allowed him to travel on trading missions to tribes several days away because his status had shifted from menial laborer to honored healer, an indication of the fluidity of status among that particular tribe. Certainly, Cabeza de Vaca also understood that he could move back down to a lower status just as quickly if he failed in his healing abilities.

During those trading journeys, Cabeza de Vaca learned about regional indigenous populations, natural foods and medicines, trade goods, intertribal politics, and even heard about cities 40 days to the north that purportedly possessed great wealth. The Spanish discovered nearly a dozen years later that these cities were the Pueblo Indian villages in and west of the Rio Grande Valley.

But the four Spanish survivors were not content to remain among the Indians forever. They longed to return to their families, friends, and Catholic New Spain. When the four survivors finally mustered enough knowledge, courage, and strength to leave their captors, they did so. They had learned a significant amount about potential allies and trade routes from talking to tribes and traveling themselves, and in the mid 1530s, they broke for freedom—for Spanish civilization—originally hoping to find Pánuco in Nueva España. With the assistance of their Indian guides, they crossed Texas and the Rio Grande, and recrossed the Rio Grande perhaps 75 miles south of El Paso.

These tribal men and women had heard of the great powers of these strangers and not only accompanied them, but also raided villages for food to feed the entourage. During their travels, thousands of Indians from various nations along the route periodically accompanied them, asking for blessings on their food, their children, and themselves. Cabeza de Vaca wrote about the frustration of not getting anything accomplished because of these important obligations. To not fulfill them would be to upset the Indians who accompanied him and provided for him; even more, it would show disrespect for others by not sharing a gift that should be shared. Ignoring his communal responsibility might also lead the native peoples to enslave him once again.

Finally by late spring of 1536, in what is now northern Mexico, they encountered a few Spaniards on horseback engaged in illegally capturing Indian slaves under the auspices of Núño Beltrán de Guzmán. As Cabeza de Vaca remembered, his countrymen "experienced great shock upon seeing me so strangely dressed and in the company of Indians. They remained looking at me a long time, so astonished that they neither spoke to me nor managed to ask me anything. I told them to take me to their captain" (Adorno and Pautz, *Álvar Núñez Cabeza de Vaca,* vol. I, 245–247). Immediately the Spaniards attempted to enslave the 600 Indians (mainly Pima) who had begun to follow Cabeza de Vaca. He refused to allow their captivity and instead urged his companions to return home. The Spanish had already dabbled in slave raiding in what would become the U.S. West, and in Núño de Guzmán's case, had shipped slaves to the Caribbean in exchange for cattle (Kessell, *Spain in the Southwest,* 19–20). After the silver lode was discovered in Zacatecas in the 1540s, Indian slaves (mostly men) would be forced to work in those mines. Therefore, western tribes spread the word about the dangers of engaging with these white men from the south.

Cabeza de Vaca's legacy would be far different than that of any Spaniard for generations. He had taken a great interest in the indigenous cultures he encountered and categorized the culture (clothing, language, food, spiritual and other rituals, housing styles, and migration patterns) of almost two dozen Indian tribes. Besides becoming a recognized healer, Cabeza de Vaca recorded what the Pima Indians had said about him and his fellow travelers in contrast to Guzmán:

> Rather, some talked with others among themselves, saying that the Christians were lying, because we came from where the sun rose, and they from where it set; and that we cured the sick, and that they killed those who were well; and that we came naked and barefoot, and they went about dressed and on horses with lances; and that we did not covet anything but rather, everything they gave us we later returned and remained with nothing, and that the others had no other objective but to steal everything they found and did not give anything to anyone. (Adorno and Pautz, *Álvar Núñez Cabeza de Vaca,* Vol. I, 249–251)

On more than one occasion, Cabeza de Vaca found himself questioning which of the two cultures was the uncivilized one. He watched five of his Spanish colleagues disappear one by one, only to learn that they had cannibalized each other. Even as a devout Catholic, he had adapted and incorporated the healing techniques of the Indian people, adding prayers and well-known Christian chants to his dancing and blowing of smoke on the injured or sick. The more he was paid for his services, the more he began to elaborate on his technique, causing even himself to question his own actions, motivations, and spiritual status. Was he a still a Christian, he wondered, or had he also become a "savage"? And what was a savage anyway, he must have pondered. Cabeza de Vaca warned Viceroy Mendoza of New Spain about the evils of enslaving Indians and, after saving the Pimas from the slave traders, spent the rest of his life speaking on behalf of native rights throughout New Spain. Much like Las Casas, he advocated for the Indians and forced Spanish authorities to improve their attempts at monitoring Spanish treatment of the Indians. Unfortunately for the native inhabitants, the Spanish empire would expand to significantly more far-flung and harder to regulate provinces. Newly arrived or expedition-leading Spaniards would be hard pressed to find quick material gain. After all, most expeditions were proprietary expeditions, and they had to return to their investors that which was due them—and there would be no more Inca or Aztec empires to find.

After Cabeza de Vaca reported to the viceroy in July 1536, he set off a firestorm of interest in those purportedly great trading cities to the north. Within three years, Fray Marcos de Niza headed an expedition into the north with the assistance of the slave Estevan, and what would later be called *la Nueva México* (reference to the new city of Mexico, *la nueva ciudad de México*) to unravel the northern mystery. Niza was a Franciscan friar who had actually accompanied Francisco Pizarro on his exploration and conquest of the Inca empire in the 1530s and had personally witnessed the great wealth of that nation. Therefore, logically, he would not likely get excited over a small store of wealth. The expedition, however, encountered numerous tribes along the path who had previously been harassed by Spanish slavers, and therefore returned the favor—making the journey north more difficult. By the time they arrived in southern Arizona, the Spaniards began to hear rumors of those trading cities again. At the same time, the American Indians in what is now Arizona and New Mexico began to hear reports that strange white men were appearing from the south, and looked very much like the slave raiders who had taken Indians from tribes to their south and west. These captives were never again seen by their families. Impatient by the slow pace of the expedition, Estevan asked for permission to take some of the Tlaxcalan Indian allies ahead to arrive first and prepare the city for Niza's arrival. Niza approved. He later learned that upon nearing the village, Estevan had boldly sent ahead a gourd decorated with jingles and one red and one white feather. One of the headmen of the six villages was enraged because the gourd and decoration were not of his people and angrily warned the intruders to depart. Estevan arrogantly ignored the warning and was captured and placed in a house outside the village. When he attempted to escape captivity, the Zunis killed him. When they were interviewed years later, Zunis reported that Estevan had demanded women and turquoise, and they interpreted him as a threat; a black man representing white men? It had to be a trick, or perhaps he was a spy for the slave hunters like Guzmán farther to the southwest. Not to mention the gourd represented something they did not know and instead they perceived it as a threat, and not as a message of friendship, as perhaps Estevan had assumed it might be interpreted.

When Niza finally did peer over the mesa to view the village, the setting sun turned the stone homes a golden hue. Satisfied, he quickly returned to report to the viceroy in Mexico City that he had found the city, and it was great indeed. He never met the native inhabitants, nor had he walked the streets, yet he elaborated on the wealth that the Indians had within the city's walls. The following year Francisco Vasquez de Coronado acquired the necessary permission from Viceroy Antonio de Mendoza to explore the northern provinces of New Spain. Coronado had to finance the expedition himself with the assistance of investors who expected a payout after Coronado returned. One of those investors was the viceroy himself. Therefore, Coronado's reputation, as well as a great deal of other people's money, was on the line. He had to find wealth to satisfy the investors and his soldiers (who expected to split the booty), as well as explore and claim the unknown north on behalf of the king and pope. Coronado knew that Niza had witnessed the great wealth of the Inca empire and had heard about the sizable riches of the Aztec empire. Certainly, this northern land that Niza raved about would yield an equivalent share to these bold and daring men.

THE CORONADO EXPEDITION

At the same time the Coronado expedition was preparing for the trip north through the mountains and deserts, the Zuni continued on with their lives, celebrating their festivals, planting their corn, and looking forward to cultivating the fruits of their labor. Yet in the back of their minds, they worried about a return of these strange and violent outsiders. Unfortunately, they would not have to wait long. Coronado's expedition arrived at Hawikuh (a Zuni village in western New Mexico) in July 1540. Coronado and his men quickly determined that Niza had lied in all he had described about the city. Perhaps expecting to see jewel-encrusted homes and gold for the taking, instead the soldiers were mightily disappointed as they approached the mesa-top community. All they found were stone and mud homes. No jewels, no gold.

To the Zuni, the Spanish soldiers looked menacing in their anger and disappointment, clad in full armor and obviously prepared for engagement. The Spanish soldiers approached the village on horseback, then surprisingly, stopped, pulled out what appeared to be very thin deerskin with marks on it, and began to shout from behind it to any of the Zunis who would listen. The Zunis who heard him tried to understand through interpreters who spoke Pima and Spanish, but the actual meaning of the document could not possibly have been comprehended. The Spanish were reading the Requerimiento, which demanded that the Indians comply with Spanish and Catholic law or a just war could be declared and the Indians would not be spared the sword or slavery. The Pueblo Indians had likely heard about the brutality of the slave traders farther south and refused to submit without a fight. Both sides prepared for war. But the Zuni were already upset with the Spaniards, for when they approached the Zuni village, the Zuni had been preparing for an important feast day that was imperative for their survival. To warn the intruders not to interrupt their ceremonies, they had prepared a line of sacred crushed cornmeal and turquoise, an obvious sign to anyone who passed by that they were preparing for a cycle of summer solstice ceremonies. Anyone com-

Ruins of Hawikuh, the largest of the Zuni pueblos in present-day New Mexico. (Historic Print & Map Company)

ing across that line would certainly understand that they should return at some other time.

When the Spaniards crossed that line of sacred cornmeal, the Zuni had no choice but to respond. In a desperate battle in 1540, the Zunis defended their homes against the onslaught of the Spaniards, who took out their frustrations against Niza on the Zuni. Niza, who had personally led the Spaniards back to the Zuni homeland, returned to Mexico in utter disbelief at the lack of wealth in the village. He left behind the innumerable insults being hurled at him by Coronado and his men.

The Zuni could not defend themselves against the harquebuses, lances, Toledo steel swords, horses, and frustrated violence behind which every thrust was hurtled toward the men and, frankly, anyone else who got in the way. To the Spaniards, it was a just war because the Zuni had refused to submit to the authority of the king and the pope as offered to them by the Requerimiento. To the Zuni, this infiltration during one of their most sacred of ceremonies, into the heart of their homes, and

against their families, could not be explained, was an inexcusable violation, and would never be forgotten. When the battle ended and Spanish
soldiers had confiscated some of the food from the Zuni, the Spaniards
remarked that the Zuni women's grinding techniques exceeded that of the
Indians to the south, and that their tortillas were "the best . . . I have ever
seen anywhere" (Calloway, *One Vast Winter Count,* 135). The Spaniards
found Zuni storehouses and took a sufficient supply to continue their
journey to the east. A few days after Hawikuh fell, Indians approached
Coronado with peace offerings of blankets and turquoise, obviously
prized possessions and recognized by the Zuni and other regional tribes
as valuable trade items. After the Spanish accepted their gifts, the Zuni returned to their homes, packed their belongings, and left.

Spaniards remained until that November, whereupon Coronado
began to send out scouts. One group headed west to the Hopi villages,
which the Zunis described as a collection of seven towns, much like their
own. When the Spanish contingent, led by Fray Juan de Padilla, confronted the first community, the Hopi approached them with clubs,
bows, and shields. They demanded that the Spaniards not come closer.
When some of the Spaniards appeared to approach the line, one of the
Hopi clubbed a Spaniard's horse. They refused to allow the Spaniards to
do to them what had occurred at the Zuni community of Hawikuh. Nevertheless, Spaniards crossed over the line, ran down many of the men, and
charged toward the community. Those who did not run away emerged
frantically from their homes offering presents. When the Spanish soldiers
found no gold, they departed and continued to search for gold under various expeditions throughout the Rio Grande Valley and environs. At
Acoma, they met warriors who quickly acceded, accepting Spanish
"friendship," certainly something they would remember 50 years later
when Spaniards came back and turned their cannons and harquebuses on
the mesa-top pueblo.

Coronado and his warriors then turned their attention eastward and
traveled to the Rio Grande Valley and its pueblo villages. At each village
that Coronado or his scouts visited, they were given gifts of clothing,
blankets, turquoise, or food. Spaniards kept diligent records of each community, describing it in detail. At Acoma, they had noted that the Indian
people could go up and down the hand-hewn staircase to the mesa top

carrying large loads, even the women, without faltering or using the walls to stabilize or aid themselves. At Pecos, the gateway to the eastern plains, Alvarado described the community as follows: "The houses are all alike, four stories high. One can walk on the roofs over the whole pueblo, there being no streets to prevent this" (Calloway, *One Vast Winter Count,* 138). More importantly, it seemed to be a village of strong people. "The people of this town pride themselves that no one has been able to subjugate them, while they dominate the pueblos as they wish" (Ibid.). In other words, the Pueblo world did not seem to be without its own conflict. The degree of violence brought by the Spaniards because of their advanced weaponry and differing ideas of protracted warfare, however, had been unmatched to that point in the Rio Grande Valley.

But in the meantime, when Coronado arrived in the central Rio Grande Valley, he attempted to negotiate with the village of Arenal for winter quarters, but the Pueblo Indians refused to give up their homes to the interlopers without a fight. And a fight they got. The villagers of Arenal quickly tired of Spanish requirements of corn, blankets, and even women. One Spaniard even demanded that a Pueblo man hold his horse while he went inside and attempted to rape his wife! The Indian boldly complained to Coronado, even going so far as to point out the abuser. Coronado did nothing to rectify the situation. Violence broke out and the pueblo of Arenal, located on the west side of the Rio Grande close to the pueblo of Sandia, rose in rebellion. A period of uncertain peace ensued, forced on the Pueblos by a contingent of cavalry and Mexican Indian allies. General García López de Cárdenas ignored the peace and charged his men to take no prisoners. Erecting posts with which to burn his captives alive, Cárdenas and his men set about killing all who attempted to escape the carnage. News of this spread like wildfire throughout the communities along the Rio Grande and the traditional trade routes toward the Plains through Abo and Quarai, north through Taos, west through Acoma and Zuni (who understood well the violent capacity of the Spaniards), south to Isleta, and east to Pecos (see Map 6).

For nearly two years Coronado searched the Plains east and north of New Mexico, up and down the Rio Grande Valley, and even to the Grand Canyon in Arizona, for any sign of wealth to reimburse the tremendous expense that he and his cohorts had expended and in hopes

Ruins of Pecos Pueblo at Pecos National Historical Park in New Mexico. (National Park Service)

of demonstrating that the region could be settled profitably. During those excursions he encountered numerous pueblos in which the people spoke a variety of languages and, because of the arid nature of the land, periodically competed for resources like water, agricultural land, timber, hunting areas, and other tools of survival. The Spaniards upset the delicate balance of power: some of the tribes sought loose alliances with the Spaniards against their enemies, and others simply tried to rid the interlopers from their lands. Pecos was nearly successful.

Pecos leaders purportedly had gold jewelry, and the Spaniards decided to investigate. After the Spanish tortured Bigotes, one of the village elders, in an attempt to learn the location of Pueblo mines, the Rio Grande erupted in violence again, but this time it did not subside until the following year. Spanish response to Pueblo Indian defiance was swift and complete. Pueblo Indians were horrified by the level of violence and abandoned more than a dozen towns, which the Spanish then destroyed to ensure that the Pueblos could no longer use them as bases of operations. Spaniards rounded up the women and children and forced them to live alongside the Spaniards for the duration.

In the meantime El Turco, a Plains Indian captive from Pecos, boasted that he knew where that Pecos gold originated. If the Spaniards allowed it, he would lead them to this place he called Quivira. As a precaution, Coronado bound El Turco in chains. With the assistance of another Pecos leader, El Turco served as Coronado's guide. They headed northeast onto the Plains where they encountered Plains Apaches, who lived in tipis and used dogs to carry their burdens. They encountered Teyas, also Apaches but enemies of the previous group, or so they were told. The Teyas had archers so strong that they could penetrate the shoulder of a buffalo with a single shot of an arrow. The Spanish learned that the buffalo serve the people in many ways and that the people use every part of the animal, even trading some of the surplus to the Pueblo Indians for corn, woven blankets, and pottery at the annual trade fair in Taos Pueblo.

Next they encountered Wichita Indians, in whose homeland El Turco had promised they would find Quivira. When confronted with the lie, El Turco admitted that he had been allowed his freedom if he would lead the Spaniards out onto the Plains until they and their horses had died. Some have speculated that, as a Plains Indian, he might have even hatched the plan himself, offering to rid the Pueblos of this new enemy while allowing him to return home to his people on the central Plains. But he paid for this deception with his life; the Spaniards garroted him and left his bones to bleach in the sun in his beloved homeland. Nevertheless, perhaps he gained his wish—at least he died among his people. El Turco had used the greed of the Spanish to negotiate with the Pueblos for his own freedom, and he would forever be remembered as single-handedly removing the Spaniards from the Pueblo Indian homelands—even if temporarily.

While out on the Plains, Coronado's men heard from the Indians about another group of bearded white men just a few days' travel to the south. Hernando de Soto's expedition had encountered tribes along the Mississippi River, and word spread about the existence of bearded white men among the astonished natives. Information spread along ancient established trade routes about the intrusions by white men and their beasts of burden from the south, the east, and the west. Like Plains tribes years later, perhaps they had visions of the impending entanglements with these Spaniards (as did Sitting Bull so many years later before the Battle of the Greasy Grass, or Little Big Horn). Either way, their world would change forever. Even though Coronado did return to the Rio Grande Valley, he would abandon the New Mexico expedition shortly thereafter in 1542 and return to Mexico City to report that little wealth existed in the north. He did add, however, that the potential for farming existed on the Plains.

But for more than 60 years, New Mexico no longer ensnared the imagination of those searching for immediate wealth like the Inca and Aztec empires had yielded. The Spaniards looked instead to the mines of Zacatecas to feed their insatiable thirst for wealth to fuel the king's quest to further his empire, to spread Catholicism, and to fund the wars of the Counterreformation in Europe.

When they returned to the heart of New Spain, Coronado's *residencia* took place, whereby the authorities heard complaints about his leadership—something that occurred at the end of every leader's or governor's term. Harsh words came from one of the three known women who accompanied the expedition, including Francisca de Hozes. She railed, for an entire day, about how he put her husband in harm's way. Fray Juan de Padilla, who simply wanted to return to the lands of the eastern plains to convert natives, find Quivira, and return the Seven Cities of Cíbola (Antilles) back to the Catholic realm, testified as well. The harshest words came against General Cárdenas, who had led the one-sided battle against the village of Arenal. Spanish law protected Indians from such abuses by Spaniards, and for his crimes and those of his expedition, the Spanish expeditionary leader was tried for crimes against the Indians and found guilty. He died in prison, but that was not much solace for the Indian people who did not know about his punishment, nor did they know about the laws that protected them from such abuses.

But for now, the Spaniards were gone from the north. They had returned from whence they came. Yet the Pueblo people would never forget the outsiders who wreaked such havoc on their lives: entering their villages and taking their food stores, spreading death and disease, chasing them from home to live on the mesa tops where they could defend themselves, and causing them to fear for their future. Now that the Spanish were gone, they could return to their lives, both the spiritual and temporal aspects, and to the pursuits of agriculture, of hunting, trading, and living. They knew the white men might return again—but they would never know when.

Coronado's expedition left an indelible footprint in the Pueblo Indian world. They learned that the Spaniards demanded obedience to an omnipotent god and king they could not see, nor would they ever meet. These outsiders expected the Pueblo people to share their already strapped resources, as well as any minerals or precious stones, whether buried below the desert floor or deep inside their sacred mountains. The Spanish brought diseases that eventually began to spread among the pueblos and left Pueblo Indians to deal with diseases that their traditional healers and local herbs and remedies could not cure. When Coronado arrived in 1540, he reported nearly 100 Indian villages. By the time the next officially sanctioned Spanish expedition arrived in 1598, many of those villages had been abandoned. It is truly impossible to know exact population figures, as Coronado did not encounter every village, nor did he accurately document the number of inhabitants that he encountered along his many expeditions based from the Rio Grande throughout the far-flung frontier. In fact, no official census would exist for New Mexico until the 1770s when northern New Spain's commandant general required it for the reorganization of the provinces. Until the Spanish returned, however, their influence continued to be felt.

For the next two generations, Spanish explorers and conquerors ignored New Mexico. In the late 1540s, the Spanish discovered a mountain north of Mexico City that yielded exactly what Spain sought: a mountain of silver. In 1548, miners struck the main veins of Zacatecas, and the rush was on. But to get to Zacatecas, Spaniards had to travel through Chichimeca Indian territory, and the Chichimeca engaged the interlopers in a war that lasted for years. Spaniards called for *guerra a sangre y a fuego* (war by blood and fire) to rid the region of what the Spanish termed heathens, even offering bounties on their heads (Kessell, *Spain in the Southwest,* 57–59). The Chichimecas had rejected the Requerimiento's offer of peace, which allowed the Spanish to engage in their religiously sanctioned war. According to the Spanish, the Chichimecas were this type of "menace," having given Sepúlveda an indisputable argument that peaceful pacification of Indian peoples was an impossible standard. While Spain found itself distracted by the Chichimeca War, continued profits from Zacatecas discouraged them from expanding farther north.

THE SPANISH RETURN TO THE RIO GRANDE VALLEY

During the mid- to late 1500s, Spain's interest in expanding trade to China and the Orient continued, and several expeditions attempted to find a logical and practicable trade route between Asia and the Americas. Unfortunately for the Spaniards, Francis Drake, a pirate extraordinaire, made his way around the southern tip of the Tierra del Fuego and appeared on the California coastline in 1579 to "take possession" of Nova Albion, or California. Within a year the English landed at Plymouth. Not realizing that these Englishmen were different than Drake's group, the Spanish thought that the English had found the mythical "Straits of Anian," reaching the East Coast from the West Coast by sailing east along the elusive straits somewhere to their north, thus allowing their English adversaries to avoid sailing around the southern tip of South America and providing quick access to trade with the Orient. Therefore, Spain's search for the straits began in earnest. Informed of the several illegal or unsanctioned expeditions into New Mexico between 1542 and 1598, New Spain's viceroy realized that the time had come for a full-fledged settlement expedition, not just for exploration.

Not to be outdone, the viceroy immediately began to search for someone to head the colony and, after a fascinating competition between two suitors that left them both out of the race, Don Juan de Oñate sought after and won the contract to settle New Mexico. The son of one of the wealthy investors of the Zacatecas mine who understood mineralogy and the potential for Indian hostility, Oñate began to convince potential investors to invest in the expedition (which took up a great deal of his time) and began to hire soldier-colonists for the journey into the north. His contract stated that he had to have 200 men and their families, but after the numerous delays during the nearly three-year preparation period, he could only muster 129 men and their families.

Allowed to head north, with the understanding that he would later recruit the additional 71 men his contract required him to have, Oñate would arrive in the Rio Grande Valley of La Nueva México in the summer of 1598. He would bring some formidable allies who served him well in his efforts to bring New Mexico into the fold of the Catholic Spanish empire. Besides the soldier-colonists and their wives, children, and servants, he also brought a host of Mexican Indian allies. Mandated by his contract, Oñate would also bring Franciscan friars to convert the Indians to the "true" faith. Dressed in drab gray robes, these friars had every intention of spreading Christianity among the "heathens." They did not care that the Indians had centuries-old religious traditions every bit as rich as the Christian tradition, complete with spiritualism and ceremony. Unlike the Coronado expedition of exploration, however, the Oñate expedition was a settlement mission. These Spaniards planned to stay and to make New Mexico return in financial gain what Oñate had spent in preparation for the expedition, as well as provide a surplus to benefit those who put their lives on the line to live among the Indians and to pay off the nervous investors.

With much pomp and ceremony near El Paso del Norte, Oñate took possession of New Mexico and everything north to the Straits of Anian on behalf of Spain's king and queen. As they struck out to the north, they encountered a 90-mile stretch of desert with precious little water (later called the *Jornada del Muerto,* or Journey of the Dead Man). And because the expedition had been delayed, their stores of food had diminished to precarious levels. They could not eat the seed grain they brought, as they needed it for the upcoming planting season. When they came upon a recently abandoned Teypana village just north of the desert, they loaded 80 pack animals with corn that they found at the site, which included numerous abandoned villages. Oñate named that main village Socorro (help) for its contribution to the Spanish settlement effort. Replenished, they continued north, finding even more abandoned villages. Eventually they encountered two Mexican Indians who had lived among the Pueblo Indians for the past five years, Tomás and Cristóbal. Swept up with the settlement expedition, these men proved to be valuable interpreters for Oñate, one translating Pueblo languages into Tlaxcalan, and the other translating Tlaxcalan to Spanish. Some have suggested that their command of Pueblo tongues lacked precision, but at least it gave the two some common ground for reaching some understanding (John, *Storms*

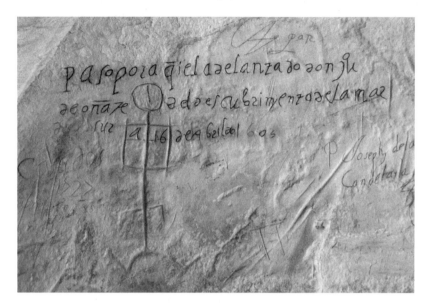

The first inscription carved at El Morro was that of Governor Don Juan de Oñate in 1605. It reads "Passed by here, the Adelantado Don Juan de Oñate, from the discovery of the Sea of the South, the 16th day of April, 1605." (National Park Service)

Brewed, 36–41). Needless to say, some of the concepts the Spanish attempted to share, whether about religion or legal issues of settlement and conquest, would no doubt be completely lost in the translation. The Spanish learned that the pueblos had been abandoned out of fear before the arrival of the intruders.

As the Spanish and their 80 carts and wagons, hundreds of people, and thousands of head of livestock traveled, the Pueblo Indians watched the caravan, remembering fearfully the disastrous two years under the last major official Spanish expedition of Coronado: villages destroyed by the wrath of the outsiders; large four-legged creatures they called stallions that stomped through their villages and fields, snorting and scaring the children; and fires, swords, and guns that killed family members, friends, and neighbors. They had tried to rid themselves of the Spaniards by sending them out on a wild goose chase to the Plains, but they had returned again. But even though this expedition seemed different, the Pueblo Indians still did not trust the hairy white men. They watched from hidden positions as the columns plodded along, stretching out for several days along El Camino Real so the natural springs' pools, drained by the Spaniards and their livestock, could replenish themselves. They watched the Spanish columns march northward along their river, past their *bosques* (small forests), and across their lands. They noticed that this time the white men had brought women and children, often a signal that this was not a war party. At the same time, they refused to trust these outsiders and vacated their villages before the Spaniards came through their lands.

The leading men of the pueblos likely joined together to consult on what to do with these intruders. As Oñate reached a village that he would rename Santo Domingo, pueblo leaders met with him in a council at the great kiva. Following the Pacification Orders of 1573, Oñate probably explained that they should voluntarily submit to King Felipe II and to Christianity. If they would kneel to kiss the ring of the governor and friar, they would live in "peace, justice, and orderliness" (John, *Storms Brewed,* 41). Obviously, the Pueblo Indians had no concept of a king who controlled so much land that the sun almost never set on his empire. Nor did they understand the idea of a single man who oversaw the religion of tens of thousands of people living in thousands of communities in many different nations. Nor did they understand the complex idea of an international colonial system of vassalage, tribute, and conversion, but they courteously agreed and watched as the Spaniards left without so much as raising a sword. These men seemed to be different from those who had come before. They did not fully comprehend the implications of kneeling to kiss the friar's and governor's rings, a symbol of absolute submission, or when the Spanish ritualistically claimed the lands, shouting "Long Live the King" and tossing sticks and dirt up in the air. But as these invaders moved north, they ritualistically took possession of every village along the way. Even though Oñate had to follow very strict rules not to harass or otherwise annoy the Pueblo Indians, whether he forced the Indians into vassalage by words or the sword, the result was the same. And what the Pueblo people saw as an inconvenient, though short, intrusion of their villages was a great "victory" to Oñate.

When Oñate finally reached the confluence of the Rio Grande and Rio Chama rivers, he encountered the village of Ohke Owinge (later he would rename it San Juan Pueblo). According to Pueblo Indian oral history and Spanish documents, its inhabitants peacefully abandoned their village for the Spaniards. Ohke Owinge tradition stated that the people felt sorry for the Spaniards because they had brought their families and were tired and hungry from the long journey. If the Spaniards had expressed an interest in living nearby, or even in their community, they certainly would have learned their lesson from Arenal and understood that their best chance at survival was to simply accede. But the Spanish kept coming, for the travelers had to separate and stretched for days along the Rio Grande. Soon the village could not house the large contingent of soldier-colonists and their families. The first Spaniards had arrived in mid-August, but others continued arriving for many days. They moved across the river to what he called San Gabriel (formerly Yunque) and proceeded to prepare their community for a permanent settlement. The settlers did not immediately recognize the bounty of the land that the Indians had come to enjoy and depend on. Even worse, they resented Oñate's orders not to loot or in other ways abuse the Indians. Within a short period, some even spoke of abandoning the colony. The whole time the Spanish settled into their homes, the Pueblo Indians watched in wonder at the animals, tools, numbers of people, and clothing the Spaniards brought. The former residents had readjusted their lives, too, for they had given up their home at Ohke Owinge, only to find that their homes did not suit the Spaniards.

Whether or not the Indians liked having such a large contingent of non-Indians living among them perhaps will never be known, because they did not complain. In fact, the day after the Spaniards arrived, they immediately recruited more than 1,500 Pueblo Indians to work alongside the immigrants to build a major *acequia*, or irrigation ditch, so that the Spaniards could grow crops the following spring. It was a major undertaking, illustrating the Indians' willingness to assist the Spanish, according to Spanish records, though whether they helped without complaint, as some historians have suggested, is debatable. If they did complain, it certainly did not make it into Spanish records. But then again, why would Oñate report the discontent of the Indians at the outset of a proprietary expedition, when he knew that he may need to assure the investors that their investment was sound? And one must remember that while the Spanish reported that the Indians were volunteers, what choice did they have? They remembered the brutality of the

Coronado expedition when Arenal refused to give up their homes and the destruction of villages. If the Spaniards could not grow crops for the following year, would they not steal more corn from their villages as they had at Socorro and Zuni years before? Moreover, if they were able to grow their own crops, perhaps they would not take their food stores during the difficult winter months. Even the women took part in preparing the Spanish community, helping mud plaster the first temporary church (an oddity to the Spanish, who saw construction as a man's job).

The Pueblo Indians then watched in fascination as the Spanish held a great festival to celebrate the building of the first Catholic mission at San Juan. During the festival, the Spanish recreated a mock battle between the Moors and Christians. No doubt at battle's end when the supposedly dead Moors, shot by Spanish harquebuses, got up laughing and dusted themselves off to enjoy the festivities, the Indians took note that these Spanish guns perhaps had only a temporary effect. After the festival, the colonists began preparing for the winter and the upcoming planting season. The Franciscan friars prepared to convert the natives and spread the influence of Christianity into the hinterlands. And the Indians returned to their traditional ceremonies and community lives.

The Catholic faith was young compared with the time-honored and well-revered structure of Pueblo Indian religion, one that honored the two- and four-legged and winged creatures, the land, the sky, and the plant life that surrounded them, among much else. As they had for generations, Pueblo Indians adopted only the manifestations of the new spiritualism that fit into their understanding of the world, adding the Christian god to their universal beliefs. They continued to hold ceremonies asking the earth for permission to plant their crops as well as asking the sky to bring rain. They continued to hold their deer dances, corn dances, buffalo dances, and pilgrimages to shrines located throughout their lands in the four cardinal directions. And many of them attended Catholic Mass as required by the resident friars. At first, this syncretism of religious beliefs was tolerated by some Franciscans because they understood it would take the Pueblo Indians time to completely convert. But to assist in their conversion, the friars would need even more missions, so they used Pueblo Indian labor to build churches throughout New Mexico. The Franciscan brothers then either lived in attached cloisters or traveled to visit missions without a friar in residence. Indians were required to tend fields to provide food for the friar, as well as tend flocks of sheep or cattle. This took time from their traditional duties and created strain between the church and the Pueblo Indians, which would explode in a few generations.

SPANISH MISSIONS

One of Spain's official goals in establishing a permanent foothold in the New World included the conversion of the indigenous people. To help them accomplish this task, the pope allowed Spain nearly full control over the Catholic Church in the New World. Numerous religious orders arrived to assist in the conversion effort, including the Franciscans, Dominicans, Augustinians, and Jesuits. The Franciscans dominated New Mexico, Texas, and California, while the Jesuits proselityzed in what is now Arizona. By 1767, however, the Jesuits found themselves evicted from Spanish holdings, and the Franciscans moved in to claim their missions, including the mission at Tubac.

Quarai, Salinas Pueblo Missions National Monument, Mountainaire, New Mexico. (Sandra K. Mathews)

The very purpose of a mission—the actual conversion of the Indians—took different forms based on which order had control over the area, as well as the local populations. In New Mexico, shortages of friars after the Pueblo Revolt until the 1820s was typical. Arizona's missions at first consisted merely of visits by Father Eusebio Francisco Kino, but the mission at San Xavier del Bac served the local communities. In California, friars rounded up Ranchería Indians from nearby areas and brought them together to live and work at the missions.

It was nearly impossible to succeed at conversion when Indians continued to live in such sparse and scattered settlements. For this reason, California's mission experience is often regarded as the harshest of all Spanish missions in North America. Whether brutal, demanding, periodic, or cautiously optimistic, the missions required the conversion of Indian people from their traditional and centuries-long belief systems to a European style of religion, Christianity, which was based on words in books and not oral tradition and communal or society-based understandings of the natural world.

Another major strain on Pueblo Indians in New Mexico (that would continue until the 1680s) developed when the Spanish implemented the encomienda in the region. This grant of Indian tribute was essentially adapted from the Muslim conquest of Spain, whereby a soldier or settler would be rewarded with an encomienda from the governor for service to the governor or crown. The owner of the encomienda, or the *encomendero,* could then travel to the Indian village granted to him or her and collect tribute based on the number of heads of households in the village as specified in the grant. Oftentimes the collection would occur two times a year, and it included such things as corn, blankets, or other woven materials. These encomiendas could be willed for one or two generations. Being in such a remote frontier region, unfortunately for the Indian communities, the encomenderos abused their right and collected more than their share, and sometimes more than just twice yearly. Sometimes Spaniards seized their tribute by force, purportedly even taking blankets off women in the dead of winter. Within a few years, Oñate and his motley band of invaders had acquired, through subversive means at times, more than a six-year supply of corn that the Pueblo people had stored—a devastating blow to the Pueblos in that unpredictable land. This increasing and unyielding demand created hostility between the Pueblo Indians and the Spaniards, the latter of whom collected what they saw as their right, through a grant by the governor according to his contract with the king or viceroy. After all, the encomenderos would argue, the tribute would reimburse their services of ensuring that the Indians converted to Christianity, as well as protecting the Pueblo people against the nomadic Indian attacks that became more common in the mid- to late 1600s—never mind that the Pueblo Indians would have preferred to defend themselves, something now prohibited by the crown. Pueblos would also have preferred to continue practicing their traditional religion and not deal with having to pay tribute for services rendered by friars. But the encomienda would continue and would become harsher as the years progressed and fewer colonists or officials exposed the abuses.

By late 1598, Oñate had initiated many explorations around New Mexico and developed a great interest in finding a less treacherous resupply route from Mexico City. The Chichimecas to the south, a combination of numerous tribes throughout the Sierra Madres, initiated conflict in response to Spanish intrusions that was termed the Mixton or Chichimeca War. The continued conflagrations that ensued between Spanish travelers along the Camino Real de Tierra Adentro to La Nueva México from Mexico City some 1,500 miles to the south caused Spanish interest in further exploration to the north to subside significantly. The Chichimecas and the numerous Apache bands that spread from what is today eastern Arizona to the hill country of Texas still threatened and harassed the supply trains that were scheduled to travel to and from New Mexico on a six-month cycle. Therefore, Oñate set about finding an alternate route to the ocean west of New Mexico, known as the Sea of Cortez, in hopes of establishing a resupply port for New Mexico to avoid the dangerous Camino Real. Not all of the soldiers left for the West at the same time, however, and when the trailing expeditionary force arrived at the base of Acoma's mesa-top village, where they had lived since the 1100s, the Indians invited them to the summit of the mesa for supplies. Once the Spanish soldier-colonists reached the summit, the Indians instructed them to split into smaller groups and accompany various Indians to the storehouses, each ominously located down different paths along the mesa-top homes. After they had been sufficiently separated, the Indians fell upon the Spaniards. The Acoma killed 13 men, including the nephew and namesake of Governor Oñate. Five men survived by jumping off the cliffside into the sand dunes hundreds of feet below. This same Acoma had previously agreed to the terms of the Requerimiento and to become vassals of Spain and live in accordance with its laws and religion. Horrified at their actions, the Spanish regrouped in San Juan to discuss the situation.

By Oñate's estimation, more than 60,000 Pueblo Indians surrounded the Spaniards. Beyond the Pueblos, innumerable other tribes lived nearby, including several Apache bands, as well as the Navajo. If the Spanish did nothing, surely they would be seen as easy targets and would be continuously challenged, and perhaps even eventually wiped out by other tribes. This type of disruption would scare off potential investors and cause the existing shareholders to fear for their investment, not to mention put the entire settlement at grave risk of attack. Spanish law was on their side, for clearly Acoma had agreed to vassalage by acceding to Spanish authority earlier. According to Acoma tradition, however, they did not recognize the sovereignty of foreign entities over their people, much less such things as a "just war" in the name of a religion they did not know or understand.

Regardless, with the blessing of the Franciscan fathers to wage a just war, Oñate sent his other nephew to lead the expedition against Acoma and force them into submission. The Acoma suffered tremendously, losing close to 800 members in battle alone—including women, children, and the elderly. Those who survived, approximately 500 women and children and some 80 men (depending on the source) were forced to march to Santo Domingo where Oñate put them on trial. According to Spanish law, they needed official legal representation and, because none of them could read or understand the Spanish legal system, their defender logically was a Spaniard. Because the Indians had broken the provisions of the agreement to which they had capitulated, even though they did not understand the full ramifications of their pledge, they suffered a miserable sentence. The two dozen men over the age of 25 were to have one foot severed and to serve 25 years of servitude (at which point they would be

Acoma Pueblo and its reflection in a pool of water, photographed by Ansel Adams during 1941–1942. The Acoma Pueblo is said to be the oldest continuously inhabited settlement in the United States and was the setting for the Acoma battles of 1598 and 1599. (National Archives)

released). Men between 12 and 24 years old would be forced into 20 years of servitude. Women older than 12 years were also sentenced to 20 years of servitude. Young girls were handed over to the missionaries and would live in the monasteries to be trained in the Christian faith and serve as servants, and the boys were sent to the soldiers, for "training." Two Hopi (Moqui) had a hand severed and were sent back to their villages to serve as a reminder that no one should resist Spanish power. Other Pueblos took note of the harshness of the sentence and an uneasy "peace" ensued, for a while. Periodic small uprisings occurred, perhaps to test the power of the Spaniards, such as later at the Tompiro villages in central New Mexico where more than 800 Indians learned the power of the Spanish sword. The 400 survivors were taken prisoner.

In the aftermath of the Acoma incident, nervous relief spread through the Spanish village as each day passed and no more "incidents" occurred. As their confidence grew, the Spanish began their expeditionary forays once again. The Spanish soldiers explored eastward to the Plains, like Coronado more than two generations before, and they resumed their quest for a supply route west from the Sea of Cortez. But dissatisfaction grew among the colonists because of increased attacks by the Apache, the lack of wealth found in the province, the harshness of the desert, and the fact that Oñate seemed to be more interested in periodically abandoning the colony to explore the hinterlands, leaving the colonists to fend for themselves. Several even contemplated abandoning the colony. Others more boldly tried to escape, but their intentions were discovered in time, and the deserters were captured en route. This infuriated Oñate, for they had signed a contract to come to New Mexico as part of his colony, and he had paid for the expedition, including the supplies they would need, with his money and that of the investors. Frustrations mounted and the disillusioned colonists finally succeeded in catching the ear of Felipe III. By 1607, Oñate had run out of money and excuses for his financiers; when Felipe III recalled Oñate, the governor had already penned his resignation and told the settlers that they could leave by 1608.

One of the most fascinating stories of the governorship of New Mexico that many historians decline to include is the aftermath. When a governor left office, the crown required a residencia. At his residencia, Oñate faced a slew of charges. He pleaded guilty to 12 counts, including various acts of cruelty against the Indians, excessive use of force in battle against the Acoma, harshness of sentence against the Acoma, and even adultery with the Spanish women of the expedition. Found guilty, he was exiled from New Mexico forever and exiled from Mexico City for four years. He also had to pay a large fine and court costs. In other words, the Spanish held their leaders accountable for their actions during their tenure, including brutality against and harsh treatment of the Indians.

THE MISSIONARY ERA AND THE BEGINNING OF DISCONTENT

Even as Oñate departed New Mexico to defend himself, leaving the colonists free to excuse themselves from the province, Franciscan friars argued that New Mexico could not be abandoned because of their successes in converting the Pueblo Indians to Christianity. They argued that they had converted some 7,000 souls (a number greatly exaggerated by zealous friars no doubt). The king agreed not to abandon the colony and his Christian obligation to continue converting the Indians and sent a new governor. From 1610 to 1680, New Mexico entered what historians have traditionally termed the Missionary Era. Fray Alonso de Benavides, the father superior of the newly created administrative unit in New Mexico called the "custody of the Conversion of St. Paul," began to lobby for New Mexico (which at the time technically included everything north of the Rio Grande, as well as west to the Pacific Ocean) to become a bishopric. He wrote a wonderfully descriptive report of New Mexico to the king of Spain in 1630 in an attempt to accomplish this task (as the king had the primary authority of the Catholic Church in the New World, according to the *Patronato Real).* He penned his first report, *The Memorial of Fray Alonso de Benavides, 1630,* to highlight the numerous missions and Indian villages that the Catholic Church serviced, likely overemphasizing the successes in converting the natives to enhance the spiritual rebirth of the Pueblo population and further his own cause to become the first bishop. When that failed to bring about the desired results, he revised his report and sent it to the pope in 1634. He never did get his bishopric, however, and instead of becoming a religious haven for converts controlled by church officials, New Mexico degenerated into a community filled with strife between civil and religious authorities bent on controlling New Mexico's population and development, but mostly bent on controlling the native populations for their own purposes (among other things). Benavides would not be around to see the disastrous effects of the confrontations that erupted between the civil and religious authorities, nor the effect they would have on the native population. And even as Benavides penned his manuscript to the king, the Pueblo Indians began discussing possibilities to effect changes in their own futures as well.

Historically, the Pueblos had accepted aspects of spiritualism from other peoples that they encountered if the newer elements enhanced their existing spiritual power. To a certain extent, it could be argued that Pueblo Indians in fact accepted Christianity through baptism. But a true understanding of the integration of Christian principles and the tenets of traditional Pueblo Indian beliefs indicates instead that they simply adapted a syncretized version of Christianity infused with their traditional native spiritual understandings, something that became increasingly unacceptable, and by the end of the Missionary Era, not tolerated at all by the ever more condemning and demanding friars. Their intolerance of a syncretized belief system became even more apparent by the end of the 1660s and 1670s.

Under the strong-handed leadership of numerous friars, New Mexico entered a difficult era where Pueblo Indians watched as civil administrators fought incessantly with religious authorities over who would control Indian labor, production, and daily activities. They watched as the Franciscan superior placed the governor under arrest, colonists were punished for siding with the church (or conversely, the civil authorities), and church officials threatened civil authorities with excommunication—even following through with excommunicating the governor on one occasion. They enjoyed Governor Bernardo López de Mendizabal, who danced with them in 1661, and reviled the friars who burned their kivas, destroyed their ceremonial masks and drums, and ordered them to cease participating in time-honored and necessary spiritual rituals, prayers, ceremonies, and offerings. They really began to resent the increasing demand on their surplus of corn, as the encomienda continued to operate in New Mexico without any apparent oversight or restraint by the authorities in Mexico City. Pueblo Indians loathed the fact they could not respond to the Apache and Navajo raids against the products of their labor, for the Spanish would not allow them to carry firearms, use horses, or leave their villages for the retaliatory raids against raiders, thereby making them appear weaker to the nomadic tribes. It seemed as if the Spanish did not have a great interest in protecting the Pueblo people, and according to Spanish law, Indians could not defend themselves against their enemies. Rather, it seemed that the Spanish had developed into disingenuous overlords and by the 1660s, the Pueblo Indians began to consider returning to their traditional ways. Some even thought about plotting retaliation.

During the 1660s and 1670s, the friars became increasingly intolerant. They moved throughout the numerous Pueblo communities and gathered up and destroyed spiritual and ceremonial masks, drums, katchinas (representations of their gods), and other religious accoutrements. In other words, they attempted to eradicate all vestiges of Pueblo religions, for the friars always recognized these old spiritual customs and accoutrements as detrimental to their ability to convert the

Hopi kachina, ca. 1890. (Bowers Museum of Cultural Art/Corbis)

Pueblo people and keep them on the path leading to heaven. But only after a few generations did friars have the boldness and daring to eradicate the native religions. In response to the increased pressure by the friars, some of the Pueblo people moved their religion underground—sometimes figuratively, and sometimes quite literally.

Their return to traditional ways did not occur simply because the Franciscan friars demanded their undivided loyalties, but also because the region had entered into a substantial dry spell. The fields had begun to dry up—crops withering before their eyes. Rivers and streams diminished, sometimes to a trickle, sometimes disappearing altogether, even during the late spring when winter melt and spring rains would have normally blessed the valleys. The Pueblo Indians began to suffer from the famine that resulted from the drought conditions, and mortality rates jumped. Unfortunately for them, the drought not only affected their pueblo villages, but also those of the Spaniards and the neighboring Apache and Navajo nations. The Spaniards who held encomiendas continued to come to the Pueblos, demanding their portions. Ever so desperate to keep their own families and communities safe from the drought and famine, the Spaniards demanded more than their share from the Pueblo villages, sometimes emptying out the pueblo's entire surplus for the winter months and spring planting. As the Spanish wagons drove off with pueblo corn, Pueblo women could be seen following the wagons, picking individual kernels of corn from the road where the kernels fell through the slats of the wagons—picking them out of the desert roads and carrying them in their baskets or dresses back to their villages. The desperation was evident, but the Spanish did not relent. As a result, Pueblo leaders began to understand that because the Spanish had forced them to stop participating in time-honored and requisite spiritual ceremonies, the earth had lost its balance, and their spirit world no longer looked at them favorably. The Spanish had forced them to forsake their belief system for another that obviously had no power to stop the drought and famine. To make matters worse, as the Pueblo people suffered from prolonged hunger and lack of proper nutrition, and as their immune systems became weaker, they soon began to suffer from illnesses that now spread more rapidly among the villages. As if they had not endured enough, what the Spaniards did not take, the Apache and Navajo demanded. The Apache suffered from the regional drought as well, and knew that the Pueblo Indians had contingency plans for droughts and famines, dependent as they were on agriculture and the natural cycles of monsoons and drought. The communities along the Rio Grande suffered, but none so desperately as the Pueblo Indians whose timeless understandings of the natural world, which in the past had prepared them for such disasters, no longer functioned. For Spanish sovereignty had taken away their security by disallowing their own defense, their participation in retaliatory raids, through the exacting price of the encomienda upon their people—oftentimes at rates far beyond what Spanish law allowed. But who would report these improprieties to the crown? Other Spaniards who also suffered from the drought, yet benefited from this unfair exaction upon their pueblo neighbors?

THE PUEBLO REVOLT

So the Pueblo Indians returned to their own gods, turning their backs on the Christian god who had either forsaken them or did not have the power to save them from these calamities. But that alone did not seem to correct the balance, so the *indio ladino* (Christianized or Hispanized Indian) governor of the Salinas and Tano villages, Esteban Clemente, planned an uprising (see sidebar on Esteban Clemente and Precursors to the Pueblo Revolt). Unfortunately, the uprising failed and Clemente suffered the consequences of plotting a rebellion.

The governor was shocked at this development because Clemente had been a trusted índio ladino, a true friend of the Spanish. Upon investigating his home later, however, they found various accoutrements of the nativistic religions that he had publicly foresworn. His deceit and trickery caused a ripple effect throughout New Mexico, for if someone like Clemente, a Christian Indian, could plot such a fiendish plan, were there others who would do the same? Perhaps the colonists should have paid closer attention.

The suffering of the Pueblo Indians, caused by the drought, crop failures, and resulting starvation, was intensified by recurring epidemics of measles and smallpox that seemed to circulate every generation and dealt a harsher blow to the Indian pueblos than to the white settlers. Moreover, they should also have recognized the impact on the Pueblo people of the increased raids by the Apache and Navajo who also suffered tremendously because of the intense and unrelenting drought. They depended primarily on hunting and gathering, and it was not just the human population that suffered, but also the animal and plant world. When the mountains experienced less snowfall during the winter, less moisture accumulated to feed the growth of forage in the mountains, the meadows fed by mountain streams, that in turn offered sustenance for the elk, deer, and animals hunted by the more nomadic tribes. Even more, that meant the nomadic tribes did not have as many goods to bring to the annual trade fairs at Taos; therefore, they could not acquire the grains they normally acquired from the pueblos and the jerked buffalo meat they acquired from the Plains tribes to the east. Instead, they turned toward those in the Rio Grande Valley whose crops they believed could sustain them until the rains began to fall again as they always had.

ESTEBAN CLEMENTE AND PRECURSORS TO THE PUEBLO REVOLT

Because Spain's main purpose in the permanent settlement of New Mexico ended up being the continued success at converting the Pueblo Indians, it came as a great surprise that their charges rose up against them with such fury. The proverbial writing was on the wall with abuses by encomenderos, illegal forced labor of the Pueblo people, increasingly difficult environmental conditions, and demands by the friars that the Pueblos completely abandon their former religious practices.

Several years before the revolt occurred, Clemente, a respected native leader of both the Tano and Salinas pueblos, renowned for his skills as an interpreter and literate in Spanish, ran a pack train for New Mexico's Spanish governors. In 1668, he witnessed as many as 450 deaths in one village alone due to starvation. So secretly Clemente and many others began to plot the destruction of the Christian kingdom that had usurped their way of life. The Spanish, after all, would never suspect him.

Fluent in Spanish and several other Pueblo languages, he truly straddled the line between the Spanish and Pueblo Indian worlds as a "cultural broker." He had operated successfully as an entrepreneur among the Spaniards, even serving in their military and gaining status as a military leader. He had been baptized as a Catholic, attended services, and on the outside, appeared to be a devout believer. But he also served as a political leader in the Pueblo world and, at the same time, as the Spanish would later learn, he had never actually abandoned his traditional Pueblo ways and continued to practice them in secret.

Frustrated at his lack of ability to effect change from the inside as a respected "Hispanized" Pueblo man floating between Spanish and Pueblo Indian worlds, he began to plot rebellion. His plan called for all Indians to drive Spanish horses into the mountains, and then on the Thursday before Easter, they would kill all the Spaniards, including the friars.

Unfortunately for Clemente, the Spaniards discovered his plot and after they hanged him, they found numerous objects in his home that suggested he had not renounced his traditional ways. Among those items, the Spanish found numerous idols, feathers, substantial quantities of herbs, and other "disgusting" things. As one of the most trusted Hispanized Pueblo Indians, the Spaniards realized that not even Clemente and his like could be trusted. New Mexico was on the verge of exploding.

By the mid 1670s, Spanish fears once again caused them to see insurgencies everywhere, and once again they wanted the Spanish governor to scrutinize the Pueblos more carefully. While their numbers had dwindled significantly in the previous 80 years, the Indian population still outnumbered the colonists by at least eight to one: only about 2,500 Spaniards lived in New Mexico, versus at least 20,000 Pueblo Indians, not to mention the hundreds of Navajo and Western and Eastern Apache that surrounded the Rio Grande Valley on three sides. When the San Ildefonso Pueblo's friar reported that Indian sorcery had caused illness to himself and others, they remembered Clemente's plot from a few years earlier and recognized the severity of allowing Pueblo Indians to go "unchecked." They had to make sure that they stopped the sorcery from spreading, or even worse, having it be used against them. Therefore, with the help of soldier-colonists, the Franciscans rounded up Pueblo Indian medicine men and leaders (whom Franciscans called sorcerers) across New Mexico. Some 47 men were brought to the capital of Santa Fe for trial. Of the men found guilty of the friars' charges, three were hanged, another committed suicide, and the rest were whipped publicly for their complicity. When word spread about the indignities that the Spanish put their honored Pueblo elders and leaders through, the Pueblo people decided that this type of infringement on Pueblo Indian culture could not be tolerated any longer. Emboldened, 70 Pueblo men showed up demanding the release of the captives. After tense negotiations, the released captives returned to their homes—except for one: Popé, a Tewa shaman and warrior. Instead of returning home, the untiring San Juan native Popé moved instead to Taos to plot revenge, a plan so thorough that it would shake the foundation of the Spanish empire's hubris, and destroy all vestiges of Spanish influence. Planned secretly in the mountain pueblo farthest from the tentacles of Spanish control, Popé and his retinue, including another Pueblo leader, Alonso Catití, and a man named Naranjo, plotted the rebellion. They engaged Pueblo Indians across the province to rise up against the Spanish on a date that would be signified by the knotted cord, the *quipu*. When two of the Pueblo runners carrying the quipu-encoded messages were intercepted and interrogated about the cords, the numerous pueblos swiftly moved into action and began to attack and kill the Spaniards on August 10, a day earlier than planned. On that fateful day, the Rio Grande Valley arose in an upsurge of violence precipitated by Spanish Franciscan friars' unwillingness to allow Pueblo Indians to continue practicing their centuries-old religion. The revolt was exacerbated by an extensive drought, which was causing the spread of disease, increased death rates, and likely lower birth rates because of disease and low birth weights.

In the earliest day of the revolt, the Pueblos diligently destroyed all vestiges of Spanish authority and culture, as demanded by Popé, by tearing down churches, destroying documents, and killing livestock. More difficult, however, was the destruction of crops the Spanish had brought, such as wheat. Pueblos had grown to depend on these European crops, and many refused to destroy them. It was nearing harvest and the people had little food as a result of the confiscations by the Spanish.

So intense was their hatred of the Franciscans and their demands on the Pueblo people that not only did they destroy the churches by setting them on fire, but they also scaled the walls to knock down the adobes, brick by brick, until the churches had been sufficiently razed, such as at Pecos Pueblo. As if that was not enough, they also covered what remained of the interior with feces, the Spanish reported as they witnessed the desecration during their exodus at Sandia Pueblo. Not all of the Pueblo Indian population, however, harbored such overwhelming resentment. In fact, some Pueblo people even refused to kill the very symbols of Spanish dominance and submission to a different spiritual authority: the friars. San Felipe Pueblo's oral tradition tells of their successful efforts to protect the friar who escaped Cochiti Pueblo upriver from them. They sheltered him until the danger was over. At one point, as they had him hidden on the mesa top, he and his protectors needed water but dared not travel down to the river and expose themselves. According to tradition, he performed a miracle and caused water to spring forth from a rock. Corroborated by Spanish records, this is one example of the unwillingness of all pueblos to act as one, with one unified goal and as one uniform army. Nevertheless, during the early 1680s, Popé and Catití attempted to unify the Pueblo Indians; but ironically, they would do so in similar fashion to the methods used by the Spanish government they would send packing. Popé would soon lose control over the movement before the Spanish truly understood the depth of Pueblo Indian hostilities.

To organize and manage the defense of the province, the Spanish authorities had divided New Mexico into two major regions: Rio Arriba (upper river, or northern) and the Rio Abajo (lower river, or southern). The governor had jurisdiction over the entire province, residing at the northern headquarters of Santa Fe, while the lieutenant governor oversaw the southern region with his headquarters in Isleta Pueblo. Overwhelmed by the Spanish population in and around Isleta, the pueblo could not participate in the revolt. During the years leading up to the revolt, they had been carefully monitored by the lieutenant governor and his military force, small though it was.

In the earliest days of the revolt, colonists in the Rio Abajo rushed to Isleta where the lieutenant governor resided, hoping to withstand assaults by attacking Pueblos until they received further instruction from the governor in Santa Fe. Before long, however, they heard about the siege of Santa Fe and were told by informants that all their compatriots to the north had been killed. Realizing the futility of remaining, they gathered up their survivors and, dejected and fearful of what might come once they left the relative security of Isleta Pueblo, ventured out and began their descent to El Paso del Norte. But had they all perished? Those Spaniards

St. Augustine Church, built in 1612, at the Isleta Pueblo in New Mexico. (iStockPhoto.com)

who were scattered across the Rio Arriba region in Santa Fe, Santa Cruz de la Cañada, and other small communities and farms along the rivers, who could make it to the capital, had gathered logically at Santa Fe to attempt to hold off the Indian assault on the community.

The Spaniards in Santa Fe closed the walls of the town and held out while the Indians assaulted the walls and taunted them from the outside. "They were saying that now God and Santa María were dead . . . and that their own God whom they obeyed never died" (Kessell, *Spain in the Southwest,* 121). In an attempt to escape, Spanish soldiers flung open and rushed the gates, catching the Pueblo Indians laying siege off guard. They took Pueblo prisoners, questioned them as to the extent of the revolt, and then set about devising a plan to escape—for they realized all had been lost. After the Pueblos cut off the water supply to the village, the Spanish recognized that they had to leave, so once again they opened the gates— but this time emptied in a procession that would lead them out of Pueblo homelands. The governor, the inhabitants of Santa Fe, and the survivors in the Rio Arriba had not all perished, and upon arriving at Isleta they were incensed when they heard that those in the Rio Abajo had given up hope and abandoned New Mexico.

As the Pueblos retreated to the mesa tops, they cautiously observed the Spanish leaving. They had no intentions of harassing them along the way or engaging them in any further military entanglements. They only wanted to rid their homelands of these demanding invaders and return to their traditional ways. The Spaniards fled with as little as the clothes on their backs, making their way from Santa Fe or Isleta, and beginning the long trek south along the Camino Real that had brought their families to New Mexico in 1598. The northern group of refugees had hoped to meet up with another contingent of Spanish colonists and soldiers that lived in a lower portion of New Mexico, and had gathered at Isleta Pueblo.

The two groups of survivors met each other just before crossing the Jornada del Muerto and made it to El Paso del Norte, the crossing from New Mexico into southern New Spain. At that time, reinforcements (most of which were convicts) led by Father Ayeta finally arrived for the New Mexico colony—but it was too late. They had abandoned the colony and would not return with colonists for more than a dozen years. New Mexico was lost.

VICTORY FOR THE RIO GRANDE TRIBES

From the native perspective, of course, they had won back their homeland. The Pueblo Revolt was the only truly successful indigenous revolt in North America where a foreign occupying nation was forced from their strongholds. When the dust from the Pueblo Revolt had settled, more than 400 Spaniards were dead, including 21 Franciscan friars. For nearly three generations, the Pueblo Indians had been pressured by the friars and soldier-colonists to change nearly everything about how they lived, how they spoke, what they called themselves, what they wore, how they married, what crops they grew, to whom they were indebted, and how they prayed. With the Spanish gone, they turned back toward their traditional spirituality, reinvigorated by the "return" of the pueblo gods whom the Spanish had tried to make them forsake during the previous decades. As much unity as it took to dislodge the Spanish authorities and their invasive and demanding settlers, the Pueblo villages had never been a single nor coherent unit. They spoke more than seven separate languages and had rituals unique to their own communities.

In his attempt to keep the Pueblos unified, however, Popé visited each village, attempting to impose his form of central authority over them. His hubris, however, seemed to his "subjects" more similar to the system they had just overthrown than to their traditional Pueblo ways. He and his lieutenant actually attempted to collect a tax of sorts to keep the rebellion strong—or perhaps to benefit his own pueblo; the true story will never be known. For not much after the Spaniards left the upper Rio Grande Valley, Popé made demands upon the pueblos, and for this, he suffered an early end for his serious misjudgment. He was killed and deposed by Luis Tupatú.

The great unified effort of the Pueblo people that succeeded in throwing the Spanish out disintegrated after the murder of Popé. It had been more than 90 years since they had practiced all of their traditional ceremonies, dances, songs, and rituals. As generations of elders had perished, few remained to recount the tales that had been told for countless generations and that held the many threads of their spiritual tradition together. The entrenchment of the Catholic friars meant that the Pueblos had to comply with their demands to adhere to the new rules and ignore their traditional and rich religious heritage. Therefore, some of the traditional ceremonies, stories, and medicines had been lost. Spaniards had destroyed all their important kivas and ceremonial accoutrements, such as katchinas, ceremonial masks, head gear, drums, prayer sticks, and other key items for their spiritual ceremonies (at least the ones the Spanish could find that Pueblos had not yet sequestered away for safe keeping). Many of the Pueblo people had become so dependent on the Spanish that they had understandably forgotten how to live entirely in the traditional way. Nevertheless, the Pueblos tried to return to their traditional ways. To most accounts, they succeeded.

The Pueblo people had watched the Spanish men, women, and children leaving New Mexico. In the rush to protect their lives, the Spanish did not have time to pack their belongings; therefore, most were on foot, some did not have sufficient clothing to keep warm, and few had enough food stores to sustain them for the duration of the journey along the Camino Real. When they arrived, the residents of El Paso had great sympathy for the bedraggled survivors. Spanish exiles may have suffered tremendously on their exodus, but things would get worse in El Paso. The drought did not relent, and the Spanish had not learned the key lesson about taking resources from those Indians who lived near them. Local tribes grew angry at the increased demands by the Spaniards on the already stressed local natural resources.

Those animals or tools that did not leave with the Spaniards, Popé had demanded be destroyed, but not everyone followed his demands. The Pueblo Indians faced very real problems after the Spanish left, and they needed the food and supplies to survive the upcoming winter and have seeds for planting. The loss of skills related to defense and warfare, nearly forgotten over the previous 90 years because lack of use, became apparent. The only weapons they owned had only recently been fashioned or taken out of storage (fearing Spanish confiscation). Because they had nearly lost the ability to defend themselves, their military stratification had also suffered. Even though most refer to the Pueblo people as nonmilitary, before the arrival of the Spanish, they did in fact have war leaders who led their men on retaliatory raids or other skirmishes that might be necessary. But for generations, they could not engage anyone militarily and therefore lost their ability to build expertise, status, equipment, and even rank.

After the Spaniards left, the nomadic tribes—in particular the Apache—took particular interest in the relative weakness of the Pueblo Indians. With the Spaniards went their firearms and horses, the protectors of the Pueblo Indians. And the Apache had also learned that the pueblos had become weak and no longer had the tools or skills to set off on a retaliatory expedition. In the meantime, the Apache had also acquired large numbers of horses, regardless of the laws that the Spanish imposed against allowing Indians to have or ride horses. They used these horses to increase the number of raids against the pueblo villages, which were now exposed without the protection of Spanish military forces, harquebuses, or cannon. Pueblos had no horses, for they were either run off or killed during the revolt. Therefore, they could not defend their stores from nomadic raids, nor could they retaliate to recover what they had lost. Within months after the Spanish left, the Apache raids began, at times with impunity.

THE HORSE

The earliest horses, the eohippus, that lived in the Americas were once believed to be ancestors to the modern horse, *equus caballus.* The eohippus were much smaller, about the size of a large dog. For unexplained reasons, however, they died out long before the Spanish brought their steeds. When the Spanish arrived in what became the U.S. West, they brought horses bred from Moorish stock that could easily maneuver, as opposed to the draft horses used throughout most of Europe for farming and warfare. By the 1598 permanent settlement expedition of Don Juan de Oñate into New Mexico, Spaniards brought both stallions and mares for the first time.

Even though Spanish law forbade Indians from owning or riding horses, continued retaliatory raids by Apache and Navajo yielded horses from the Spanish. They developed animal husbandry skills, and soon their horse herds grew. Through intertribal trade and raids, the horse culture expanded beyond the Apache and Navajo, to include the Comanche, Ute, Kiowa and Kiowa-Apache, who in turn traded horses to Plains and mountain tribes, until they spread as far as the Nez

Indians Hunting the Bison *painted by Swiss artist Karl Bodmer, 1832–1834. (Library of Congress)*

Percé by the mid- to late 1700s. When the Nez Percé acquired horses, they interbred selectively to create a phenomenal breed well adapted to the mountainous and rugged terrain of the Rocky Mountains: the Appaloosa.

Acquiring the horse transformed only one major Plains tribe from sedentary to migratory: the Pawnee. For most nomadic and seminomadic tribes, horses made them more mobile and therefore more capable of following buffalo herds for much longer distances. They could drag longer lodge poles as they traveled, meaning that their lodges were larger as well. Also, acquiring horses allowed the development of a culture based on possession of horses as a designation of wealth. As Pretty-shield, a Crow medicine woman, said about the acquisition of the horse during the 18th century, it made life easier. The horse revolutionized American Indian cultures throughout the American West.

The adoption of the horse by tribes also changed the ecology of the region. As horse herds grew, less forage was available for the native species, likely causing shifts in migratory and feeding patterns. It also allowed horse-bound American Indians to hunt more effectively, which also had an impact on native animal populations.

Surrounding the Pueblos on the west, the south, and the east lived various bands of Apache Indians. Like the Pueblo Indians, they were not one unified force, but rather numerous independent bands of culturally and linguistically distinct Apache whose lifestyle varied according their home range. The Chiricahua, White Mountain, and Tonto Apache lived to the west near the current border between New Mexico and Arizona; the Suma lived to the south. To the north lived the Jicarilla Apache, and to the south the Mescalero. On the east, the Lipan Apache existed as Plains people who found themselves forced south after the arrival of the Comanche.

By the late 1600s and early 1700s, the Comanche appeared in the region. They had originally lived farther north and east, but like many tribes in this volatile colonial period, they found themselves forced west and south as the pressure from the English and French on the coast and along the Saint Lawrence River and the expansion of the fur trade forced such powerhouse tribes as the Algonkin and Iroquois farther west in search of furs. As a result of their westward and southward expansion, their pressure pushed other tribes from the East and Midwest farther west. Some tribes were forced west while others moved voluntarily out of economic necessity or simply for survival. An excellent example of this westward movement is the confrontation between the Chippewa-Ojibwa and the Lakota Sioux in Wisconsin and Minnesota, which lasted until the mid-1700s. Most of the Sioux were forced out and moved onto the plains of the Dakotas. This shift caused other tribes to relocate south and west as well. While the Pueblo Indians had no direct contact with either of those European colonial powers, their actions in the east had a direct effect on Indian life and ability to survive traditionally in the west.

These shifting populations would wreak havoc upon the balance of power on the southern Plains and desert Southwest. Conditions became more challenging for the Pueblo Indians in the Rio Grande Valley and farther west into Laguna, Zuni, and Hopi territory during the 1680s. The drought and subsequent famine did not end, so competition for resources became more intense. The Spanish had taken what they could with them, but they could not take their diseases with them. There are no records of the number of deaths caused by the European diseases that continued to spread among the Indian people between 1680 and 1692, but influenza, a variety of European viruses, and smallpox would continue to devastate the Indian populations.

For the next few years, several Pueblo Indians ventured south to the Spanish holdout of El Paso del Norte to ask the Spanish colonists and their military to return and help protect the Pueblos against their emboldened enemies, including the Apache and Navajo, and soon the Comanche and Ute. Spanish military contingents led raids into New Mexico, including one led by the governor who had lost New Mexico, Antonio de Otermín (1681), and another led by his replacement, Don Domingo Jironza Petris de Cruzate (1688). They were as much reconnaissance missions as they were an attempt to reassert Spanish authority. They hoped to learn about the condition of the pueblos and determine whether a reconquest was possible.

In 1681, Otermín marched north with an army of more than 250, including Spanish soldiers and Indian allies. They brought horses, carts, mules, ammunition, and harquebuses. This was a carefully orchestrated reconnaissance mission, and he hoped to learn as much as he could about the state of the revolt, the will of the Pueblo peoples as a whole, and the possibility of reconquest. Both governors wanted to be the one to reunite New Mexico with New Spain. Otermín sent an advance guard under Juan Domingo de Mendoza who, upon encountering Pueblo Indian villages, burned them and destroyed their food stores, something that Otermín later protested—for the Spaniards could have used that food in El Paso and on the expedition. Mendoza made another mistake for which Otermín admonished him: upon encountering a force of Pueblo Indians preparing for war, he allowed them to go home after repenting of their actions, instead of engaging or disarming them. However, Mendoza followed the letter of Spanish law requiring the Spanish to offer contracts of fealty to the crown and pope before engaging in a "just war," something the Pueblos by this point clearly understood. Perhaps the Spaniards could have retaken New Mexico in 1681, perhaps not. But Otermín, having made no real gains in New Mexico, returned to El Paso by the end of the year.

In just over a month, Otermín had tried and failed to reconquer New Mexico. Interestingly, some members of Isleta Pueblo, who had had a long relationship with the Spaniards (not by choice), quickly accepted the return of the Spaniards under Otermín when the Spanish force appeared at their pueblo. Because of their perceived complicity (and the failure of the Spaniards to retake New Mexico), those Isletans who had so readily accepted the Spanish soldiers' return feared reprisals and asked the Spanish to take their villagers back to El Paso so they could establish a community there (known today as Ysleta del Sur). More than 350 Isletans made the journey and established Ysleta del Sur, which still exists today. Not all Isletans welcomed the Spaniards, however, and oral history illustrates this quite aptly. Even today, Isleta tribal members talk of how parents dug holes in the walls of their adobe homes and hid their children inside, plastering them closed until the Spanish departed. Some of the others fled into the hills, while the collaborators negotiated with the conquerors. Perhaps the retaliation that those 350 feared in part came from within their own village, not only from neighboring tribes. Fleeing south with Otermín, the Isletans must have feared their lives away from family and friends, their traditional lifeways, their kivas, and their sacred shrines.

Otermín, however, was more concerned about his own future and how this failed expedition would tarnish his record and hopes for a better appointment in the future. Two years later, the Spanish crown replaced him with a motivated soldier, whose legacy has proven elusive to future researchers.

Otermín's replacement as governor, Don Domingo Jironza Petris de Cruzate, would look north, too, in hopes of reestablishing the renegade colony and getting the glory and honor for restoring the frontier province. In office from 1683 to 1686, and again from 1688 to 1691, Jironza put plans in motion to recover New Mexico. His expedition into the Rio Grande Valley took place in 1688. He and his rather small army traveled up the river, somewhat untouched by confrontation, through the Rio Abajo to Zía Pueblo, just west of the Rio Grande in central New Mexico for the glory of the Spanish crown (and potentially a better governmental position). Jironza and his men razed the village of Zía, killing approximately 600 natives and capturing more than 70, which he intended to sell as slaves. Even though outnumbered by ten to one, it is thought that this bloody foray weakened the resolve of future rebellions against invading Spaniards.

Jironza interrogated the captives he took from Zía, who shared stories of pueblo life without Spain's presence. He hoped to find out about the unity of the Pueblo Indians and to remind the pueblos of their proximity. Jironza learned that the pueblo coalition had disintegrated, that Popé had met an early end, that crop failures had continued, and that the nomadic raids had intensified when the Pueblos' protectors left. Moreover, they learned that some of the Pueblo people actually wanted the Spaniards to return. Those who had converted and did not wash off their baptism in the Rio Grande with soapweed watched family members die without the last rites and new babies born and growing up without the rite of baptism or communion and other important Catholic sacraments. While Popé called for husbands and wives who married under the aegis of the Catholic Church to disband their unions, many did not. And others continued to want the blessings of the Christian God for their partnerships. Records illustrate the numbers of Pueblo baptisms and marriages in the missions after the Pueblo Revolt, thereby indicating that these were indeed not false rumors. As Jironza fought to get reappointed to the governorship of New Mexico after his successful reconnaissance of 1688, he did what he could to prepare the ragtag band of leftover colonists for the reconquest of New Mexico. He would not win the bid for the governorship, however, until after Don Diego de Vargas had taken over in 1692, making his bid moot. It would not be until 1692 under the leadership of Vargas that the Spanish would successfully reclaim the northern frontier.

RECONQUEST OF NEW MEXICO AND A PHILOSOPHY OF ACCOMMODATION

Vargas's bold and royally sanctioned reconquest in 1692 involved only soldiers, horses, and supplies—not the families and supplies necessary for resettlement. But before he could lead his reconquering expedition north, he first had to subdue tribes in the El Paso area that had harassed the local Spanish and Pueblo Indian populations, among them the Sumas and Mansos tribes. After he had sorted out a tenuous peace, he began to look toward building his little army to move north. By the summer of 1692, he and approximately 200 soldiers, as well as some Franciscan friars, headed north to retake New Mexico for the Spanish king.

After much preparation and recruiting, Vargas marched north across the Rio Grande, planning to use his small military force to demand the submission of the tribes—but through peaceful means. He would offer the Pueblo Indians a pardon and ask them to once again pledge their fealty to the crown and the Catholic Church. If necessary, however, he would take New Mexico "by force of arms." As they marched north along the 100-year-old *Camino Real de Tierra Adentro,* he noted that pueblo after pueblo lay abandoned, even if just temporarily. When he arrived at the former headquarters at Santa Fe, he found it inhabited by Pueblos who had converted the former governor's palace into a pueblo-styled village. Shocked at seeing these white strangers in and near their village streets once again, they listened to Vargas's appeal and watched his bold and daring reentry, accompanied by just a single friar and without weaponry to illustrate his genuine desire to regain their trust. The Pueblos acquiesced, and Vargas unfurled the banner of Spain and retook New Mexico. Even one of Pope's former lieutenants arrived at Vargas's camp to pledge his loyalty. To illustrate his fealty, he raised a small contingent of "friendly" Indians to assist the Spaniards and provided Vargas with useful intelligence regarding the many of the other pueblos. During his expedition, Vargas had reconquered Santa Fe, potentially gaining the respect of the Indians he encountered by not resorting to the sword, and he gained the loyalty of a major and respected Pueblo Indian who had actually led the fight against the Spanish a dozen years before. While in New Mexico with Vargas, friars baptized more than 2,000 Indians at the request of their parents (mostly children younger than 13 years). For some of these children, Vargas would stand as godfather to cement the relationship between himself and each of the pueblo communities, one of mutual obligation and responsibility. After accomplishing what two others before him could not, Vargas returned to El Paso by Christmas, and the news of his success quickly spread throughout New Spain.

The Pueblo people had to wonder to what end this Spanish soldier had come with an army, yet had not asserted its military might even while demanding their loyalty to the king and pope, and ultimately turning around and leaving the province. Certainly they understood that he would soon return, and this time he would come with more than just a small army. Some Pueblos knew they could use the assistance and protection of the Spanish men, their horses, and their guns. As the Pueblos pondered the future of their beleaguered state of affairs, finding their villages besieged by the ever-more emboldened nomadic warriors, Vargas set about preparing for his return to New Mexico, this time with soldiers, colonists, livestock, supplies, and seed. Some of the recruits he enlisted had lived in New Mexico previously, and were no doubt curious about the state of their land grants, fields, herds, and homes. By September 1693, Vargas returned north, this time with 800 settlers, livestock, and supplies.

The pueblos, Vargas heard, had begun to ready themselves. Reports from some cooperating Indians indicated that some of the northern tribes planned to rise up again. Hearing the same intelligence reports unceasingly as he traveled north, he wondered what he would face as he arrived at Santa Fe. When they arrived at Santa Fe, they saw that Tano and Tewa Indians still occupied the former capital. Vargas learned that they refused to vacate the capital to the Spaniards; after all, it had been their home for a dozen years. The unwavering occupants became even more resolute when the Spaniards began making demands on their food supply. The Spanish settlers who had accompanied Vargas had established a camp outside the walls of their former capital, waiting for Vargas to succeed in his negotiations. But at more than 6,000 feet in elevation, Santa Fe could get very cold and snowbound in the winters, and by December, conditions had grown so precarious that the Spanish settlers began to suffer from hunger and cold. The settlers demanded that Vargas remove the Pueblo inhabitants from Santa Fe so that the Spanish colonists could have their homes restored, leaving behind the makeshift camp they occupied. The belligerent Pueblo people had had enough opportunity for negotiating a peaceful settlement.

To force the Indians to vacate their former home and capital, Vargas laid siege to Santa Fe just as the Pueblos had done 13 years before to extricate the Spanish defenders, by cutting off the water supply to the village. With pressure from Vargas, the Pueblos eventually relinquished their hold on the former capital, and the chaos that ensued would later cause Vargas to face charges for unnecessary use of force for the firing squad executions of 70 Indians, as well as the enslavement of around 400 women and children. In the end, the Spanish retook the former capital and demanded that the Pueblo Indians live once again under Spanish rule, as they had promised in 1692 during Vargas's earlier reconquest expedition. But the Indians had won an improbable victory: the encomienda would never return to New Mexico. While the crown had granted an encomienda to Vargas, he never put it into operation. As historian Elizabeth A. H. John put it, "thus vanished the greatest economic grievance of the Pueblos and the worst source of friction between Spanish and Pueblo populations" (John, *Storms Brewed*, 149).

Religious friction remained, albeit much diminished. Franciscan friars no longer held the power they had commanded during the Missionary Era, and therefore they did not implement the force they had overzealously used during the 1660s and 1670s. Pueblo Indians held steadfast to their ancient religious spiritualism, and Franciscans conceded to the coexistence of both belief systems among the Pueblo Indians. In a word, they had arrived at accommodation between the two disparate worlds, and that principal would guide them throughout the end of the Spanish colonial period.

Besides religious toleration, which led to more syncretization between spiritual worlds, the Spanish also relaxed some of the rules relating
to military issues. Before, Pueblo Indians could not retaliate against nomadic Indian (or any other) raids or incursions against their homes or
persons. But after Vargas retook New Mexico, Pueblo Indian auxiliaries
could begin to fight alongside Spanish soldiers in retaliatory raids and
battles they encountered against their common adversaries the Navajo
and Faraon Apache, as well as the Comanche who had moved down into
the southern Plains after tribes pushed out of the Great Lakes region
shifted to the west.

An excellent example of the military partnership that formed between the Spanish and the Pueblo Indians occurred in 1720. Vargas had
not been governor for almost 20 years, but his spirit of accommodation
and mutual existence continued to permeate the colony and develop into
a more meaningful relationships, even beyond military. The Spanish had
heard that French expansion and influence had crossed the Mississippi
River and into regions clearly claimed by the Spanish. Rumors stated that
the French had begun trading with the Pawnee, a potentially dangerous
enemy on the upper Plains. Lt. Pedro de Villasur, a young soldier from
Santa Fe, organized and led the expedition that consisted of 42 men,
pueblo auxiliaries, and some private Spanish colonists, to march north to
find out if the French indeed posed a threat to Spanish hegemony. Upon
arriving in the evening in mid-July at the confluence of the Loup and
Platte rivers, they encountered a band of Pawnee. After short negotiations, both sides agreed to rest the evening and parlay in the morning. Before dawn, however, the Pawnee flooded into the Spanish encampment
and began attacking the Spanish contingent with French muskets and
bows and arrows. Villasur was among the first to fall, and with him more
than 30 other Spaniards perished. Those survivors limped back to Santa
Fe to report that indeed the French had established a trade relationship
with the Pawnee. Because of the great distance and lack of resources, the
Spanish never attempted to reclaim the central Plains. While the Villasure
Massacre certainly tarnished the image of Spain's strength on the frontier,
the Spanish would continue to assert its superiority among Indian populations close to Spanish settlements. And this event taught the Spanish
that they should keep a wary eye on tribes to their north and east.

Over the past 100 years, these nomadic Plains tribes had learned the value of horses that could improve their ability at warfare and raiding, as well as sheep and cattle for dependable sources of food. Beyond that, nearly all the tribes engaged in the practice of taking captives. Indians used captives for a variety of purposes, including to replace tribal members lost because of warfare or captivity. They also used them to trade to the Spanish for items they could not acquire through raids, including the return of their own family members taken in raids by the Spanish. By the 1700s, Spanish officials created a classification for Plains Indian captives who had lived for a generation or more among the Spanish and become "Hispanized" (that is, Christian, adapting to Spanish culture and language): *genízaros*. In the 1700s, Spanish authorities would even encourage genízaro land grants and settlements around the fringes of the Rio Grande communities, to serve as a buffer zone against nomadic incursions—a sort of front line of defense against nomadic raiding.

Even though tensions grew between the nomadic communities and the settled villages along the Rio Grande and its environs, a unique experience occurred yearly at Taos Pueblo: the annual trade fair (historically, the Pecos experienced these, too). The trade fairs became an important feature of occupied New Mexico for Indian people from many different regions (mountains, plains, deserts, for example). The Spaniards and Pueblo Indians traded agricultural goods, products from their domestic livestock herds, Spanish-made goods, and Indian captives to primarily Apache, Ute, and Comanche Indians, but other tribes were represented as well. While the Ute and Apache had raided Spanish and Pueblo villages in the early 1600s, the Comanche began to raid and take captives too. Nomadic tribes brought buffalo and deer hides, jerked meat, and other products of the plains and mountain regions, as well as Spanish and Pueblo Indian captives. And, in an attempt to effect the return of Spaniards from the nomadic tribes during these trade fairs, the governor of New Mexico set up a recovery fund whose purpose it was to purchase back captives so they could be reunited with their families. The Comanche, incidentally, oftentimes brought horses bearing Spanish brands from Texas to the trade fairs.

As the Comanche moved onto the southern Plains, they acquired horses from the Apache and then directly from raiding Spanish settle-

In the late 1950s, about 1,300 Indians lived here in the Taos Pueblo in practically the same buildings and under the same conditions as in the 16th century under Spanish rule. (National Archives)

ments. Known for their expertise in horsemanship, they were feared by Spaniards who found themselves fighting off the Comanche attacks all too often. But the Comanche, Apache, Ute, and Navajo had not originally started the raiding cycle that spiraled into the 18th century. Some of the first raids that took place between the northern frontier's various Apache bands and Spaniards occurred before New Mexico's settlement when Spanish slave raiders captured Apaches to be sold into slavery, a result of Nuño de Guzmán's slave raids into Sonora as early as the beginning of the 1500s, for example. The retaliatory raids continued throughout the 1500s and 1600s, and would proceed into the very end of the Spanish colonial period.

For generations, the authorities in New Mexico had attempted to put an end to the incessant nomadic attacks, some of which drove off entire herds of horses or sheep (and by the late 1700s and early 1800s a herd of sheep could number in the tens of thousands). Nothing seemed to work. But by the late 1700s, one New Mexico governor attempted to stop the raiding. Juan Bautista de Anza quickly recognized the futility of the continued retaliatory raids that the Spanish had practiced since their arrival in the late 16th century. He conceded that the Comanche were the biggest threat and hatched a plot to eliminate that particular threat. Because the Comanche operated not as one single band but as numerous smaller bands based on kinship, Anza had to figure out which band seemed to hold the most prestige and power among the rest and then to confront and subdue that band by use of force. Of all the bands living on the east slope of the Rockies and out onto the Plains, one leader, Cuerno Verde (Green Horn), appeared to have the most power and respect among all bands. After a well-conceived surprise attack on his camp, Cuerno Verde's men were defeated. News of his demise spread rapidly. By 1785, 400 Comanche showed up in New Mexico to ally themselves with the Spaniards. The formal agreement allowed the Comanches access to Santa Fe and the trade fair in Taos. The Spanish also enlisted their assistance in New Mexico's war against the Apache. With the Utes, the Apache had waged war on the remote Hopi Pueblos, reducing their population from more than 8,000 in the 1770s to fewer than 800. The Comanche Peace opened up a new chapter in Indian relations in the region and of extended warfare between the Apache and Comanche, sanctioned and supplied by the Spanish.

The Comanche were not the only threat in the 1780s, however; by 1780 and 1781, a smallpox epidemic ravaged the Southwest. Spaniards, Pueblos, and nomadic Indians as far out as the northern Plains alike found their populations affected, and for the Comanche, they likely lost half of their population. As a result of the shifts in population, the Comanche and Kiowa ended up forming an alliance. After the Spanish subdued Cuerno Verde, and for at least 20 years, a relative peace ensued between the Spanish and Comanche as both renewed their efforts against the Apache on all sides. Incidentally, the Apaches continued to defend their homelands and to cause disruptions for non-Apaches in the region until the U.S. military finally forced the last of the nonreservation Chiricahua Apaches into prisoner of war status and removal to a Florida prison with the final subjugation of Geronimo and his small band in 1886.

As New Mexico's Spanish population grew, the Pueblo Indian population dropped. While a number of Pueblo Indians were lost to death or capture in Indian raids, it was not the major cause of the decline of their population. Proximity to Spanish settlers caused diseases to spread quickly between populations, and numerous epidemics spread throughout their communities. Borderlands historian John L. Kessell tells of the epidemics, for example, that hit Pecos Pueblo every 10 to 15 years: "1696 (fever), 1704, 1728–29 (measles), 1738 (smallpox), 1748, 1759, 1780–81 (smallpox), 1800 (smallpox), 1816 (smallpox), and 1826. None exceeded the severity of North America's smallpox pandemic of 1779–1781" (Kessell, *Spain in the Southwest,* 297). These epidemics were not limited to New Mexico, but spread throughout the entire West along the traditional trading trails that had existed from years long before the Spanish had even become a nation. Indigenous populations withered as more Spaniards headed north and natural population increase caused Spaniards to outnumber Indians in New Mexico by the mid-1700s. No other northern colony of New Spain would reach that number.

In the 1700s, New Mexico's borders stretched from the Rio Grande to Florida, west to the Pacific Ocean, and north to the fabled Straits of Anián, in its earliest years. But as the Spanish realm expanded, and more colonists and explorers arrived in the northern provinces and as people learned more about these disparate regions, Spaniards began to take an interest in regions never before permanently occupied by them. For example, southern Arizona, which was technically still considered part of New Mexico until the middle of the U.S. Civil War in the 1860s, found itself a "target" of the Jesuit missionaries in the late 17th century. Texas, which had been traversed by Spaniards in search of the ill-starred La Salle expedition's survivors in the 1600s, became a buffer zone against French expansion by the early 1700s. California, the last of the northern frontier settlements settled by Spanish colonists, came about as an attempt to control the western boundaries, assist in the defense and food resupply of the Spanish galleons, and provide a base of operations for further expansion if necessary. Moreover, all of these recent acquisitions sported friars of some denomination to convert the nations. For Arizona, this was the primary purpose for establishing a presence, and it would be the Jesuits under the leadership of Father Eusebio Francisco Kino, not the Franciscans of New Mexico, who would take the challenge of establishing a permanent presence without the assistance of a military force.

BIBLIOGRAPHIC ESSAY

Colin G. Calloway's *One Vast Winter Count: The Native American West before Lewis and Clark* (Lincoln: University of Nebraska Press, 2003) and *First Peoples: A Documentary Survey of American Indian History* (Boston: Bedford/St. Martin's, 1999) are excellent overviews for all periods of Indian subjugation, as are Roger L. Nichols's *American Indians in U.S. History* (Norman: University of Oklahoma, 2004) and *The American Indian: Past and Present,* 5th ed. (New York: McGraw Hill, 1999); Barry M. Pritzker, *A Native American Encyclopedia: History, Culture, and Peoples* (Oxford: Oxford University Press, 2000); the somewhat dated but useful Alvin M. Josephy, Jr., *The Indian Heritage of America* (New York: Alfred A. Knopf, 1969); and Arrell Morgan Gibson, *The American Indian: Past and Present* (Lexington, MA: D.C. Heath and Company, 1980). Other useful sources include Alvin M. Josephy, Jr., *500 Nations: An Illustrated History of North American Indians* (New York: Gramercy, 2002); Frederick Hoxie, *Indians in American History: An Introduction* (New York: Harlan Davidson, 1998); Wendell H. Oswalt, *This Land Was Theirs: A Study of Native Americans* (Oxford: Oxford University Press, 2001); Philip Weeks, ed., *"They Made Us Many Promises": The American Indian Experience 1524 to the Present,* 2nd ed. (Wheeling, IL: Harlan Davidson, 2002); Roger L. Nichols, *American Indians in U.S. History* (Norman: University of Oklahoma Press, 2003); Clifford E. Trafzer, *As Long as the Grass Shall Grow and the Rivers Flow: A History of Native Americans* (Belmont, CA: Wadsworth Group/Thompson Learning, 2000); Angie Debo, *A History of Indians of the United States* (Norman: University of Oklahoma Press, 1970); Vine Deloria, Jr., and Clifford M. Lytle, *The Nations Within: The Past and Future of American Indian Sovereignty* (Austin: University of Texas Press, 1984); Joel W. Martin, *The Land Looks After Us: A History of Native American Religion* (New York: Oxford University Press, 2001); Laurence M. Hauptman, *Tribes & Tribulations: Misconceptions about American Indians and Their Histories* (Albuquerque: University of New Mexico, 1995); and finally, Alice Beck Kehoe, *North American Indians: A Comprehensive Account,* 3rd ed. (Upper Saddle River, NJ: Prentice Hall, 2006). For an interesting discussion about cultural brokers, see Margaret Connell-Szasz, ed., *Between Indian and White Worlds: The Cultural Brokers* (Norman: University of Oklahoma Press, 1994). Standard texts on American Indian history include James Axtell, *The Invasion Within: The Contest of Cultures in Colonial North America* (New York: Oxford University Press, 1985); Robert E. Berkhofer, Jr., *The White Man's Indian* (New York: Alfred A. Knopf, 1978); Francis Jennings, *The Invasion of America: Indians, Colonialism and the Cant of Conquest* (Chapel Hill: University of North Carolina Press, 1975); Richard E. W. Adams and Murdo J. MacLeod, eds., *The Cambridge History of the Native Peoples of the*

Americas (Cambridge, UK: Cambridge University Press, 2000); Karen Olsen Bruhns and Karen E. Stothert, *Women in Ancient America* (Norman: University of Oklahoma Press, 1999); Colin G. Calloway, *New Worlds for All: Indians, Europeans, and the Remaking of America* (Baltimore: Johns Hopkins University Press, 1997); Jared Diamond, *Guns, Germs, and Steel: The Fates of Human Societies* (New York: W. W. Norton, 1997) and *Collapse: How Societies Choose to Fail or Succeed* (New York: Viking Press, 2005); Thomas D. Dillehay, *The Settlement of the Americas: A New Prehistory* (New York: Basic Books, 2000); James E. Dixon, *Bones, Boats, and Bison: Archaeology and the First Colonization of Western North America* (Albuquerque: University of New Mexico Press, 1999); Francis Haines, *The Buffalo: The Story of American Bison and Their Hunters from Prehistoric Times to the Present* (1970, reprint, Norman: University of Oklahoma Press, 1995).

The excellent series *Handbook of North American Indians* is published by the Smithsonian Institution in Washington, D.C., under the general editorship of William Sturtevant: Robert F. Heizer, ed., *California*, vol. 8 (1978); Alfonzo Ortiz, ed., *Southwest*, vol. 9 and vol. 10 (1979); Warren L. D'Azevedo, ed., *Great Basin*, vol. 11 (1986); DeWard E. Walker, ed., *Plateau*, vol. 12 (1998); Raymond J. DeMallie, ed., *Plains*, vol. 13, parts 1 and 2 (2001); Bruce G. Trigger, ed., *Northeast*, vol. 15 (1978). Other volumes deal with additional regions, such as the Southeast, Indian-white interaction, and languages.

A variety of excellent sources were used, including John L. Kessell, *Spain in the Southwest: A Narrative History of Colonial New Mexico, Arizona, Texas, and California* (Norman: University of Oklahoma Press, 2002); David J. Weber, *The Spanish Frontier in North America* (New Haven, CT: Yale University Press, 1994); Elizabeth Ann Harper John, *Storms Brewed in Other Men's Worlds: The Confrontation of Indians, Spanish, and French in the Southwest, 1540–1795* (Lincoln: University of Nebraska Press, 1975); Edward H. Spicer, *Cycles of Conquest: The Impact of Spain, Mexico, and the United States on the Indians of the Southwest, 1533–1960* (Tucson: University of Arizona Press, 1976); Max L. Moorhead, *The Presidio: Bastion of the Spanish Borderlands* (Norman: University of Oklahoma Press, 1991). In addition, there are the following works by Oakah L. Jones, Jr.: *Los Paisanos: Spanish Settlers on the Northern Frontier of New Spain* (Norman: University of Oklahoma Press, 1996); *Nueva Vizcaya: Heartland of the Spanish Frontier* (Albuquerque: University of New Mexico Press, 1988); and *Pueblo Warriors & Spanish Conquest* (Norman: University of Oklahoma Press, 1966). For Pueblo histories, see Alfonso Ortiz, *Tewa World: Space, Time, Being, and Becoming in a Pueblo Society* (Chicago: University of Chicago Press, 1972); Joe S. Sando, *Nee Hemish: A History of Jemez Pueblo* (Albuquerque: University of New Mexico Press, 1982) and *Pueblo Nations: Eight Centuries of Pueblo Indian History* (Santa Fe, NM: Clear Light Publishing, 1992); W. W. Hill, *An Ethnography of Santa Clara Pueblo, New Mexico* (Albuquerque: University of

New Mexico Press, 1982); Michael Adler and Herbert W. Dick, eds., *Picuris Pueblo through Time: Eight Centuries of Change in a Northern Rio Grande Pueblo* (Dallas: William P. Clements Center for Southwest Research, 1999); Ward Allen Minge and Simon J. Ortiz, *Acoma: Pueblo in the Sky* (Albuquerque: University of New Mexico Press, 1991); Laura Bayer, Floyd Montoya, and the People of the Pueblo of Santa Ana, *Santa Ana: The People of the Pueblo, and the History of Tamaya* (Albuquerque: University of New Mexico Press, 1994); William Whitman, *The Pueblo Indians of San Ildefonso: A Changing Culture* (New York: AMS Press, 1969); E. Richard Hart, ed., *Zuni and the Courts: A Struggle for Sovereign Land Rights* (Lawrence: University Press of Kansas, 1995); Charles H. Lange, *Cochiti: A New Mexico Pueblo, Past and Present* (Albuquerque: University of New Mexico Press, 1959); R. C. Gordon-McCutchan, *The Taos Indians and the Battle for Blue Lake* (Santa Fe, NM: Red Crane Books, 1995); G. Emlen Hall, *Four Leagues of Pecos: A Legal History of the Pecos Grant, 1800–1933* (Albuquerque: University of New Mexico Press, 1984); and John L. Kessell, *Kiva, Cross & Crown: The Pecos Indians and New Mexico, 1540–1840* (Tucson, AZ: Southwest Parks & Monuments Association, 1995).

Several excellent sources exist covering the region claimed by the Spaniards. Primary sources include Eleanor B. Adams and Fray Angélico Chávez, trans. and eds., *The Missions of New Mexico, 1776: A Description by Fray Francisco Atanasio Domínguez with Other Contemporary Documents* (Albuquerque: University of New Mexico Press, 1956); Rolena Adorno and Patrick Charles Pautz, *Álvar Núñez Cabeza de Vaca: His Account, His Life, and the Expedition of Pánfilo de Narváez,* 3 vols. (Lincoln: University of Nebraska Press, 1999); Cyclone Covey, trans., *Adventures in the Unknown Interior of America* (Albuquerque: University of New Mexico Press, 1983); J. Manuel Espinosa, trans. and ed., *The Pueblo Indian Revolt of 1696 and the Franciscan Missions in New Mexico: Letters of the Missionaries and Related Documents* (Norman: University of Oklahoma Press, 1988). Other excellent primary sources include Charles Wilson Hackett, ed., *Historical Documents Relating to New Mexico, Nueva Vizcaya, and Approaches Thereto, to 1773,* 3 vols. (Washington, D.C.: Carnegie Institute, 1923–1927), and *Revolt of the Pueblo Indians of New Mexico and Otermín's Attempted Reconquest 1680–1682,* trans. Charmion Clair Shelby, 2 vols. (Albuquerque: University of New Mexico Press, 1942); Cleve Hallenbeck, *The Journey of Fray Marcos de Niza* (Dallas: Southern Methodist University Press, 1964) and *Spanish Missions of the Old Southwest* (Garden City, NY: Doubleday, Page, and Company, 1926); and Fray Alonso de Benavidez, *The Memorial of 1630,* trans. Mrs. Edward E. Ayer (Albuquerque: Horn and Wallace, 1965). See also George P. Hammond and Agapito Rey, eds., *Don Juan de Oñate: Colonizer of New Mexico, 1595–1628,* 2 vols. (Albuquerque: University of New Mexico Press, 1953), *Narrative of the Coronado Expedition 1540–1542* (Albuquerque: University of New Mexico Press, 1940), *New Mexico in 1602: Juan de Montoya's Relation of the Discovery of*

New Mexico (Albuquerque: Quivira Society, 1938), and *The Rediscovery of New Mexico* (Albuquerque, University of New Mexico Press, 1966); Fritz Leo Hoffman, trans., *Diary of the Alarcón Expedition into Texas, 1718–1719,* by Fray Francisco Céliz (Los Angeles: Quivira Society, 1935); John L. Kessell, ed., *Remote Beyond Compare: Letters of Don Diego de Vargas to His Family from New Spain and New Mexico, 1675–1706* (Albuquerque: University of New Mexico Press, 1989), with Rick Hendricks, eds., *By Force of Arms: The Journal of Don Diego de Vargas, New Mexico, 1691–93* (Albuquerque: University of New Mexico Press, 1992), with Meredith D. Dodge, eds., *To the Royal Crown Restored: The Journals of Don Diego de Vargas, New Mexico 1692–94* (Albuquerque: University of New Mexico Press, 1995), *Blood on the Boulders: The Journals of Don Diego de Vargas, New Mexico 1694–97,* 2 vols. (Albuquerque: University of New Mexico Press, 1998), and with Larry D. Miller, eds., *That Disturbances Cease: The Journals of Don Diego de Vargas, New Mexico, 1697–1700* (Albuquerque: University of New Mexico Press, 2000). These numerous Vargas volumes are classic representations of a key period of transition in New Mexico history from one of dissension and distrust to one of collaboration, cooperation, and accommodation between the Spaniards and the Pueblo Indians. Other excellent sources for Pacific exploration include Herbert Eugene Bolton, *Spanish Exploration in the Southwest, 1542–1706* (New York: Charles Scribners Sons, 1916), and Herbert E. Bolton, *Guide to Materials for the History of the United States in the Principal Archives of Mexico* (New York: Kraus Reprint, 1965).

See also John Meares, *Voyages Made in the Years 1788 and 1789, from China to the North West Coast of America* (London: The Logographic Press for J. Walter: 1790); Spanish Archives of New Mexico, 1621–1821, Microfilm reels, State of New Mexico Library and Archives Records Center, Santa Fe (see also Ralph Emerson Twitchell, *Spanish Archives of New Mexico: Compiled and Chronologically Arranged with Historical, Biographical and Genealogical Annotations and Translations,* vols. 1 and 2 (Albuquerque: Horn and Wallace, 1965); Ted J. Warner, ed., *The Domínguez-Escalante Journal: Their Expedition through Colorado, Utah, Arizona, and New Mexico in 1776,* trans. Fray Angélico Chávez (Salt Lake City: University of Utah Press, 1995); Fray Alonso de Benavides, *The Memorial of Fray Alonso de Benavides, 1630* (Albuquerque: Horn and Wallace, 1965).

For information on Bartolomé de las Casas and the Black Legend, see his own *Short Account of the Destruction of the Indies* (New York: Penguin Classics, 1999); Philip Wayne Powell, *Tree of Hate: Propaganda and Prejudices Affecting United States Relations with the Hispanic World,* reprint ed. (Fort Worth, TX: Stella Maris Books, 1971).

For two standard secondary sources on the Pueblo Revolt, see Andrew Knaut, *The Pueblo Revolt: Conquest and Resistance in Seventeenth-Century New Mexico* (Norman: University of Oklahoma Press, 1997), and Robert Silverberg,

The Pueblo Revolt (Lincoln: University of Nebraska Press, 1994). See also Joe S. Sando and Herman Agoyo, eds., *Po'pay: Leader of the First American Revolution* (Santa Fe, NM: Clear Light Publishers, 2005), and Stefanie Beninato, "Pope, Pose-yemu, and Naranjo: A New Look at Leadership in the Pueblo Revolt of 1680," *New Mexico Historical Review* 65 (1990).

James L. Brooks, *Captives and Cousins: Slavery, Kinship, and Community in the Southwest Borderlands* (Chapel Hill: University of North Carolina Press, 2002); and Ross Frank, *From Settler to Citizen: New Mexican Economic Development and the Creation of Vecino Society, 1750–1820* (Berkeley: University of California Press, 2000); Philip Wayne Powell, *Soldiers, Indians, & Silver: The Northward Advance of New Spain, 1550–1600* (Ann Arbor, MI: University Microfilms, 1968); Robert Himmerich y Valencia, *The Encomenderos of New Spain 1521–1555* (Austin: University of Texas Press, 1991). Finally, for two excellent sources on the administration of the colonies, see Charles R. Cutter's *The Protector de Indios in Colonial New Mexico, 1659–1821* (Albuquerque: University of New Mexico Press, 1986) and his *The Legal Culture of Northern New Spain, 1700–1810,* reprint ed. 1995 (Albuquerque: University of New Mexico Press; 2001).

Finally, for an interesting discussion about the impact of the horse on American Indians during this early colonial period, see James Sherow, "Workings of the Geodialectic: High Plains Indians and Their Horses in the Region of the Arkansas River Valley, 1800–1870," *Environmental History Review* 16 (Summer 1992): 61–84, and Pretty-shield's discussion of the shift to horse culture in Frank B. Linderman, *Pretty-shield, Medicine Woman of the Crow* (Lincoln: University of Nebraska Press, 1974).

CHAPTER THREE

FROM THE PACIFIC TO THE GULF OF MEXICO

THE GILA AND SALT RIVER VALLEYS

In the northern reaches of New Spain, just to the west of El Paso and the *Jornada del Muerto,* that 90-mile stretch of desert through which the Camino Real passed, lived the Opata, Jocome, and Jano; the Papago and upper Pima; and the Western Apache Indians (a conglomeration of various bands of Apache more simply known as the Western Apache; see Chapter 1). Along the Colorado River lived the Maricopa, and the Cocopa surrounded its mouth at the Sea of California (or the Sea of Cortez).

The Pima and Papago took up the greatest land mass between Apache Pass (southeastern Arizona) and nearly all the way to the mouth of the Colorado River to the west. They ranged north to the Salt River and the homeland of the Maricopa Indians. The Jocome and Janos were their eastern neighbors, and the Western Apache were just to the northeast. Above them sat the Maricopa and the Yavapai, and to their west the Cocopa. To the southeast were the Opata. Indeed, Jesuit Father Eusebio Francisco Kino did not enter into an uninhabited place. These tribes based their lifestyles on perhaps thousands of years of learning to adapt to the difficult desert climate. The Pima and Papago spoke one of the Pima languages, derived from the Uto-Aztecan family. They had a linguistic family living to the south, called the Pima Bajo by the Spaniards. The upper Pimas derived from numerous bands that survived as farmers on the river banks as well as those that lived farther from rivers. Recognized

Women of the Papagos, a group of people who lived on the border of the United States and Mexico, from Report on the United States and Mexican Boundary Survey, *1857–1859. (National Oceanic and Atmospheric Administration)*

as different by the Spanish, they called themselves the Tohono O'odham, or "we, the people" (Fontana, "Pima and Papago," 125). Those descended from the upper Pima Indians during the Spanish period are now called the Pima and Papago.

In one of the driest places to which the Spaniards laid claim, these tribes survived with sometimes as little as less than one inch to three and a half inches of average annual rainfall. They learned to depend on the annual rainy seasons in midsummer and early winter. Temperatures soared as well, sometimes reaching as high as 120°F in the summer. Therefore, food and water were precious resources because of the low yearly rainfall, and these tribes learned to depend on food gathering and hunting as their main source of sustenance. They must have known or learned that depending entirely on cultivated crops invited disaster. Certainly, they had access to the trade routes to Mexico City and, like the Mogollón peoples, would have acquired various seeds for planting or grinding into meal. Therefore, they had a seminomadic existence, moving from one camp (called *rancherías*) to another, always searching for water; plants that yield fruits, roots, or other sustenance; and animals to hunt. Plant life lived precariously in the arid environment, as did humans and animals. The region also hosted mountain ranges, which provided some access to cooler temperatures and potentially snowfall in the winter. Therefore, everything from bighorn sheep to antelope to white-tailed and mule deer existed, as did various foxes, pack rats, javelinas, coyotes, badgers, cottontails, and ringtails (Ibid., 129). In other words, there was food; one just had to be able to relocate periodically to follow the bounty and the cycles of gathering (see Map 6).

Into this arid region a Jesuit friar would arrive in the late 1600s to spread the message of the Catholic faith among any who would listen. Father Kino arrived in Mexico City nearly a year after the Pueblo Revolt in northern New Spain, which had claimed the lives of nearly 400 Spanish citizens, including more than 20 friars—by far a majority of the entire complement for the frontier colony. Certainly, Father Kino pondered the massive death toll in New Mexico, learned the circumstances under which the deaths had occurred, and this knowledge played a role in his methods of conversion in the Baja and the Pimería Alta (southern Arizona). Northern New Spain had not seemed this dangerous since the

Mixton Wars in the 1540s, but that did not deter Father Kino from his goal of converting his native charges.

Nearly 200 years had passed since Spain first arrived in the New World, and it had been 160 years since Cortés had subdued the Aztecs. The population of Mexico City had changed in composition, and the layout of the town, based on European designs and with its magnificent buildings and great plazas, awed the newcomer. Father Kino visited the enormous cathedral and pondered the Pueblo Revolt not one year before. He had not been chosen to remain in Mexico City, however; he was more interested in that which drew him to become a Jesuit in the first place: selfless service on behalf of the Lord to those who did not know the Christian God. He found his first calling in Baja California, across the Sea of Cortez from that region that Álvar Núñez Cabeza de Vaca first encountered Spanish slavers after his travels from La Pascua Florida. By the mid-1680s, he and Isidro de Atondo had set up a permanent settlement for the first time in Baja and had established missions on the southern end. But by 1686, after several attempts, the missions at Baja and farther north had to be abandoned. Yet Father Kino and his colleague, Father Juan María Salvatierra, refused to give up a potential foothold for the Jesuits in northern New Spain, which would help them compete with the Franciscans for control of the New World. This time, he landed among the Pima in northern Sonora and southern Arizona.

Thus, Father Salvatierra and Father Kino had chosen a challenging realm, yet one not without promise. Father Kino set up his mission, which he called Dolores, at one of the Tohono O'odham rancherías. He had arrived with the blessing of the Catholic Church, and without the assistance of the military; but he also provoked the consternation of his other Spanish neighbors, who saw Kino's missions as a threat to their economic survival. Mining and ranching enterprises had traditionally used the labor of Indian people, mostly against their will. Abuse of Indian labor could only continue as long as the Indians remained heathens, and officials, who did not benefit from the existing economic system, continued to have no interest or oversight in the region. To bring Christianity into the region threatened the labor base for the already challenging economic enterprises. Moreover, the land the missions occupied was land that could not later be acquired by the miners and ranchers.

Kino would find himself in the midst of accusations by nearby Spanish miners and ranchers that he was removing Indians for forced impressments into the *repartimiento* (conscription of labor) from which it would personally benefit when his four reinforcements arrived in December 1690 to establish four new missions. Kino recognized the potential predicament, and planned ahead, bringing with him a royal decree from the Guadalajara *audiencia* (similar to a supreme court) indicating that any Indians baptized by the missionaries would be exempted from the repartimiento for 20 years. Unfortunately for Kino, this did not make the conversion come more easily. In fact, reports came to Mexico City that the Indians had abandoned the missions because of the requirement that they remain in permanent habitation. How were they to survive living in merely one location? They would become entirely dependent on the Spanish for food and shelter because, after all, the harvest of different plant types varied by season, meaning that the tribes required movement or they would starve.

Therefore, to hasten the conversion process and add to the protection of Indians from the often abused repartimiento system, Kino intended to go on a *visita,* or tour, of the region in early 1691. During this tour, several Indians came with him (either Opata or Yaqui Indians from farther south), and at the first village they encountered, they set up three different shelters to aid them in their stay. One would serve as a location for Mass, another for sleeping, and another as a kitchen. The tribe was the Tumacácori; Kino described them as friendly native people, who were gentle and interested. They were curious about the black robes the friars wore in the hot desert heat, and gathered around as Kino and his helpers gestured and attempted to communicate with them about the Holy Gospel.

Kino succeeded in his conversion attempts, by most accounts, and by the early 1700s, reports came back about Kino's missions to Mexico City via Captain Juan Mateo Manje (the nephew to former New Mexico Governor Jironza, now alcalde mayor and military governor of Sonora). Manje marveled at the spread of Catholicism across Pimería Alta, which reported some 16,000 converts. He applauded the meticulous maps generated, as well as the detailed ethnocultural information that the Jesuits had recorded. Even more, Kino had expanded the operation so much that to feed the growing converts, he had to begin raising cattle to

Father Eusebio Francisco Kino (1645–1711), Jesuit missionary. (Arizona Historical Society/Tucson, AHS 44478)

feed his charges. His livestock operations, perhaps, were exactly what the neighboring Spaniards had feared. For the Indians lived along the most productive river valleys, making the rich, fertile, and irrigable soil off limits to Spanish acquisition. Spanish law continued to protect the landholdings, particularly those of sedentary Indians.

While Kino had succeeded in establishing missions, complete with an organized system of outreach, the building of missions, and cattle herds, the Jesuits would not remain in control of Arizona. For political reasons, the Spanish crown ejected the Jesuits from all Spanish holdings in 1767, leaving Arizona open to the efforts of another order. The Franciscans arrived shortly thereafter and, under the leadership of Aragon native Francisco Garcés, the missions found a rebirth. Garcés seemed to enjoy the austere life and was often found around the campfires of Indian peoples sharing in their traditional foods. He ventured to the valley floor of the Grand Canyon to interact and attempt the conversion of the Havasupai. He traveled up and down the Gila and Colorado rivers, often alone or only with a Pima guide. He asserted that a trail could be forged across the region between New Mexico and California, enticing the presidio's captain, Juan Bautista de Anza, to eventually venture out to attempt to establish that trail. While the trail did not succeed in bridging the gap between the two colonial outposts, other trails to the east became priorities—especially after the French relinquished control over their territorial claims west of the Mississippi River in 1762 after they failed to defend themselves against the British during the French and Indian War (1754–1763). The French had not always seemed an ally to the Spanish, however, as the Texas experience illustrated.

XENOPHOBIA LEADS SPAIN TO THE INTERIOR

Spain's first real interest in Texas occurred on the heels of the voyage of a Frenchman, Robert Cavelier, Sieur de La Salle, into the Gulf of Mexico in an attempt to find the headwaters of the Mississippi River, to which the French had laid claim in the mid-1680s. La Salle had convinced King Louis XIV that expansion into Spanish-held territory would be beneficial to New France, with the mines in Nueva Vizcaya (just to the south and west of Texas). The French had already traveled nearly the entire length of the Mississippi River a few years earlier, but they hoped to establish a firm foundation at the mouth of the river by finding it via a sea route. Unfortunately, La Salle and his men overshot the Mississippi's mouth and instead found themselves near Matagordo Bay (in what is now Texas) and set up a rudimentary post, Fort St. Louis, in 1685. La Salle hoped to use the fort as a base to then find the Mississippi River.

When the Spanish accidentally happened upon a French deserter and learned of the French attempt to establish a permanent presence in what they clearly termed Spanish territory, they sent out reconnaissance missions to find the French expedition and remove it from Spanish territory. Even though Spain had clearly claimed all territory north of the coast of Florida and the Rio Grande more than 100 years earlier, they did not move against the French when the competing European power claimed New France along the Saint Lawrence River in the 1530s and then permanently occupied it by the early 1600s. They attempted to move against the French trade relationship with the Pawnee along the Platte River in the 1720s, but failed to stop their expanding influence among Plains tribes. This new intrusion, however, was too close to their mines and shipping routes across the Gulf of Mexico, not to mention that the French could galvanize the support of the native populations against the Spaniards and have ready allies in a battle for extending territorial claims. By the time the Spanish forces finally found Fort St. Louis, however, with some guidance from the Tonkawa Indians (who told them it had been abandoned), they found the fort in disarray. They learned later that the Karankawa Indians (who lived along the coast between the Nueces and Colorado rivers) had quickly become enraged at the French for having stolen their canoes. They paid back the French by ravaging the post and killing those who had not died during the earlier mutiny against La Salle, or from disease and overexposure to the elements.

The Spanish then quickly organized a plan to occupy Texas permanently, to halt any further advances by the French. To do so in a cost-effective manner, they integrated the two major goals that had mandated the direction of settlement in post-Revolt New Mexico—religious and military, but with the added purpose of having the region serve as a buffer zone against further French (and later British and U.S.) encroachment. The Caddos seemed eager to have the Spanish arrive near their communities. Of great interest to the Spaniards was the story they told that, in the absence of the French and the Spanish, a nun had visited them all dressed in blue and had brought them the yearning for Christianity. María de Jesús de Agreda, known as the blue nun, according to her story had bilocated from Agreda, Spain, where she lived in a convent, to visit the Indian peoples of the Americas. Other Indian farmers whom the Spanish encountered besides the Caddos did not speak of the blue nun, but had similar lifestyles to the Spanish.

The Caddos lived in small communities scattered along the bottoms, fertile lands along the river's edge. Like the Natchez and the Creeks, the Caddos lived in wooden houses, gathered together in recognizable towns. They grew the "three sisters" (corn, beans, squash), as well as various types of melons. They had also developed a governmental structure, as well as something that the Spanish even described as a "civilization." In other words, they had developed into a highly organized, stratified sedentary community with a strong religious component. They had a political organization that consisted of loose confederations: the Hasinai, Kadohadacho, and Natchitoches. Successful in agriculture and trade, their reputation for being a great nation spread far beyond their own regional borders.

Besides the Caddos, other tribes inhabited Texas. In the panhandle region (beyond the reach of Spanish settlements and missions) lived the Kiowa and sat the northern reaches of the Comanche in Texas. South of the Comanche in southwestern Texas toward the current New Mexico border were the Kiowa, the Mescalero Apache (who also resided in New Mexico), the Lipan Apache, and the Jumano. In the far south of Texas lived the Coahuiltecans, and above them the Karankawa, and to their north the Tonkawa. Farther east along the Brazos River lived the Tawakoni and above them the Waco. Above the Waco at the headwaters of the Trinity lived the Wichita, and to their east lived the Caddo confederated tribes. In other words, the Spanish did not enter a region uninhabited, rather one that had started undergoing a shift in population and alliances because of the recent arrival of the Comanche. The first census of the region listed a nonmission Indian population of more than 7,000 in the 1770s.

Indians who lived along the coast seemed to harbor more interest in becoming converts, although their motivations in converting involved acquiring Spanish protection from neighboring tribes rather than the more eternal goals of salvation. As was typical throughout frontier regions where Indians encountered non-Indians, some tribes (such as the Coahuiltecans) would seek out the powerful outsiders at a large cost for the built-in protections they offered. Other tribes sought out the outsiders as a way to escape certain death from disease and its companion, starvation. New skill sets learned from the Spanish (new systems of farming, animal husbandry, manufacture of soaps, adobe, footwear, and more) also offset the friars' demands that they attend Mass, learn the catechism and stations of the cross, and participate in Catholic festivals and ceremonies. Finally, they stood to gain from the irrigation ditches and dams (such as those that are still visible at San Juan Capistrano mission). In fact, San Juan Capistrano mission was entirely self-supporting. The acequias diverted water to the Indian fields, which grew a variety of foods: corn, beans, squash, sweet potatoes, and sugar cane. The Indians also had orchards and nonirrigated fields that produced melons, pumpkins, grapes, and peppers. The Indians also raised sheep and cattle, which they then processed into woolen and leather goods and food. Their artisan skills also produced iron tools, which, together with the other products of the mission, they traded as far as Louisiana and Coahuila in the south. They tolerated Christianity because of the skills, tools, and technologies that they gained; but perhaps it went even beyond that. Many of them adapted to Spanish work ethics and cultural character, even intermarrying with local Spanish populations. Such high levels of integration, however, also led to the abandonment of tribal cultures. For example, the Coahuiltecans disappeared as a tribal entity because they assimilated so effectively into Spanish society.

When the Spanish arrived permanently after their initial exploration missions in the 1680s, they chose to build their first outpost in the region near the Caddos (who lived in northeast Texas along the Sabine River) and the Trinity River, instead of closer to the New Mexico colony or the strategic coastline. By 1690, the Spanish had established two missions, the Santísimo Nombre de María and San Francisco de los Tejas. It would not be until 1716 that the Spanish would establish a series of other missions and forts along the Camino Real in Texas that led from the farthest eastern fort, Fort San Francisco de los Dolores, and Los Adaes Mission, then heading westward to the missions Nuestra Señora de los Nacogdoches, San José de los Nazones, Purísima Concepción, and in 1718 (and much farther west) San Antonio de Valero and San Antonio de Béjar (presidio, town, and mission), and in 1702, San José Mission. Finally, in 1721, the Spanish answered La Salle's challenge by building a presidio very close to the site of the original Fort St. Louis, Nuestra Señora de la Bahía de Espíritu Santo. But by then, the French had already established their own strongholds on the Red River in central Louisiana, a fort at Natchitoches, and other forts at the mouth of the Mississippi River, Mobile Bay, and along the coast between the two. The French had also established the Arkansas Post at the confluence of the Arkansas and Mississippi rivers, as well as Fort New Orleans. The French threat would continue until 1763 (see Map 8).

In the meantime, the Spanish set about establishing a permanent foothold in Texas, hoping to continue their missionary work among the Caddos and expand their missionary efforts to the other tribes that surrounded them, but the missionaries complained that they needed more forts to protect their charges from the nomadic Indians (and Frenchmen). The southern Plains had indeed become a "hot" zone of Indian activity. The Lipan Apache, Kiowa, and Kiowa-Apache found themselves under new pressure from the Comanches who had recently moved south into the southern Plains, as a result of shifting Indian populations to the north. As a result of acquiring the horse, the Comanche had become what many termed later the "Lords of the Southern Plains," wreaking havoc on Spanish missions and prefatory Spanish settlements.

Instead of sending more troops, however, the Spanish viceroy instead simply sent a governor with gifts to placate the tribes. Within a year, the governor left and was replaced by another governor who did even less to assist the friars. As a result, the missions had no defenses against the growing hostility of nomadic Plains tribes. With the Spanish, of course, came their diseases, and in 1692–1693, the Caddos experienced a major outbreak of smallpox. When the Caddo asked the friar about the high death rates, he told them that it was "God's will," and if he willed it, the Spanish would die too. Obviously, this did not bode well for future conversions, and by 1693, the Caddos demanded that the missionaries leave. The friar ordered the mission bells to be buried, then returned to the Rio Grande (where he was killed five years later by another Pueblo uprising).

Illustration of a Comanche village by George Catlin, 1844. (Hulton-Deutsch Collection/Corbis)

Like the Caddos, the Karakawas had no interest in converting to Christianity and rebuffed the Spanish efforts of converting their people. Similar to the Coahuiltecans, the Karakawas also lived along the Gulf Coast, but they refused to give up their economic independence by living at a mission and working in mission fields and raising mission livestock. The Jumanos found no great draw to live in the missions, but instead chose to placate the Spanish so that they would protect the Jumanos during their trade missions to the Caddo peoples in eastern Texas. The Jumanos, unfortunately, found themselves swallowed up by the Apache, and by the 1850s, the Caddos had lost their land claims in Texas because of continued encroachment by first Spaniards, then the arrival of U.S. citizens under the auspices of the empresario program, which began officially in 1821.

Other Texan tribes that the Spanish encountered provided a stiffer challenge, as they were more firmly resolved not to allow these infiltrators to alter their lifestyle and instead held the Spaniards at bay. The Apache, Wichita, and Comanche, of course, fall into this category. In the earliest days, the Spanish had a distinct advantage over the nomadic, non-Christianized Indians, or *índios bárbaros:* the horse. It was not long, however, before the índios bárbaros began stealing Spanish goods and supplies so that they could continue their nomadic life unimpeded. To equal the advantage, the nomadic tribes also began to steal Spanish horses, which gave them even more speed and mobility, and improved their ability to feed and defend themselves. As they became more agile and effective, the nomadic warriors began to expand their raids against more disparate Spanish communities and missions to discourage their continued advances. Besides horses, they also took tools, weapons, and other supplies, thereby improving their ability to survive and making the Wichita (*norteños*), Apache, and Comanche even more formidable adversaries.

The Spanish policy of continued collusion with the Comanche and Wichita against the Apache actually succeeded in limiting Apache raiding on Spanish missions and communities, which did soon end. A new administrator, Teodoro de Croix, became the first commandant general of the Provincias Internas, a new administrative jurisdiction that included all of the northern frontier provinces and had its headquarters in Chihuahua. Croix fully intended to wage open warfare against the Apaches, but instead, in 1779 he was ordered to placate them by giving commissions and gifts to the Apache. Unfortunately, this was a failed strategy as well.

The missions in Texas, as well as New Mexico, faced the next major change: secularization, or the process of turning over control of the missions from the friars (missionaries or regular orders like Franciscans, who focused on converting the native peoples) to the secular priests and turning the missions into parishes instead (therefore focusing on the maintenance of faith, not conversion). The conversion to secularization also meant that local communities would support the parishes, not the colonial government. It would not be until 1820, however, that the secularization process would be complete. Besides this "assault" on the missions from an administrative standpoint, the missions also faced other pressures. Anticlericalism, an outcropping of the philosophies of enlightenment, which had begun to circulate in the colonies as early as the late 1700s (even though the dissemination of such literature was banned by the crown), affected clerics even as far into the hinterlands as Texas.

Finally, frustration by mission Indians of the heavy-handed intimidation and outright demands on their labor mounted. The mission Indians argued that the friars had been physically cruel, demanding that they leave behind their traditional ways and sacred beliefs, and that they had put themselves at the mercy of a friar who rarely answered to his superior personally after he had arrived on the frontier. They began to rebel in Texas by acts of sabotage, work stoppage (or slowing down their labors), pretending to be ill, gambling, destroying sacred Catholic objects, and demeaning the friars. In the long run, the friars' success in converting the Texas natives, therefore, was minimal.

Regarding the índios bárbaros, the Spanish had even less success. They had attempted to establish a mission at Santa Cruz de San Sabá for the Apaches in 1757 on the San Sabá River, as well as a fort (San Luis de Amarillas) some three miles away, in an attempt to quiet the Apaches. It would house up to 400 people (including women and children). The Apaches refused to come to the mission, however. Comanche were incensed at Spanish overtures to their enemies, the Apaches, and together with the Tonkawas and Hasinai, destroyed the mission not quite a year later. While only a few Spaniards died (including a missionary), the Spanish retaliated the following year to teach the Indians a lesson. They gathered a force and penetrated deep into the Red River territory, only to find a Wichita village flying the French flag and using their French guns to rout the Spanish expedition. Farther west, the Franciscans had attempted to build missions to help convert the Lipán Apaches, but it also failed as a result of the harassment by Comanche in that region. Realizing the power of the Plains Indians, the Spanish recognized that the Indians felt they owed no loyalty to Spain, but instead had obviously established a strong trade relationship with the French, where they acquired their guns, powder, shot, and even a few uniforms. The southern Plains Indians, who now had horses and technology, could hold their own against the Spanish who did not know the geography or have the alliances that the Plains tribes had established. San Sabá was the last mission the Texans attempted to establish for the Apache or northern tribes. In fact, the Spanish recognized the futility of occupying the northern frontier, which was part of the reason the empresario program would occupy the regions north of Spanish settlements in Texas.

NEW PURPOSES FOR THE FRONTIER

As Texas entered the second phase of Spanish conquest in the mid-18th century, the French threat disappeared. In 1762, the French ceded all land west of the Mississippi River to Spain in their attempt to keep it from falling into the hands of the British at the end of the French and Indian War (1754–1763). Also during the mid-18th century, a new king occupied the Spanish throne who had new ideas for the colonial provinces of the Americas. King Carlos III (1759–1788) believed that to reestablish Spain's preeminence globally, as well as to reorganize the provinces, he would need to dispatch an official to study the Americas and come up with a new administrative plan. Under the leadership of José de Gálvez, the Spanish frontier would undergo a series of changes that attempted to wrest the colonies from under the control of home-grown American administrators, who were oftentimes reported as inefficient, took advantage of their position to become wealthy, and benefited themselves through bribes and kickbacks. Under the new system, the highest-level officials would come from Spain, trusted and worthy administrators who could eliminate corruption and the skimming of colonial profits. While taxes were lowered, the new administrators actually collected them. Also, the crown finally encouraged intercolonial economic development and trade, but to benefit from the increased internal economic opportunity, the crown enforced the *alcabala* (sales tax) even as it lowered duties.

Specifically regarding the Indian people of Texas, a directive came to limit the military and missionary presence in eastern Texas and to relocate the Spanish settlers who had lived there to San Antonio. Because of the new policy directed at the Comanche under the leadership of Governor Juan Bautista de Anza of New Mexico, the Texas administrators and military officials would treat the Comanche with more respect, and even friendly engagement, while the Apache saw Spanish retaliation and hostility unleashed against them. Until that point, though, the Comanche and Wichita had grown tired of and complained about the Spanish missionaries indulging the Apaches at the missions, and they demanded that it stop. As a result, the Spanish allied with the Comanche and Wichita against the Apache.

Even though the Spanish settlers from the Los Adaes region had to move to San Antonio, they did petition to return. And within a few years, they were allowed to return. The settlers were a mixture of Spanish settlers, Frenchmen left over from the previous failed settlements in Louisiana, and even some Indians and Africans. Their return allowed for this miscegenated community to provide a line of Spanish civilization and defense against the ever-expanding British empire, which now shared a border with the Spanish north. Their proximity to the Caddos and Wichitas allowed for those relations to continue to develop. After the settlers returned, they established what Texas historians Calvert and de León termed the "only successful civilian settlement in East Texas" (Calvert and de León, *The History of Texas,* 36–38).

Because the previous Comanche policies had now failed, in large part because of Spanish overtures to the Apache through commissions and gifts, the Spanish changed their policies toward the Comanche and the Wichitas and began offering them gifts and rewards as well. For the next three decades, a relative peace fell over the Texan communities. The policy succeeded in dividing and conquering, reducing the Indian forces to becoming dependent on handouts, and disrupting traditional tribal alliances. The infusion of Spanish trade goods into the native economies also helped allay their determination to acquire those goods through raiding (Calvert and de León, *A History of Texas,* 38–45; and Weber, *The Spanish Frontier,* 191–214). The Spanish would find yet another different experience in California, where so many disparate groups of ranchería Indians lived in sparse and shifting settlements.

THE PACIFIC COAST

California first gained the interest of Spaniards as early as the 1540s, resulting from Cabeza de Vaca's voyage into the interior of North America, but also as a result of the quest for a strait that would connect the Atlantic with the Pacific Ocean. As early as 1533, the first Spanish sailor identified Baja, California, but until 1539, they still believed Baja was an island. In 1542, the crown charged Juan Rodríguez Cabrillo with exploring the western coastline of the Americas, north of Baja, and then to sail across the ocean to China. His three ships sailed north and encountered San Diego's bay, which he asserted would provide a good port for vessels.

When they landed, the native peoples scattered. Those few who remained behind expressed through sign language that they had heard of
other men who appeared as these Spaniards had, but overland—and they
had killed many Indian people. Although some hostilities did erupt,
Cabrillo attempted to buy off the Indians' anger through gift-giving, a
gesture he would use again farther to the north. At Santa Catalina Island
and San Pedro, he paused for the winter, then his men continued the
journey north without him. Upon leaving his ship to rescue some of his
men from an Indian attack while on some slippery rocks, he shattered a
leg bone, which became infected. He later died of the injury and resultant infection. The expedition, now under the leadership of Bartolomé
Ferrer, then headed as far north as the 42nd degree latitude, or the Cali-
fornia-Oregon border. Because of the tempestuousness of the seas and the
lack of supplies, he decided to abandon the quest to reach China and instead returned to Mexico. The expedition had charted more than 1,200
miles of California coastline, and although some members of the expedition suggested that California could host ports or forts, no permanent
Spanish settlement would occur in California for another 200 years.

By the 1760s, however, all that would change. Gálvez was instrumental in establishing a permanent stronghold in Nueva California. Brought
to the Americas under the Bourbon reforms that continued under the
reign of Carlos III, Gálvez envisioned threats to the Pacific Coast of
northern New Spain from many places. Of course he feared the Russians,
who had already made inroads into Russian Alaska and had traveled as far
south as the Tlingit stronghold in the archipelagos. It was only a matter
of time before the Russians appeared in California to harvest the sea lions
there. In fact, by 1812, the Russians had established a fort in northern
California, forcing the Pomos to labor in their fields so that they could
supply Alaska with fresh produce. Moreover, Gálvez feared the approach-
ing British Empire, which already had a firm base of trade in the north
with the Hudson Bay Company, established in 1670 (by 1820 the Hudson Bay Company would merge with one of its rivals and control almost
all of western Canada). In other words, the threats perceived by Gálvez
were real and would manifest within the next two generations. To the Indians, none of this mattered, as California Indians did not depend heavily on long-distance trade with outsiders, Indians or otherwise. Therefore,

this international maneuvering had little impact on their daily life until the intrusions became personal and permanent.

Part of Gálvez's plan for fortifying the northern border of New Spain involved establishing a firm hold over Monterey Bay, a location Cabrillo had indicated was well suited for the purpose. While on his way to Monterey, Gálvez was overtaken by a Spanish official who warned him that the Russians had in fact arrived in California, and that he should figure out some way of dislodging them from Spanish territory. He well knew that the settlement of Baja had not gone as planned (starting with Kino's failed mission at Loretto); furthermore, the Jesuits who had retained spiritual control over the region found themselves evicted from all Spanish-held territory in 1767. The Jesuits, unfortunately, had spearheaded the missionization process in Baja, and now that they had been forced out by Carlos III, the other orders scrambled to gain control over the newly abandoned regions.

The permanent settlement of California would fall to a Franciscan, Junípero Serra, and a military leader, Gaspar de Portolá. Father Serra, a hard-nosed penitent friar who insisted on suffering to toughen his religious zeal, would become perhaps the most controversial father in northern New Spain. His bachelor compatriot, Portolá, who had 30 years of military service, would head north in 1769 with Serra to bring California under Spanish control and to show the Russians they were not welcome. When the Spanish contingent arrived at San Diego Bay, they encountered the other prongs of the expedition that had come by sea, and another overland from the formerly Jesuit-held missions of what is now Arizona. When they arrived, they learned of the diseases that had immobilized the early arrivals. As Spanish Borderlands historian David J. Weber described in his *The Spanish Frontier in North America* (1992), instead of seeing a fort and mission, they saw instead a hospital and cemetery. Scurvy had taken its toll. The Spaniards regrouped and headed north once again. While they did not find San Francisco harbor (until 1775) or Monterey Bay, they returned to San Diego and established the first mission, San Diego de Alcalá. The local Indians, the Ipai, who had first had contact with Cabrillo some 200 years before, were not interested in the mission, but they were interested in the goods the Spanish had brought. They pilfered Spanish supplies, a task made easier as the Spanish fell once again

Mission San Diego de Alcalá, founded by Father Junípero Serra in 1769, was the first of the California missions. (National Oceanic and Atmospheric Administration)

to scurvy, further weakening their numbers. Portolá recognized the futility of remaining in San Diego, with its pilfering Indians and recurring diseases, and he demanded that his men find Monterey, which they did in 1770. Portolá himself did not remain in California and expressed grave doubts as to the ability of the Spanish to maintain a firm hold on the coastal province.

Although some the natives stole from the Spanish at San Diego, farther north the natives seemed curious, but cautious. Within months, however, that would change as Spanish settlers began to steal indiscriminately from the Indian peoples and violate their women. When asked to stop the abuses, the Spanish soldiers complained vehemently; after all, they had arrived on this frontier far from home (or other Spanish settlements) without any of their own women. To alleviate the Spaniards' grumblings, and to keep them from sinning so openly, Serra performed marriage ceremonies between Spanish men and captive Indian women. Other men simply continued to rape Indian women with impunity. Indeed, the earliest days of Spanish conquest in California proved unbearable for the local native populations. Because they had no tradition of warfare or warrior cultures, the native populations had few defenses against the open hostility of the Spanish conquerors. And if Indians killed Spanish soldiers, the Spanish officers could replenish their forces by bringing more soldiers and colonists from New Spain. They also had horses, guns, cannon, and other instruments of war that native people did not. This open challenge to the traditional way of life of the native cultures made the friars' task of converting their charges exceedingly difficult. Perhaps as challenging, the Indians did not live in large, settled permanent villages, so the friars constantly had to travel to the villages instead. While the military had constructed two presidios (San Diego and Monterey) by 1770, the friars had five missions constructed by 1774. Eventually, Serra's missions would number 20 and would stretch from San Francisco to San Diego, but even with gifts as distributions, the friars converted relatively few of the entire California Indian population. In fact, by 1821, only 21,000 Indians resided at the missions—or approximately 10 percent of the whole native population of California by that time (Weber, *Spanish Frontier,* 263).

Hoping to make California more accessible overland, Juan Bautista de Anza forged a trail from Sonora to California in 1774, thereby connecting older, established northern communities with California—and connecting the latter with the sea. Only two years later, Father Silvestre Vélez de Escalante and Fray Francisco Atanásio Domínguez led an expedition headed west from Santa Fe, New Mexico, in which they hoped to connect an overland route to Monterey in order to open the newly permitted trade between colonies. During their journey they mapped new portions of the northern interior reaches, including parts of Colorado, Utah, and northern Arizona. The Utes, whom they used as guides when they encountered them along the route, purposely led them astray, thereby diverting the Spanish expedition away from their homes on their northwestern route. Members of the Domínguez-Escalante expedition were the first Europeans to hear about the Great Salt Lake and the first to cross the Grand Canyon (at the Crossing of the Fathers, which is now submerged). While their expedition failed to find another overland route to connect the colonies, thanks to the opening policies, the Spanish charted lands previously unknown to them, had friendly encounters with numerous Great Basin tribes, and described wondrous landscapes that would later become U.S. national parks or monuments.

A few years later, Anza would open yet another route along the Gila and Colorado rivers, establishing two missions and a presidio to demonstrate a firm presence among the Yuma peoples in what is now southern Arizona. The Yuma had first experienced missionaries under Father Kino in 1698, but they loathed the overzealous behavior of the Franciscans in attempting to control their lives. Spanish soldiers, greedy for Indian land, had allowed their horses and cattle to run rampant through Yuma fields and mesquite trees (from which they collected mesquite beans, crushing them into a powder for sustenance). They rebelled, destroyed the Spanish missions, settlements, and even the presidio—thereby cutting off the Gila-Colorado route to California. Even though the Spanish managed to muster a devastating retaliation against the Indian insurrection, they never regained control over the Yuma, who continued to defend their lives, land, and traditional culture well beyond the period of Spanish sovereignty.

Unfortunately for the California tribes, it would not be so easy to throw off the yoke of Spanish control. While the California Indian population exceeded 300,000, they did not operate as a single entity, nor did they have a warrior tradition overall. As a result of their inability to defend their traditional way of life against the Spanish enforcers, Spaniards forced many ranchería tribes to relocate into missions situated closer to the Spanish communities, in order to better control their population, labor, and conversion (much like the English and later French had done). While at the missions, the Indians learned the new trades suited to a "civilized" people: weaving, herding livestock, pottery, blacksmithing, farming, brick making, and other like tasks. Friars oftentimes sold the fruits of their labor to provide funds to purchase the food and supplies needed to house the large numbers of Indians, but they also used the income to fund new missions and even provide profit for the church itself. Mission herds reached nearly a half million cattle, 60,000 horses, and more than a quarter million sheep and goats at its height.

To ensure that the Indians continued their labor, they were not allowed to leave the missions. Friars had complete control over their lives, and when they refused to work or attempted to flee, the friars punished

*Native American with a fish slung over his shoulder in Southern California, ca. 1790.
(National Oceanic and Atmospheric Administration)*

them severely with whippings or by placing them in irons or in stocks. As if to accentuate the brutality that already existed, the mortality rates at the missions were excessive. Indian populations at just two missions dropped by 75 percent because of disease, sanitation issues, lack of traditional medical care, change in diet, and the social disruption of missionary discipline. In all, the California Indian population likely dropped by more than 33 percent between 1769 and 1821 (White, *It's Your Misfortune,* 32–33; Weber, *Spanish Frontier,* 263). While on the one hand treatment of the Indian people in the California missions was deplorable, on the other hand, the Franciscans continued to maintain their stranglehold because they argued they were protecting the Indians from the degenerate behaviors of the lascivious Spanish soldiers who would see the released Indian women as targets of their uncontrollable lustful behaviors.

Although life in the missions proved beyond the pale for Indian people who found themselves corralled, life for the Spanish population was difficult as well. One of the biggest issues for Spanish colonists involved the lack of Spanish women, and therefore the men periodically paid unwanted sexual attention on Indian women. Therefore, in an attempt to assist these men to adapt to life in California more adequately, the Spanish governors sent for women and families to join the Spanish soldiers on the northern frontier, in an attempt to create some form of normalcy. Another key to the survival of the Spanish in California involved Anza's establishment of the overland resupply route, another *camino real de tierra adentro,* to dependably resupply the California colonies with tools, supplies, food, seed, clothing, trade goods, horses and other livestock, building materials, religious vestments, and other objects necessary for expanding the missions in California. Even with the concerted efforts of the Spanish government, California's civilian population failed to grow at rates New Mexico experienced, however. In fact, by the 1750s, New Mexico's Spanish population finally outnumbered the Pueblo Indian population. In the end, nearly 40,000 Spaniards lived in and around New Mexico, with 6,000 living in Santa Fe alone. Texas would see a mere 7,000 or so at the end of the Spanish colonial period, and California would achieve only around 3,200 by 1821—most of whom were descended from the original immigrants from before the 1780s.

Mexican Independence Elicits Change

New Mexico, Arizona, Texas, and California would not remain within the Spanish empire forever, however. After the Grito de Dolores, issued by Father Hidalgo in 1810, started the Mexican Revolution, Mexico finally gained its independence from Spain in 1821. Under the new Mexican constitution of 1824, all permanent inhabitants of Mexico would be considered *vecinos,* or citizens—including American Indian populations who would receive all the rights and privileges guaranteed a vecino under the constitution. While this would pose great difficulties for the United States in 1848 with the terminology found in the Treaty of Guadalupe Hidalgo (1848), which allowed citizens of Mexico to choose to become citizens of the United States in territories confiscated by the United States, the new constitution gave American Indians equal status among the other inhabitants of Mexico. Indians throughout New Spain, however, had long dealt with Spanish colonial law and used the provisions within it to defend themselves in the face of Spanish colonization, ill treatment, encroachment, and much more. They defended themselves locally with the governor, and even traveled as far as Mexico City to defend their claims at the audiencia set up by the king for the New World. They successfully defended their claims, sought justice, and gained respect in society. Some even became military officers or administrators within the Spanish system. They adjusted, as they always had, to those newcomers who had infiltrated their homelands. Unfortunately, unlike those cultures who had previously insinuated themselves into the lands long held by the native peoples, the Spanish were there to stay and intended to dominate all they encountered. Indians within the French- and Russian-held realms would experience such penetrations by outsiders, but the realities of those experiences were far different, as will be shown in other chapters.

Bibliographic Essay

For the overview on the Spanish frontier as a whole, see the bibliography at the end of the previous chapter. In addition, see Howard R. Lamar, *The New Encyclopedia of the American West* (New Haven, CT: Yale University Press, 1998); Richard White, *It's Your Misfortune* (Norman: University of Oklahoma Press, 1991); Edward H. Spicer, *Cycles of Conquest: The Impact of Spain, Mexico and the*

United States on the Indians of the Southwest, 1530–1960 (Tucson: University of Arizona Press, 1962); Elizabeth Ann Harper Johns, *Storms Brewed in Other Men's Worlds: The Confrontation of Indians, Spanish, and French in the Southwest, 1540–1795*, 2nd ed. (Norman: University of Oklahoma Press, 1996); Bernardo de Gálvez, *Instructions for Governing the Interior Provinces of New Spain, 1786*, Donald E. Worcester, ed. (Berkeley: Quivira Society, 1951); and David J. Weber, *Índios Bárbaros: Spaniards and Their Savages in the Age of Enlightenment* (New Haven, CT: Yale University Press, 2005), and *The Spanish Frontier in North America* (New Haven, CT: Yale University Press, 1992).

More specifically, for Arizona, consult Lawrence Clark Powell, *Arizona: A History,* reprint ed. (Albuquerque: University of New Mexico Press, 1990); Andrew Wallace, *Sources and Readings in Arizona History* (Tucson: University of Arizona Press, 1965); Jay J. Wagoner, *Early Arizona, Prehistory to Civil War* (Tucson: University of Arizona Press, 1975); Ross Santee, *Arizona, a Guide to the Grand Canyon State* (New York: Hastings House, 1940); Odie B. Faulk, *Arizona, a Short History* (Norman: University of Oklahoma Press, 1970); Madeline F. Paré and Bert M. Fireman, *Arizona Pageant: A Short History of the 48th State* (Tempe: Arizona Historical Foundation, 1970); George P. Hammond, Agapito Rey, Vivian C. Fisher, and W. Michael Mathes, eds., *Apostolic Chronicle of Juan Domingo Arricivita: The Franciscan Mission Frontier in the Eighteenth Century in Arizona, Texas, and California,* 2 vols. (Berkeley, CA: Academy of American Franciscan History, 1996); Iris H. W. Engstrand and Donald C. Cutter, *Spanish Settlement in the Far Southwest: Arizona, California, and New Mexico, 1530–1821* (Golden, CO: Fulcrum Publishing, 1996); Peter Gerhard, *The North Frontier of New Spain,* rev. ed. (Norman: University of Oklahoma, 1993), and *Pirates of the Pacific, 1575–1742* (Lincoln: University of Nebraska Press, 1990); Stephen Trimble, *The People: Indians of the American Southwest* (Santa Fe, NM: School of American Research, 1995); Henry R. Wagner, *The Spanish Southwest, 1542–1794,* 2 parts (Albuquerque: Quivira Society, 1937); Josef Espinosa y Tello, *A Spanish Voyage to Vancouver and the Northwest Coast of America,* trans. Cecil Jane (London: Argonaut Press, 1930); and Alfred Barnaby Thomas, ed., *The Plains Indians of New Mexico, 1751–1778* (Albuquerque: University of New Mexico Press, 1940). See also the following by Robert S. Weddle: *The French Thorn: Rival Explorers in the Spanish Sea, 1682–1762* (College Station: Texas A&M University Press, 1991), *San Juan Bautista: Gateway to Spanish Texas* (Austin: University of Texas Press, 1968), *The San Sabá Mission, Spanish Pivot in Texas* (Austin: University of Texas Press, 1964), *Spanish Sea: The Gulf of Mexico in North American Discovery, 1500–1685* (College Station: Texas A&M University Press, 1985), and finally, *Wilderness Manhunt: The Spanish Search for La Salle* (Austin: University of Texas Press, 1973); Bunny Fontana, "Pima and Papago: Introduction," *Handbook of North American Indians,* vol. 10 (Washington, D.C.: Smithsonian Institution, 1983).

For Arizona, see Herbert Eugene Bolton, ed., *Anza's California Expeditions,*
5 vols. (Berkeley: University of California Press, 1930), and *Kino's Historical
Memoir of Pimería Alta, 1683–1711,* 2 vols. (Cleveland: Arthur H. Clark, 1919).
Other good sources include Elliott Coues, ed., *On the Trail of a Spanish Pioneer:
The Diary and Itinerary of Francisco Garcés in His Travels through Sonora, Arizona,
and California, 1775–1776,* 2 vols. (New York: F. P. Harper, 1900); Ernest J.
Burrus, ed., *Kino and Manje, Explorers of Sonora and Arizona: Their Vision of the
Future* (Rome: Jesuit Historical Institute, 1971); Kieran McCarty, ed., *Desert
Documentary: The Spanish Years, 1767–1821* (Tucson: Arizona Historical Society,
1976); Frank McNitt, *The Indian Traders* (Norman: University of Oklahoma
Press, 1962; Jack D. Forbes, *Apache, Navaho, and Spaniard,* 2nd ed. (Norman:
University of Oklahoma Press, 1994); John L. Kessell, *Mission of Sorrows: Jesuit
Guevavi and the Pimas, 1691–1767* (Tucson: University of Arizona Press, 1970);
Phillip Wayne Powell, *Soldiers, Indians, and Silver: The Northward Advance of
New Spain, 1550–1600* (Berkeley: University of California Press, 1952); Joseph
P. Sánchez, *Explorers, Traders, and Slavers: Forging the Old Spanish Trail,
1678–1850* (Salt Lake City: University of Utah Press, 1997); Mark Santiago,
Massacre at the Yuma Crossing: Spanish Relations with the Quechans, 1770–1782
(Tucson: University of Arizona Press, 1998).

For references to Texas, see Robert Calvert, Arnoldo de León, and Gregg
Cantrell, *The History of Texas,* 3rd ed. (Wheeling, IL: Harlan Davidson, 2002);
Donald E. Chipman, *Spanish Texas, 1519–1821* (Austin: University of Texas
Press, 1992), and with Harriett Denise Joseph, *Notable Men and Women of Spanish Texas* (Austin: University of Texas Press, 1999). See also William C. Foster,
Spanish Expeditions into Texas, 1689–1768 (Austin: University of Texas Press,
1995), and William C. Foster, ed., *The La Salle Expedition to Texas: The Journal
of Henri Joutel, 1684–1687,* trans. Johanna S. Warren (Austin: Texas State Historical Association, 1998), and William C. Foster, ed., *Texas and Northeastern
Mexico, 1630–1690 by Juan Bautista Chapa,* trans. Ned F. Brierley (Austin: University of Texas Press, 1997); Jack Jackson and William C. Foster, eds., *Imaginary
Kingdom: Texas as Seen by the Rivera and Rubí Military Expeditions, 1727 and
1767* (Austin: Texas State Historical Association, 1995); Jesús Frank de la Teja,
San Antonio de Béxar, A Community on New Spain's Northern Frontier (Albuquerque: University of New Mexico Press, 1995); Marion A. Habig, *Spanish
Texas Pilgrimage: The Old Franciscan Missions and Other Spanish Settlements of
Texas, 1632–1821* (Chicago: Franciscan Herald Press, 1990); Nancy P. Hickerson, *The Jumanos: Hunters and Traders of the Southern Plains* (Austin: University
of Texas Press, 1994); F. Todd Smith, *The Caddo Indians: Tribes at the Convergence of Empires, 1542–1854* (College Station: Texas A&M University Press,
1996); Kay Hindes, Mark R. Wolf, Grant D. Hall, and Kathleen Kirk Gilmore,
*The Rediscovery of Santa Cruz de San Sabá, A Mission for the Apache in Spanish
Texas* (Austin: Texas Historical Foundation and Texas Tech University Press,

1995); Jack Jackson, *Los Mesteños: Spanish Ranching in Texas, 1721–1821* (College Station: Texas A&M University Press, 1986); Noel M. Loomis and Abraham P. Nasatir, *Pedro Vial and the Roads to Santa Fe* (Norman: University of Oklahoma Press, 1967); W. H. Timmons, *El Paso: A Borderlands History* (El Paso: Texas Western Press, 1990).

For California (and the Northwest Coast), see Warren L. Cook, *Flood Tide of Empire: Spain and the Pacific Northwest, 1543–1819* (New Haven, CT: Yale University Press, 1973); Donald C. Cutter, ed., *The California Coast: A Bilingual Edition of Documents from the Sutro Collection* (Norman: University of Oklahoma Press, 1969), *California in 1792: A Spanish Naval Visit* (Norman: University of Oklahoma Press, 1990), and *The Defense of Northern New Spain: Hugo O'Conor's Report to Teodoro de Croix, July 22, 1777* (Dallas: Southern Methodist University Press, 1994). See also Harry W. Crosby, *Antigua California: Mission and Colony on the Peninsular Frontier, 1697–1768* (Albuquerque: University of New Mexico Press, 1994); Peter M. Dunne, *Pioneer Black Robes on the West Coast* (Berkeley: University of California Press, 1940); Maynard Geiger, *Franciscan Missionaries in Hispanic California, 1769–1848: A Biographical Dictionary* (San Marino, CA: Huntington Library, 1969), and *The Life and Times of Fray Junípero Serra, O.F.M.*, 2 vols. (Washington, D.C.: Academy of American Franciscan History, 1959); Harry Kelsey, *Juan Rodríguez Cabrillo* (San Marino, CA: Huntington Library, 1986); Michael W. Mathes, *Vizcaíno and Spanish Expansion in the Pacific Ocean, 1580–1630* (San Francisco: California Historical Society, 1968); Cynthia Radding, *Wandering Peoples: Colonialism, Ethnic Spaces, and Ecological Frontiers in Northwestern Mexico, 1700–1850* (Durham, NC: Duke University Press, 1997); Richman, Irving Berdine, *California under Spain and Mexico, 1535–1847; A Contribution toward the History of the Pacific Coast of the United States, Based on Original Sources, Chiefly Manuscript, in the Spanish and Mexican Archives and Other Repositories*. Reprint, 1911. New York: Cooper Square Publishers, 1965); Michael E. Thurman, *The Naval Department of San Blas: New Spain's Bastion for Alta California and Nootka, 1767–1798* (Glendale, CA: Arthur H. Clark, 1967).

Chapter Four

FROM THE
SAINT LAWRENCE AND
GREAT LAKES TO THE
ROCKY MOUNTAINS

While documentation about the French in the western portions of what is now the United States is not as extensive because of the nature of French activities on the Plains and in Rocky Mountain region, understanding the precursors to their appearance on the western frontier is paramount to placing the French and Indian experience in the West in its proper historical context. Unlike the Spanish, who marched into Indian lands in large groups and settlement expeditions, demanding obedience to the crown and pope, threatening war for noncompliance, and sometimes working out an uneasy peace; or the English, who often devastated Indian homelands, offering bounties for their scalps and forcing them to find new homes farther west; history tends to remember the French differently. The French were known for integrating into Indian-held territories through mutually beneficial trade relationships, engaging in political negotiations as almost reciprocal partners, and integrating into Indian families through intermarriage and acceptance of the progeny of those relations. Yet the story of the French, like that of the Spanish and English, in the Americas is much more complex, one that depends on an understanding not only of the interaction between individual traders but also of shifts, strains, breaks, and wars in French colonial and Indian history.

EXPLORATION IN THE SAINT LAWRENCE

Even as the Spanish empire expanded, thanks in part to its expectations of finding great wealth like the Inca and Aztec empires and in part because

French explorer Jacques Cartier ascends the Saint Lawrence River in Canada. Cartier's voyages from June 1534 to May 1536 were the beginning of France's efforts to exploit Canada. (Library of Congress)

of the blessing of the pope, France began to explore westward as well, engaging peoples indigenous to the Gulf of Saint Lawrence, such as those living in Newfoundland and Cape Breton islands, in trade by the early 1500s. Jacques Cartier had visited the region as early as 1534 and was awed by the beauty and abundance of the lands, dotted by farmland and orchards along the banks of the Saint Lawrence River. He saw where the Ottawa River flowed into the Saint Lawrence as he peered at it from a distance, and claimed it all for the king of France. While permanent French colonial settlements did not occur at the outset, trade initiated by the Mi'kmaq Indians in beaver pelts would begin a long relationship between the Saint Lawrence and interior tribes and the French colonial power. Periodically, French ships arrived and continued trading in the Saint Lawrence and surrounding environs; therefore, when the French arrived permanently in the early 1600s, the trade relationship had been secured.

Unlike the Spanish empire, which at its very outset arrived in the New World hoping to find a route to the Orient, the French arrived and almost immediately established as its sole purpose to engage in trade with the Montagnais and other coastal tribes in the Gulf of Saint Lawrence. Even though the French occupied portions of New France itinerantly from the 1530s on, a more permanent presence was not established until 1604 when King Henri IV asked the Society of Jesuits to send two missionaries to accompany a French fishing fleet to the Grand Banks. Shortly thereafter, the Jesuits established a permanent base of operations in the Bay of Fundy. Their efforts did not see immediate success, however, for it was not until 1610 that some 21 Indians were baptized—and this by a secular priest (as opposed to a member of the regular orders, missionaries like the Jesuits, Dominicans, and Franciscans). This, however, was all the motivation the Catholic Church and French crown needed to begin the push to convert the "heathens" of New France. While the missionaries had aspirations of converting large numbers of indigenous peoples, some French traders and colonists would soon decide that the missionaries were more bother than benefit.

The French government required trading missions into the interior to take missionaries with them, much to the frustration of the Indians they encountered. If they wanted the trade goods, however, they had to "tolerate the obnoxious black robes in their midst" (Eccles, *Essays on New France*, 27). Other complications created stumbling blocks for the Jesuits, including periodic captures of French bases by Anglo-Scots in 1628–1629, as well as the continuous threat of attack by the enemies of their Huron and Algonkin trading partners—the Iroquois Confederacy, who lived across the Saint Lawrence River and consisted of the Seneca, Cayuga, Onondaga, Oneida, and Mohawk (and after 1711, the Tuscarora) tribes. Resupply and funding afforded another major disadvantage to conversion, as the Saint Lawrence froze in the winter—disallowing any river travel and thereby ships with supplies or troop reinforcements from France. Moreover, the Thirty Years' War (1618–1648) caused the Jesuits to seek funding for their missionizing ventures from other sources, such as wealthy individuals and the Compagnie de Saint-Sacrement.

One of the greatest successes that the Jesuits initially claimed was the Huron mission. Located in present-day Ontario, Huronia was inhabited by people who called themselves Wendat. They lived at a strategic location between two major trading and ecological zones, giving them the status of intermediaries, in trade. Moreover, they had soil suitable for domesticated agriculture and grew and harvested crops such as corn in abundance. Speaking a branch of the Algonquian language, they traded tobacco, shells and wampum, raccoon pelt robes, and other items. Their trade served as an extension of the relationships they had established and that had developed and grown over time. The Huron recognized the Iroquois as their enemies and periodically attempted to get the French to support them in their wars against the Iroquois, or at the very least give them guns as trade goods to use against the Iroquois.

As Samuel de Champlain continued to expand French fur trade in the early 1600s throughout the Saint Lawrence River watershed and explore their relationship with these Algonquians, the Iroquois became more nervous about the developing alliance. Tension began to build between these age-old adversaries. But the Huron had trapped out the fur-bearing animals in their homelands by the 1630s, thereby forcing them to trade with other tribal trading partners farther west to supply France's insatiable thirst for furs. With an eye to expansion, Champlain sent out Jean Nicollet, the first European to see Lake Michigan, to establish rela-

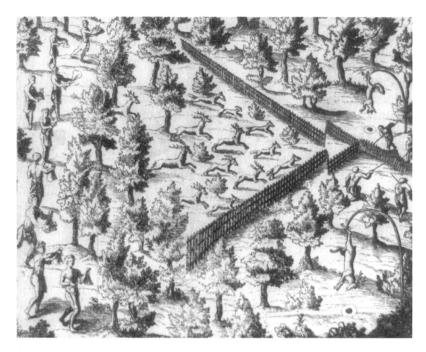

Bird's-eye view of a Huron deer hunt in New France (present-day Canada), showing Indians driving deer toward fences into a narrow enclosure to be killed, and two dead deer hanging from bent trees, ca. 1619. (Library of Congress)

tionships with those Indians he encountered in the west in hopes of engaging them in the fur trade. Interestingly, Nicollet believed that if he traveled far enough west, he would encounter China. However, instead of engaging with the Chinese, as he hoped, he encountered the Ho-Chunk. He brought back news of the Sioux Indians, some of whom would later be taken into captivity by the French. The West did not provide a quick route to China, but the French did establish a rapport with western Great Lakes tribes. For the Huron, however, their days were numbered. As disease spread and their numbers dwindled, Champlain pressed them to accept Jesuit missionaries and become Christians.

The Huron, skeptical of these black-robed individuals whom they felt chastised and admonished their culture, tried to maintain their traditional way of life. The Jesuits understood the importance of respecting traditional lifeways of tribal peoples—especially at the outset—and actually endeavored to adapt somewhat to Indian culture. They traveled in canoes with various tribes and lived by the Indians' rules of the water. The Jesuits clearly delineated these rules in their records (*The Jesuit Relations*), for example: do not paddle unless you intend to continue for the duration of the journey—sometimes up to 30 or more miles; do not let your hat interfere with other paddlers; and carry your share in the portages. They ate native foods, used native lodges, respected native traditions and women, and did not steal Indian lands. Yet the Huron were not motivated to adapt to the odd religion. They had their own, which had served them well for untold generations. When smallpox struck in 1639–1640, however, Huron resolve began to weaken. The epidemic probably caused some of them to seek a new spiritual power that could fight this intractable disease. But as their numbers dwindled even more, some began to equate baptism as the actual impetus for death (probably because the friars insisted on baptizing the Indians when they realized they would die soon). To make matters worse, by the mid-1600s, the Huron felt the wrath of the Iroquois who had finally acquired guns from the Dutch upon their arrival in the region by the 1610s, as well as the English. The Iroquois had more than three generations of vengeance to direct at the Huron as a result of the unbalanced fight of the previous 60 or more years. And because only Christianized Indians could acquire guns from the French, it put non-Christian Hurons and Algonkins at a great disadvantage.

Unfortunately, by that point, Huronia and the Huron missions—the only great success story in New France's conversion efforts, had failed after devastating epidemics ravaged the community, and then the Iroquois attacked, completely destroying the Hurons as a unified and coherent nation with a defined homeland. This had a devastating effect on other nations as well, for they witnessed that the French would not or could not protect the Huron from their enemies. And, potentially more insidiously, the French God was not powerful enough to protect his new charges from the "heathen" nations. News of the destruction of the Huron nation and the powerlessness of the French God must have had a negative impact on the Jesuits' ability to continue their successes in converting natives and spreading Catholicism. Even as the French failed to convert native peoples, French traders continued to show great interest in expanding the fur industry, whether or not the Jesuits succeeded in the spiritual realm. By the end of the 1600s, converting the natives was no longer a main concern of the French crown. The Indians could not effectively defend themselves any more as a result of the ravages of disease, high mortality rates, and resulting social disjunction that occurred in its wake. By the 1660s, the Huron had dispersed throughout the Great Lakes region, been taken captive by the Iroquois, or moved to live among various other tribes as far west and south as the Eries or Neutrals. As the Great Lakes region deteriorated into warfare because of overtrapping and controversies over hunting rights, some eastern tribes began to filter into more western regions. France's king began to ponder the logic of maintaining such a far-flung and contentious frontier at such a great expense.

With those tribes formerly allied with New France dispersed across the West and their lands ravaged and abandoned, and French posts beleaguered by constant fear of Iroquois attacks, *coureurs de bois* ("runners of the forest," or fur traders who lived among the Indians in the remote regions of New France) moved farther west to engage the fur trade again. Huron intermediaries no longer served to bring furs from the West. Instead, the Ottawa replaced the Huron as intermediaries in the fur trade, establishing their base at Chequamegon Bay on Lake Superior in what is now northern Wisconsin. Some tribes began to move farther east to escape assaults by the Sioux, who attempted to defend their homelands in the western Great Lakes region against the immigration of eastern tribes. They regrouped near Sault Sainte Marie, where the Great Lakes came together. From this base, the Ottawa engaged in trade with tribes as far west and north as the Cree, Assiniboines, and Sioux. To the south, the French engaged the "Sauks, Foxes, Potawatomis, Winnebagos, Menonimees, Mascoutens, Miamis, and Illinois" in the fur trade, thereby supplying more than 60 percent of all the furs to France (Calloway, *One Vast Winter Count*, 235).

In the Great Lakes region, the French encountered the numerous Ojibwa, or Chippewa bands, that lived throughout the region to the south and west of the Great Lakes. With a population of nearly 25,000, they had established themselves mostly as hunters or fishermen. Their location in the north made dependable agriculture an impossibility. By the end of the 1600s, the French (and some British) had made forays into the region, and some of the Ojibwa had even acquired guns. With the traditional balance of power upset in the region, the Ojibwa allied with the Cree to their north and began exerting pressure on the Dakota tribes. The latter, traditionally farmers who also collected wild rice, moved westward to escape the pressure of the expanding power of the Ojibwa and Cree (except for the Santee Dakota, who remained in what is now Minnesota).

NEW FRANCE SOLIDIFIES ITS HOLD

Settlement patterns in New France did not occur with the precision or order that they did in the Spanish empire. Instead of large expeditions with 10,000 head of livestock and a thousand Indian allies, as well as harquebuses and cannon trained on Indian communities—just in case—French settlement patterns proceeded at a much more relaxed and perhaps disorganized fashion. New France slowly established the communities of Quebec, Montreal, and Three Rivers by the early 1600s, and they remained small. By 1663, however, the French crown would declare New France a "royal colony" by taking it out of the proprietary realm and making it a "ward" of the crown. Accomplished only because of the relative peace and quiet in France, this allowed the crown to control the settlement and potential development of New France more deliberately and with far greater oversight—theoretically.

Some 70 years after Cartier's initial voyage, Samuel de Champlain followed Cartier's route. But instead of seeing rich communities along the Saint Lawrence, replete with the orchards and fields that Cartier had described as serving the needs of local tribes of Mi'kmaq, Abenakis, Montagnais, Huron, and Algonkin, instead he saw fields overgrown and villages abandoned. Disease, brought by the French, as well as competition for trade, which likely led to intensified warfare, had caused populations to drop and exposed villages to abandonment. Nevertheless, Champlain reestablished a French presence permanently when he founded Quebec City as a year-round settlement in 1608. This gave France a firm foothold in the Americas and an advantage with the northern fur trade. For the French, the Quebec City settlement could not have come at a better time, for farther south the English seemed to have finally succeeded in permanently occupying the James River (although, of course, neither the French nor the English knew whether or not Jamestown would succeed, or if it would disintegrate and disappear as Roanoke had in previous years).

Unlike the Spanish who, once they figured out that they had in fact run aground on a whole new continent, had come in large groups intent on extending the aegis of Spanish and Catholic control over the indigenous peoples that they found, the French came in small numbers. The French came without armies, but with fine-quality trade goods and hopes of establishing trading alliances with the many well-organized and seemingly powerful tribes along the Saint Lawrence River. They hoped to corner the market on the fur trade in North America and therefore become the main supplier of furs in Europe.

With fits and starts, the French empire attempted to expand, but because no mountains of silver or cities of gold appeared, immigration to New France remained but a mere trickle compared with that of their European counterparts. New France had far more challenges environmentally with establishing settlements resulting from the difficult and frigid northern climate. The French depended on river travel along the Saint Lawrence for resupply—but the river froze for half of the year, leaving the colonists snowbound and with no hope of communication or assistance from France. While a major barrier for half the year, the Saint Lawrence River also provided a path westward, to which the French traveled in birchbark canoes, something they learned about from the local tribes such as the Huron, Montagnais, and Algonkin. Tribes that the French encountered based their existence on or near the water, which made up nearly one-quarter of all the regions claimed by France. Birchbark canoes, being the primary and most dependable mode of transportation, were quickly adapted from the Indians. Using the rivers gave Indian people access to trade with other riverine tribes, to harvest the wild rice that grew in coves or small bays along the streams and lakes, to a dependable method of transportation (people and supplies), and to communication. Around that water-centered lifestyle, they also hunted, fished, collected maple sap and made sugar, and traveled to different campsites depending upon the season. When the French encountered the many different Algonkian or Iroquoian-speaking tribes, they quickly understood that if they intended to live among the native people successfully, they would need to learn their language, and to a certain extent they would need to learn how to adapt to aspects of their Indian hosts' lifestyles that would help them survive the long winters. As easily as some of them did adapt to Indian methods of transportation, trade, foodways, and even housing styles, in some ways, the excitement and potential financial gains of living on the "frontier" did not capture the imagination of large numbers of Frenchmen. For the first several generations, few Frenchmen, much less their families, actually ventured into this unfamiliar and "new world."

The French population in the Americas stayed low, and by the 1660s, a mere 130 years into the colonization process, only 3,200 French colonists even lived in the entire region. Three settlements did emerge along the Saint Lawrence River: Quebec, which served as the headquarters for the region, Trois-Rivières (1634) or Three Rivers, and Montreal (1642). The settlements were not strongly defended, well populated, or self-sufficient, even though that was a requirement of any company that contracted with the French crown to have a monopoly over New France. Like the companies that founded Virginia, the French also sanctioned monopolies to run the new ventures overseas, yet all of them failed in their primary purpose—to bring Frenchmen and their families to create permanent communities, raise their families, establish a permanent foothold for France, and perhaps most important, grow crops in order to make New France self-sufficient. That way, New France could survive without having to rely on the resupply vessels that could travel only when the Saint Lawrence was not frozen.

One such company that attempted to live up to its contract with France was the Company of 100 Associates of New France. The crown hoped that New France would be a proprietary colony, but it was far too difficult to manage, and the contracts of company after company were dissolved by the crown until finally, in 1663, King Louis XIV established New France as a royal colony under the control of Jean-Baptiste Colbert, the minister of marine. For the first time, the French government made an official attempt to organize and integrate New France into the French colonial system. For nearly a dozen years, Louis XIV funded New France at a rate it had never experienced, providing funding for more soldiers, traders, missionaries, and missions of exploration throughout the Saint Lawrence Valley, but also beyond—to the Mississippi River and points farther west. For the first time, the French began to look west and engage with tribes as far away as Minnesota, Iowa, Missouri, and Arkansas.

INDIANS AND THE FRENCH FUR TRADE

The French engaged in the fur trade with Indian people before even setting foot on North America. By the time the French reached the region west of the Mississippi River, they had been trading with many tribes throughout the Great Lakes region for more than 100 years. Their trading partners included the Mi'kmaq and Huron in the east and the Ojibwa and Pawnee to the west and south.

The fur trade benefited the French, who supplied European markets with desirable, high-quality, dense furs. It also benefited the tribes who established trade with the French because the Indians wanted to use the firearms and other metal tools against their enemies and to expand their trapping territory and stature among tribal neighbors. When the Huron and Algonkins acquired guns, the Iroquois suffered tremendously at the hands of both. But later the Huron would suffer a far worse fate when the Iroquois acquired their own firearms from the Dutch in the early 1600s.

As they spread west, the French also brought their steel knives, axes, firearms, metal cooking utensils and vessels, wool products, glass beads and mirrors, and linen, to name a few of the items. These items proved more than useful to both native men and women. Tribes grew dependent on these objects of European culture and could not, or would not, return to life as they had lived it before.

The fur trade also brought contagious diseases, like smallpox, the common cold, and influenza that Indians had no immunities to fight. Alcohol acquired from French traders tore apart Indian society at its very core. The fur trade also brought heightened tension and a realignment of the traditional balance of power in the regions the fur trade affected. It also created a whole new race: the métis—children born to French fur trappers who married Indian women to cement a trade relationship. Was the fur trade a positive influence or a harbinger of the destruction of Indian sovereignty?

NEW FRANCE REALIGNS RELATIONSHIP WITH TRIBES

After 1663, the number of settlers began to grow ever so slightly, and missionaries began to focus more on the French colonists and less on converting the Huron, Algonkin, and Montagnais. The pressure on indigenous cultures and spiritualism, therefore, had been released somewhat, though it would never completely disappear. By 1673, the French understood the importance of continued expansion and permanent settlements to quell the expansion of the English, even if Christianity was not the primary goal in their expansion.

Jesuit missionary Father Jacques Marquette and Canadian fur trader Louis Joliet set out from the Wisconsin River to follow the length of the Mississippi River to find its mouth, wholly depending on their abilities at interacting with tribes that they encountered for their sustenance and survival. Joliet spoke six native languages and Marquette held the calumet, given to him by tribes in the Michimilimackinac region, where their journey had originally begun. They used native transportation—birchbark canoes—survived on Indian foods they had acquired, and planned to trade for the supplies they needed along the route. During the journey, Joliet planned to collect and record information about the tribes they encountered, as well as their propensity toward trade. New France hoped to create trading alliances with as many western tribes as they could before the English had the opportunity, and the Mississippi River provided New France an excellent barrier to stop continued English advances westward. Moreover, between the Fox River, which formed a part of the Saint Lawrence watershed, and the Wisconsin River, which formed a part of the Mississippi River watershed, lay a mere 1.28 miles of portage that strategically connected the two major segments of the French empire. As long as the French maintained that portage and the access to the mouths of the Saint Lawrence and Mississippi rivers, they would control a vast majority of North America.

The French explorers created extensive maps of the Mississippi River Valley and its tributaries where they could discern that information from informants. Similar to the early Spanish maps, they recorded the location of rivers and which ones were navigable, geographical landmarks, and tribes (location, population, livelihood, and more) that they encountered on the journey. Upon his return during a portage to Lake Michigan from the Illinois River, Marquette even suggested digging a canal between the two great water systems of the North, thereby linking the Saint Lawrence through the Great Lakes, to the Mississippi River and the Gulf of Mexico to aid in the export of furs from the interior and to ease travel throughout New France. Most important, perhaps, they learned that the quality of the furs farther south seemed far inferior to those of the north, obviously because of the more temperate climate. And even though they technically did not make it all the way to the mouth of the Mississippi, they had gathered key information about potential for trade, travel, and a southern water route that would allow for the resupply of the colony throughout the winter months.

THE CALUMET

Often known improperly as a peace pipe, the calumet proved invaluable in France's movement westward. Throughout the Midwest, tensions flared as competition for furs, depleted in the northeast by the 1640s, caused many tribes, including both the Huron and Iroquois, to move westward and either establish alliances with the Great Lakes tribes for furs or, in the case of the Huron, attempt to disrupt the Iroquois' alliances.

Calumets—whose holders decorated the stems with various colored feathers, which indicated whether the holder sought peace or battle, or perhaps some other purpose—were carried by both Indians and Frenchmen. Held out by Marquette and Joliet as they encountered tribes along the Mississippi, the calumet signaled peace and allowed for calm and unaggressive engagements between the explorers and the cautious (and at times defensive) Indians they encountered.

Marquette, who was saved on more than one occasion by using the calumet as a "free pass" through Indian territory, wrote that "there is nothing more mysterious or respected among them. . . . It seems to be the God of peace and of war, the Arbiter of life and of death." He remarked that they used

Dakota Indian with calumet kneels inside a tipi in in 1907. (Library of Congress)

the calumet to establish peace, negotiate an end to disputes, and engage in conversations with strangers. Other Frenchmen described the calumet as having the "authority to confirm everything, and which renders solemn oaths binding" (Calloway, *One Vast Winter Count*, 237).

The knowledge gathered from this expedition would prove invaluable, and less than a dozen years later, René Robert Cavelier, Sieur de La Salle, would attempt to find the mouth of the Mississippi River. Minister of Marine Colbert had given La Salle a contract for a monopoly on trading posts in the Mississippi Valley if he would locate the mouth of the Mississippi. In 1682, La Salle and Henri Tonti did reach the mouth by traveling down the river, claiming the mouth and its vast watershed that stretched from roughly the Continental Divide in the west to the Allegheny and Appalachian mountains to the east (the largest watershed in what would become the United States) for the French crown, naming the area west of the Mississippi Louisiana.

When La Salle was commissioned to return by sea a few years later to locate the mouth from the Gulf of Mexico, he did not find the same success, however. According to King Louis XIV's minister, Marquis de Seignelay, "The principal purpose of Sieur de la Salle in making this discovery was to find a port on the Gulf of Mexico on which could be formed a French settlement to serve as a base for conquests upon the Spaniards" (quoted in Kessell, *Spain in the Southwest,* 125). Yet far more was at stake in this venture than the attempted takeover of Spanish holdings. At the same time, the French had a great interest in holding back the tide of English expansion, finding a warm-water port, and expanding their territories for the benefit of the fur traders and the French crown. Unfortunately, during his sea voyage La Salle and his men overshot the mouth by leagues, and ended up near in what is now Matagordo Bay, Texas. In a vain attempt at demonstrating command over his crew, which seemed on the cusp of mutiny from the sheer frustration at being driven ashore and losing a vessel on the difficult seas, he landed and established a base in 1685.

La Salle declared that from this base they would search overland to find the mouth of the Mississippi and claim it for the crown. Needless to say, La Salle's expedition was a great failure, one in which he and his nephew met an inauspicious end at the hands of the murderous and mutinous crew. Some mutineers commandeered the one remaining vessel and sailed it out into the harbor to escape Texas, but the ship was likely caught in a storm and sank to the bottom of the Gulf of Mexico (where it was excavated in the 1990s under a major grant from the National Geographic Society). For two disastrous years, those who survived the mutiny eked out a living on the coast, where they eventually met their end. According to a Jumano Indian, coastal tribes had killed all of the Frenchmen, except for a few who had been away on a trading mission with the Tejas. Two of the French survivors appeared later in New Mexico, and another apparently "turned Native."

Regardless of whether or not La Salle's expedition was a failure, coureurs de bois took full advantage of the knowledge gained from the Marquette and Joliet expedition as well as from La Salle's first voyage. Even though Colbert, New France's minister of marine, had issued orders to stop westward travel and exploration, he could not control the coureurs de bois, nor curtail their activities. Instead, Colbert attempted to impose control by initiating a licensing system, whereby a mere 25 canoes (which could hold up to five tons of cargo) would have an annual right to trade in the western regions. Without government outposts and controls throughout the far-flung reaches of the West, however, the coureurs de bois ignored regulations, and instead of bringing their wares to posts in New France at the end of the season, they employed intermediaries and remained in the West, some with their native families. Unfortunately, the Indian people and the environment would be adversely affected by the fur trade, as would the European market, which soon became flooded with western furs.

The French continued to watch the British advances and feigned shock when an English ship arrived at Hudson Bay and initiated trade with the northern tribes, in particular the Cree, who had previously been a staunch French trade partner. The French reacted slowly, however, as they knew ships could traverse the straits into Hudson Bay for only a few weeks of the year. Furthermore, western tribes, with whom the English hoped to establish trade relations, much preferred to trade with the French who lived in their midst (even though the cost of shipping supplies from France to the Americas, along the Saint Lawrence and up the vast river systems throughout Canada, was more than the costs the British incurred shipping goods from England to Hudson Bay). And, as previously mentioned, the goods from France were of better quality. But the English presence in French-dominated regions had begun, and soon the

English would be in the Far West, along the California to Alaska coastline, attempting to entice coastal tribes to engage in trade with Great Britain and forsake their former European partners.

As French traders and their Indian allies began to move west, they encountered resistance from various tribes. Nevertheless, La Salle, had previously established a series of trading posts on the Illinois River by the 1670s; thus, by right of occupation, he had claimed suzerainty over the lands of both the Illinois and Miami Indians for the French crown. But the tribes did not acquiesce so easily. To make matters worse, by the 1670s, the English had already made advances from their settlements along the Atlantic Coast and had begun to establish inroads with the Iroquois as trading partners. Thus, when the Iroquois showed up in the Illinois region in the 1680s to stake their claim on the fur trade, one of the first battles for the West occurred between Indians and their European allies.

On this occasion, the Iroquois had bested the Illinois and the French, whom they promised to destroy. A humiliating peace ensued for the French, who learned that the Iroquois Confederacy intended to control all of the tribes south of the Great Lakes—all the way to the Mississippi River—and then to divert any furs from the region from Montreal to Albany, all under the direct control of the Iroquois. European wars again interceded and had a major effect on the success of the Iroquois to bring their plan to fruition, however. And just as the French began in earnest their attempts to draw the western tribes into fur-trading alliances, a glut of furs hit French storehouses, forcing New France's authorities to call for the abandonment and destruction of all of the posts, save one in the Illinois region. But by then the beaver trade had been suspended, and by the 1690s, French merchants had little interest in acquiring more furs from the Americas.

SAINT LAWRENCE TRIBE REALIGNMENT AND EXPANSION SOUTH

The French had other problems that took their attention away from the Americas. Conflicts had grown between the northeastern English colonies and the French, and by the late 1680s, the English had attacked Port Royal and destroyed buildings, desecrated churches, and looted the community. Their allies, the Iroquois, were to join with other English

Eighteenth-century depiction of an Iroquois warrior. (Library and Archives Canada/Bibliothèque et Archives Canada (R9266-3492) Peter Winkworth Collection of Canadiana)

colonists and soldiers to make an assault on Montreal, but due to overall incompetence, this expedition fell short, and by 1697 the Iroquois sued for peace.

To counterbalance the negative news for traders, tribes in the Great Lakes region, the Ojibwa and Ottawa, affirmed that by 1700, the Iroquois had been defeated once and for all. The French had seen this coming. Regardless of the ignominious defeat, the Iroquois remained staunch in their demands under the terms of the treaty. According to the agreement crafted, the Iroquois would serve as a buffer zone between France's Indian allies to the north and the English to the south. The Iroquois had learned that they could not depend on English military support, just as the Hurons had learned two generations before when they believed that the French had abandoned them when the Iroquois decimated their village. The Iroquois were in a special position to play the French off the English to get what they wanted. Most important, the Iroquois had the right to remain neutral in all future wars between the European powers. In 1701, representatives from 28 different tribes traveled to Montreal where they negotiated a peace, once and for all, with the Iroquois. The delegation included the French and many Great Lakes tribes: Ottawa, Ojibwas, Potawatomis, Sauks, Foxes, Winnebagos, Menominees, Kickapoos, Mascoutens, Miamis, Illinois, Nipissings, and the remnants of the Huron, among others. Perhaps of greatest interest to the French was the Iroquois' promise not to become involved in wars between France and England. These successful negotiations with the Iroquois opened the door for the French to focus their energies elsewhere.

This new opportunity to focus elsewhere was important because in the late 1690s, Louis XIV heard rumors that English traders had begun to cross over the Alleghenies and were attempting to establish trade relations with Indians along the Mississippi River. Because the Iroquois no longer posed a threat, Louis XIV became interested in expanding French authority into the Mississippi basin on a permanent basis, and in 1700 New France looked to the south in an attempt to prevent the English from expanding westward (see Map 9). From the European perspective, the Indians in those regions seemed relegated to becoming merely pawns in the international fur trade, but they certainly gained significantly from their trade relationship, whether it was acquiring tools and guns or gaining prestige among area tribes. Their status as independent and sovereign nations, however, was challenged by the growing international battle for sovereignty over their homelands—sovereignty that the Indians had never given up, nor had they any inkling that they would lose their sovereignty in the next 100 years.

To justify their claim on the Mississippi River and its basin, the French authorities sent Pierre Le Moyne d'Iberville south with secret orders to destroy any English outposts and establish a settlement at the mouth of the Mississippi River. After all, the nation that controlled the mouth of the Mississippi also controlled its watershed, and therefore the interior. While the fur trade and conversion still carried some influence in the expansionist philosophy of Louis XIV, he was mostly interested in expansion as a political tool to quell English power in the Americas. Technically, expansion for New France was nothing new, for since the 1650s, French fur traders had begun pushing deeper into the continent as the furs played out along the Saint Lawrence River. His interest in denying the English more territory would also be his primary reason for handing over Louisiana and everything west of the Mississippi River to the Spanish in 1762 when the French found themselves confronted with signing the Treaty of Paris and rescinding control over all of New France.

ENVIRONMENTAL CONSEQUENCES OF THE FUR TRADE

The French used the fur trade to bring Hurons and Algonkins into the French trade network and make them dependent on (and thus allies to) the French. Therefore, they would be less likely to trade with and create alliances with other foreign powers.

Unfortunately, to remain a trade partner, tribes had to find furs that they could trade. As the years progressed, Indian tribes trapped all of the available beaver pelts in their rivers and drainage basins, forcing them to either enlist other tribes farther west or south into trading and then becoming middlemen in the trade system themselves, or forcing them to uproot from their traditional homelands and move farther upriver to hunt and trap. However, the lands to which they relocated were not unoccupied, and intertribal conflict arose between tribes competing for resources.

With French guns, the westward-moving tribes easily dominated the tribes they encountered, and those tribes joined the trade network, fought and paid dearly for their unwillingness to join, or relocated (thereby causing other displacements or potentially uniting tribes that had been diminished by the diseases that also came with French trade goods). Besides disrupting entire communities and river systems, the long-established balance of power throughout the western regions had to be rebalanced. Often those that came out on top were those with French guns and trade goods.

Moreover, the balance of nature was also irreparably damaged. Beaver no longer built their dams, and existing dams eroded, thereby causing water systems to be greatly affected in each watershed. The food chain, or rather pyramid, was irrevocably altered, and the lasting impact of that on the region cannot be overstated. The result was a shift in plant and animal life that is still being studied by botanists and zoologists.

After the 1701 treaty with the Indian nations was signed, Louis XIV gave orders to create the new colony of Louisiana. This plan was meant both to stop English and to establish a southern port to potentially allow for the transport of supplies to the colonies in the winter via the Mississippi River. France needed to have two access points to the inland empire for both strategic and economic reasons.

To secure the west, Louis XIV also ordered a new French settlement to be established at a point between Lake Erie and Lake Huron—Detroit. Its foundation would serve as a barrier to English expansion into the Old Northwest and allow for continued French control over the Great Lakes, and therefore the interior and the Mississippi River's headwaters. Indian peoples who lived in those western regions shifted from becoming potential trade partners with the French, as had the Montagnais, Huron, and Algonkins, to becoming willing (or unwilling) pawns in an international game of chess. French authorities would now recognize Indian nations as partners only to make certain that they would not establish trade relations with the English, and therefore would not side with the English in future wars against France in the Americas. To accomplish this mission of separating Indians in French-held territories from the English, the French government planned to use French missionaries and fur traders to establish a close commercial union.

By the early 1700s, the church in New France had become rather ineffectual among indigenous peoples, especially after the bishop of New France chose to make his residence in Paris, thereby illustrating his disinterest in the daily operations in New France and rendering him incapable of restoring dominance, order, and even discipline among his charges in the New World. As a result, the duty fell to the *Troupes de la Marine* (colonial regulars) and the fur traders. The fur trade had officially taken on a purely political purpose: to keep England at bay. It no longer served a purely commercial function. The newly organized western expansion took place under the auspices of post commandants. These men formed companies, oftentimes in partnership with Montreal merchants who had easy access to incoming trade goods on the Saint Lawrence, and hired *voyageurs* (traders) to travel among the Indian people trading for furs. Montreal would be the trade center, but furs taken by allies of the Iroquois from French-held regions sometimes found their way to English-controlled Albany. Although sometimes Indian tribes allied with the French provided the furs to the Albany merchants, the French could do little to stop it. Clandestine trade frustrated the French authorities, but the Christian Indians of the Sault Saint Louis and Lake of Two Mountains mission tribes, both located close to Montreal, were important to the success of continued French control of the region, and the French authorities could not afford to alienate the tribes. Farther north and west, control over the fur trade became even less certain.

France was incapable of holding back the tide of Englishmen, however, and by the end of the War of Spanish Succession (1702–1713), which began just as the peace was signed with the Iroquois that would purportedly end hostilities on that border, Louis XIV had ceded Newfoundland and Acadia to England. But France refused to acquiesce on England's claim to the south shores of the Saint Lawrence, and instead asserted its dominion over the Saint Lawrence waterway and all the Indians who lived there (Mi'kmaq, Abenaki, Malecites). Even more unfortunate for France, however, they could not maintain their control over Hudson

Bay. The British claimed that the Treaty of Utrecht (1713), which had ended the War of Spanish Succession, also allowed them the right to Hudson Bay and the lands and rivers that drained into it, which included a large portion of North America. For the American Indians in the West, the Treaty of Utrecht had little consequences, other than the likelihood that the French would turn an interested eye in their direction once again—not for trade, but for political purposes: to stop further expansion by the English.

As a result, the French renewed their efforts at engaging tribes across the West in peace negotiations and working them into alliances that would help end the threat of English advances. Where it behooved the tribes, they joined the French alliance in the westernmost portions of New France. They had become emboldened by their access to guns and control over the fur trade as far west as the northern Ohio River Valley. If they chose not to involve themselves in the fur trade, they could avoid the wars that the Iroquois and New France brought into the West as a result of their demands for fur or the trade goods that came with the exchange. Even though French expansion did proceed westward, it never reached the Pacific Coast, or even west of the Rocky Mountains. But French expansion did bring with it large numbers of French settlers, as did Spanish expansion throughout Mexico, the Caribbean, and South America; but it did not prevent English expansion as the East Coast and the English colonies continued to grow even more rapidly as the slave trade and cotton plantations began to take hold.

While all of these negotiations occurred, the indigenous peoples continued to trade with the French at their posts throughout the western regions, not realizing that the negotiations might have a profound effect upon their lives. And according to French records, the Indians appreciated having the French trade partners actually located throughout the West in their own homelands. Except for the Sioux, who kept an appreciable distance between themselves and the French (who tended to capture them for use as slaves throughout New France), tribes engaged in lively trade until the French government officially left the Americas in 1763.

Unlike the English who, when they established their "factories" (trading posts), claimed the land upon which it resided for the crown, the

French claimed title to only the land upon which the post sat as a deterrent to English claims, but their claim did not impinge upon native rights to that same or surrounding land. According to French Borderlands historian W. J. Eccles, claiming Indian lands was "something they did not dare do" (Eccles, *Essays on New France,* 85). In fact, the French did not have complete sovereignty throughout their West, nor would they ever. And to be fair, they did not choose to make domination of tribes a goal of their colonization efforts. The Indian people never considered themselves French subjects, nor did they consider themselves vassals to the French crown. The French simply did not have the military might, large populations of settlers relocated from France, or the ability to extend the same control over their scattered settlements as did the Spanish or English (both of whom came originally in large "clumps" of settlers with contracts to permanently settle). Therefore, the French never attempted to treat their trading partners as vassals, subjects, or second-class citizens or worse. (Of course, this ignores the fact that the French did take Sioux captives and sell them into slavery.)

NEW FRANCE LOOKS WEST

Indian people from the Saint Lawrence River to the Great Lakes, down the Mississippi River, and up to the far northern reaches of what are now the Northwest Territories in northern Canada, continued to trade with the French instead of the English for two reasons. The first, of course, was the proximity of the French trading posts and the willingness of French traders to come into their regions with trade goods. While the English had established some bases along the Hudson Bay region, they were located in regions far off the beaten path for many Indian trappers (although some did make their way to the Hudson Bay region). Second, and perhaps more importantly, the French had far superior trade goods. Only with woolen cloth and blankets did the English have an upper hand. The Hudson Bay Company, chartered on May 2, 1670, by English King Charles II, manufactured blankets with thin black lines on the sides of approximately two to four inches, indicating how many beaver pelts (or half pelts) one blanket would cost. Until 2006, the English-owned Hudson Bay Company continued to operate, manufacturing blankets in England (it was recently sold to a U.S. company).

Then again, the French had a clear advantage when it came to spirits. French traders brought brandy, not the gin and rum of far lesser quality that the English brought (often called rotgut for obvious reasons). Liquor became a standard trade item for two major reasons. First, the Indians demanded it, and according to some traders, the Indians could not seem to resist it. Second, it was a trade item that would need to be resupplied indeterminately. Although one could have enough pots and pans, knives, and guns, liquor would be used up and a consistent need developed. The desire for liquor made tribes dependent on the French traders who brought the better-quality product, keeping them in the trade cycle. And in the words of one trader, Duncan McGillivray, "When a nation becomes addicted to drinking it affords a strong presumption that they will soon become excellent hunters" (Eccles, *Essays on New France,* 86). To learn about the impact of alcohol on a native community, one needs only to study the oral histories coming from the Shawnee Confederacy during the late 1700s and early 1800s.

TENSKWATAWA, THE SHAWNEE PROPHET

While not as famous as his brother, Tecumseh, Tenskwatawa (also known as Elskwatawa) provided the spiritual foundation for the Shawnee uprising, which is mostly credited to his older brother. Given the name Lalawethicka in his early life (meaning "He Who Makes a Loud Noise"), Tenskwatawa's early life revealed the frustrations of the Ohio Valley tribes.

The boys' father died when they were young. His father's brothers raised Tecumseh, which was customary upon the death of a father, so he could follow clan lineage and continue learning the skills and knowledge consistent with his clan and gender. On the other hand, aunts raised Lalawethicka and therefore he never learned the skills assigned to men. For a time, he lived with his sister, but after the Treaty of Greenville was signed in 1795, which limited the size of Shawnee homelands, he moved out and married. However, he was incapable of supporting his family and instead turned to whiskey.

A Shawnee elder, a medicine man or healer, befriended Lalawethicka and began to share his wisdom. After his friend's

A Shawnee mystic and the brother of Tecumseh, Tenskwatawa was the first of two influential Indians to be called The Prophet, appointing himself prophet in 1805. Lalawethicka was his given name, but he adopted the name Elkswatawa, and later Tenskwatawa, The Prophet. (McKenney, Thomas L. and James Hall, The Indian Tribes of North America, 1836–1844)

death, Lalawethicka attempted to heal his tribe's people of the various illnesses brought on by contact with Europeans, but he had no power and his medicine was weak. Frustrated, he realized that his people thought of him as powerless because of his transgressions and worthlessness as a provider.

On one occasion while lighting a pipe, purportedly after having been drinking, he fell unconscious. Thought to be dead, his wife and family were preparing his funeral arrangements, when he astonished everyone by sitting bolt upright. He had had a vision, the one thing that had

> previously eluded him. His vision told him to forsake all that the Europeans had brought and to teach his people to return to traditional lifeways.
>
> Beginning in 1805, Lalawethicka began to spread his vision and message with great success—not just among the Shawnee, but also among other Ohio Valley tribes. Known from this point as Tenskwatawa (Open Door), he began the movement that one historian has argued was usurped by his older brother and turned into a military movement, which then fed the Shawnee uprising.

Traders defended their use of alcohol in the fur trade, as did some important officials, such as Governor-General Louis de Buade, comte de Frontenac, who himself was also engaged in the fur trade for profit. He made light of the incidences where Indians would become drunk and, enraged by the liquor, kill unsuspecting family members, traders, or standers-by, something that happened often among the Shawnee during Tenskwatawa's era. Downplayed by those who stood to gain personally from the continued trade, Frontenac and others argued that Indians behaved no worse than any other European. The missionaries knew better, however, and only the missionaries took a virulent stand against the trading of alcohol to American Indians, but it was of no use. American Indians made choices in what they traded and how they lived their lives, and many Frenchmen, as well as the Jesuit fathers, understood that it would be foolhardy to impose their moral authority over the numerous tribes upon whom they depended for trade and security.

When the French did expand westward, the coureurs de bois and later voyageurs did so with the unspoken license of the Indians whose territory they traversed. Between 1719 and 1750, the number of military, voyageurs, traders, clerks, and merchants fluctuated from 200 to around 600 at most by mid-century. In other words, with fewer than 1,000 people, the French maintained control of nearly half of the North American continent. Such a small population made it difficult for the French to control the interior as the English began moving west. While the French clearly occupied forts in the Ohio Valley, westward to the Great Lakes, down the Mississippi River, and to the north, the westernmost portions of French-held territories were not as clearly defended.

But as furs became more and more scarce in the Mississippi Valley, the French needed to expand farther west, perhaps as far as the Pacific. More importantly perhaps, interest in science and expanded knowledge about the Americas increased the crown's interest in continued exploration. Furthermore, for the French, finding a route west to the ocean was of particular importance. So under the guise of expanding the fur trade, France intended to send out major expeditions into the western hinterlands. However, the Fox Indians who lived on the south side of the Great Lakes blocked their path, leading to wars that cost the French dearly.

By 1734, the Fox resistance had been crushed, but the Sioux posed an equally difficult challenge, forcing the expedition of Lt. Pierre Gaultier de Varennes et de La Vérendrye to attempt to reach the western ocean via a more northerly route, where he finally came upon the Rocky Mountains along the Saskatchewan River. La Vérendrye had previously established a post in the northern frontier in his attempt to be the first Frenchman to reach the western ocean, but he was mostly interested in fame for himself. Most frustrating to him involved the logistics and time constraints of having to resupply his far western posts from Montreal via Michilimackinac to the west by canoe. His men developed morale problems, however, and the isolation of being so far removed from New France caused excessive frustration over even the smallest personal infractions. Furthermore, illnesses and lack of medical personnel and supplies caused a major problem for them. But they had two important tasks to execute: to keep the Cree from attacking the Sioux and to attempt to end intertribal warfare in the West. The Cree, incidentally, had established themselves as the predominant culture on the northern Plains. In fact, Cree was the lingua franca of the northern Plains.

The calmer the western frontier was, the fewer hostilities would be directed at the French settlements and travelers. Furthermore, wars cost money. In other words, the goal of peace had more to do with self-preservation and cost-effectiveness than concern for the native peoples. When La Vérendrye attempted to lend support to the northern tribes in their campaign against the Sioux, they exacted revenge—killing his nephew and 20 of his men. When the Illinois rose up against two tribes in their area (hacking a Canadian blacksmith to pieces in the process), the beleaguered two tribes asked for assistance from their allies, which included

La Vérendrye explores what is today western Canada. (Library and Archives Canada/Bibliothèque et Archives Canada)

the Iowa and the Sioux. Only after a large disbursement of trade presents did the Illinois call off their aggression. Other tasks for the western posts involved making sure that the Indians had no contact or interaction with the English colonists along the coast. The English, incidentally, were often blamed for the Indian uprisings in western regions of New France.

One major result of the Indian conflicts that had developed in the West involved the capture of Sioux Indians by the Cree and Assiniboine. The French traders purchased the captives and sold them at a high price in Canada. For example, while beaver sold for a mere four livres at auction in Quebec, one Sioux slave sold for 351 livres in 1733. La Vérendrye, obviously proud of his part in the trafficking of human slaves, bragged about the number of slaves he had shipped to Montreal from the western frontier. In the 1730s, one governor-general attempted to stop the purchase of slaves from the Assiniboine, but it had little affect, for by the 1750s, the slave trade had picked up: as many as 60 Pani (Pawnee) a year were sold at Fort des Prairies alone. Apparently not all slaves were poorly treated, physically abused, or used for heavy physical labor, and some found themselves at Jesuit missions for conversion.

Another group of Sioux had interactions with the French, but in a more positive vein: the Dakota who lived at the headwaters of the Mississippi River. When the French moved into their region, the Dakota tolerated them because they brought trade goods and skilled workers (blacksmiths, for example) whose services were now needed to repair the metal tools they had previously acquired from the French. They considered the French inferior in many ways, not the least of which was that the French were smaller and less physically capable than the Indians. In fact, the Indians believed that if they had not shared their knowledge of travel by canoe, routes, food sources, hunting, and medicinal herbs, the French would certainly have either starved to death or found some other quick end. They distrusted the black robes, or the Jesuits, and the French even more.

The Indian people questioned the establishment of new posts in the West, and they grew frustrated at increased prices without logical causes. Moreover, the French sometimes did not offer the same value of tribute for permission to cross their homelands or for permission to establish posts on their lands (the French considered the items gifts, not tribute, of course). Overall, however, so few Frenchmen lived out West that the Indians could tolerate them, unlike the English, who arrived in droves and demanded that the Indians give up their land and move away into other tribal homelands where they were oftentimes not welcome—something the Indians who found themselves on lands recently claimed by the English would experience firsthand within a few generations (Eccles, *Essays on New France,* 100–108).

The tribes that moved west affected tribes already living on the Plains and in the western Great Lakes regions, and when the expeditions under the La Vérendrye arrived as far west as the Red and Assiniboine rivers, they witnessed the effects of those earlier shifts. La Vérendrye headed farther south onto the Plains, witnessing firsthand the farming communities of the Mandan and Hidatsas, who still lived in their traditional round earthen lodges along the Missouri River. They had only just begun to acquire horses by the 1740s from other Plains tribes, such as the Cheyenne

Mandan village, ca. 1832, painted by Karl Bodmer. (Library of Congress)

(who had recently moved south because the Sioux had moved onto the Plains and become increasely bold). Beyond the Mandan and Hidatsa, La Vérendrye encountered the Crow and the Shoshone, the latter of which had already amassed a large number of horses. Returning via the Black Hills, La Vérendrye's expedition learned that the Assiniboine and Cree had established trade relations with the British at Hudson Bay. As a result, the French increased their efforts in the West, building more trading posts to convince the tribes to forgo trade with the British.

SHIFTING GOALS

By the mid-1750s the future of New France became less certain. In fact, by 1753 the king had become shocked at the expenditures that the western posts demanded and threatened to abandon the colony. French military forces and Indian allies had begun to go on the offensive (or defensive, depending on one's historical perspective) and attack English colonies from north to south, causing a strain on French military logistics and, even worse, on the colonial expenditures. The Indians, who had always fought alongside the French when it suited them, were allies in these incursions against the English. Moreover, they used the French as allies against their own enemies, the Iroquois, to maintain control over the Ohio Valley tribes like the Miami, Kickapoo, Wyandots, and the relocated Lenni-Lenape (Delaware); that is, they were able to do this until the English colonial authorities in the Americas forced a truce on the Iroquois, Shawnee, and Delaware tribes, whose lands they had decimated during their relentless campaigns against the tribes.

At this point, tribes in the southern Great Lakes region generally stopped allying with the French. Perhaps they saw the large numbers of British regulars, as well as the growing numbers of English colonists. The British learned of the new posts that La Vérendrye established as a result of his trip through the Plains and responded by sending Anthony Henday to go beyond French control on the Plains to establish relations with tribes even farther west. Traveling as far west as Calgary, Henday met Blackfeet, Bloods, and Piegans (a Blackfoot confederacy that would periodically trade, hunt, and travel in the northern United States), as well as the Atsinas. Henday likely traded guns to the Blackfeet, which they in turn used against the Shoshoni, Flathead, and Kutenais, forcing them back into the Rocky Mountains. While Henday tried to engage the Blackfeet in the fur trade empire, they had no interest in it, and instead continued hunting buffalo on the Plains. Henday's mission proved unsuccessful, not simply for the recalcitrance of the Blackfeet and their growing power and interest in exerting their dominance on the northern Plains, but also because his travels occurred in mid-1750—coinciding with the French and Indian War, which broke out in 1754.

By 1759, the French and Indian War had turned, and Quebec and Niagara fell to the English. When Quebec was occupied the following year, the future of France in the New World was doomed. Largely as a result of a failure in the French leadership, the French would abandon all of its holdings in North America, turning them over to the Spanish and the British. In a secret agreement with Spain the year before the official treaty ending the French and Indian War (also known as the Seven Years' War), the French gave Spain all of the lands that fell west of the Mississippi River. Lands to the east, as well as all holdings north of the Great

Lakes and Saint Lawrence, fell to the English with the Treaty of Paris of 1763.

With this shift in suzerainty in formerly French-held areas, however, came a new policy toward American Indians—one that would lead to suffering, usurpation of their homelands, and even their ultimate removal to Indian Territory, a region set up by the United States in the 1830s to put Indian people who were "in the way" of civilization. To the great frustration of the Indians who had previously dealt with the French, they learned that the British had little interest in establishing strong alliances with them, nor did the British have any interest in providing the high-quality trade items the Indian people had grown accustomed to during the previous 100 to 200 years. Even worse, they learned that the English had little respect for indigenous land holdings and had no intentions of continuing the habit of trading with Indians to achieve political alliances. If England had no need for trade items from the Indians, they simply stopped trading. The days where Indians could expect reciprocal respect and mutually beneficial trade arrangements were gone. After all, with France out of the picture, no other Europeans were in contention for the region. Even though Spain had acquired the region west of the Mississippi River, Spanish authorities were in no position to actually occupy the region, much less exert influence eastward and beyond the Mississippi River. They could do relatively little to stop the westward advances of the English, and later the United States as it began to expand ever westward into the American West in its push to the Pacific Ocean.

Much farther west, and to the north of the Spanish holdings, a relatively recently arrived power began flexing its muscle and expanded across the Bering Sea into the Aleutian Chain, toward south central Alaska, and down the Pacific Coast: the Russians. And the Russians would soon find themselves head to head with England and Spain with claims on the Pacific Northwest.

BIBLIOGRAPHIC ESSAY

Excellent primary sources on later periods include Elliott Coues, ed., *New Light on the History of the Greater Northwest: The Manuscript Journals of Alexander Henry and David Thompson, 1799–1814*, 2 vols. (Minneapolis: Ross and Haines, 1965); E. E. Rich, ed., *Cumberland House Journals and Inland Journals,*

1775–82 (London: Hudson's Bay Record Society, 1952), *Moose Fort Journals, 1783–85* (London: Hudson's Bay Record Society, 1954), and *Observations on Hudson's Bay by James Isham* (Toronto: Champlain Society for the Hudson's Bay Record Society, 1949). Excellent sources on New France include W. J. Eccles, *The Canadian Frontier, 1545–1760* (Albuquerque: University of New Mexico Press, 1969), *Essays on New France* (Oxford: Oxford University Press, 1987), *The French in North America, 1500–1783* (Markham, Ontario: Fitzhenry and Whiteside, 1998), and *Frontenac: The Courtier Governor* (Lincoln: University of Nebraska Press, 2003); and Alan Greer, *The People of New France* (Toronto: University of Toronto Press, 1997). Other excellent sources on New France include Stewart L. Mims, *Colbert's West Indian Policy* (New Haven, CT: Yale University Press, 1912); Raymond Du Bois Cahall, *The Sovereign Council of New France: A Study in Canadian Constitutional History,* Studies in History, Economics, and Public Law (1915, reprint, New York: Lawbook Exchange, 2005); Jean Delanglez, *Some La Salle Journeys* (Chicago: Loyola Press, 1938), *Frontenac and the Jesuits* (Chicago: Institute of Jesuit History, Loyola University, 1939), and *Life and Voyages of Louis Jolliet, 1645–1700* (Chicago: Institute of Jesuit History, Loyola University, 1948); and Joseph P. Donnelly, *Jacques Marquette, S.J., 1637–1675* (Chicago: Loyola Press, 1968).

For a more general history of the American Indian experience, see Harold E. Driver, *Indians of North America* (Chicago: University of Chicago Press, 1961). For more specific Canadian histories regarding native people, see R. Cole Harris, *Canada Before Confederation* (1974, reprint, Montreal: McGill Queens University Press, 1991); W. J. Healy, *Women of Red River* (Winnipeg, Manitoba: Russell, Lang & Company, Ltd., 1923); Harold A. Innis, *The Fur Trade in Canada: An Introduction to Canadian Economic History* (1962, reprint, Toronto: University of Toronto Press, 1999); C. Jaenen, *Friend and Foe; Aspects of French-Amerindian Contact in the 16th and 17th Centuries* (Toronto: McClelland and Stewart, 1976); Ruth Landis, *The Ojibwa Woman* (1971, reprint, Lincoln: University of Nebraska Press, 2006); D. Geneva Lent, *West of the Mountains: James Sinclair and the Hudson's Bay Company* (Seattle: University of Washington Press, 1963); Oscar Lewis, *The Effects of White Contact upon Blackfoot Culture with Special Reference to the Role of the Fur Trade* (1942, reprint, Seattle: University of Washington Press, 1966); J. G. MacGregor, *Peter Fidler: Canada's Forgotten Explorer, 1769–1822* (1966, reprint, Saskatoon, Saskatchewan: Fifth House Publishers, 1999); Cecil W. Mackenzie, *Donald Mackenzie: "King of the Northwest": The Story of an International Hero of the Oregon Country and the Red River Settlement at Lower Fort Garry (Winnipeg)* (1937, reprint, Ontario: Stewart Publishing & Printing, 2001); William Christie MacLeod, *The American Indian Frontier* (1928, reprint, New York: Routledge, 1996); A. G. Morice, *The History of the Northern Interior of British Columbia*

(Toronto: William Briggs, 1904); A. S. Morton, *A History of the Canadian West to 1870–71: Being a History of Rupert's Land (The Hudson's Bay Company's Territory) and of the North-West Territory (including the Pacific Slope)*, 2nd ed. (Toronto: University of Saskatchewan by University of Toronto Press, 1973); Yoland Murphy, *Women of the Forest* (New York: Columbia University Press, 1985); Walter O'Meara, *Daughters of the Country: The Women of the Fur Traders and Mountain Men* (New York: Harcourt, Brace & World, Inc., 1968); Ann Pescatello, *Power and Pawn: The Female in Iberian Families, Societies, and Cultures* (London: Greenwood Press, 1976); Arthur J. Ray, *Indians in the Fur Trade: Their Roles as Trappers, Hunters, and Middlemen in the Lands Southwest of Hudson Bay, 1660–1870* (Toronto: University of Toronto Press, 1974); Lewis O. Saum, *The Fur Trader and the Indian* (Seattle: University of Washington Press, 1966); Roy St. George Stubbs, *Four Recorders of Rupert's Land: A Brief Survey of the Hudson's Bay Company Courts of Rupert's Land* (Winnipeg, Manitoba: Peguis Publishers, 1967); and W. S. Wallace, *The Pedlars from Quebec and Other Papers on the Nor'Westers* (Toronto: Ryerson Press, 1954).

Other useful books include Burt Brown Barker, *The McLoughlin Empire and Its Rulers: Doctor John McLoughlin, Doctor David McLoughlin, Marie Louis (Sister St. Henry): An Account of Their Personal Lives, and of their Parents, Relatives, and Children: in Canada's Quebec Province, in Paris, France, and in the West of the Hudson's Bay Company* (Glendale, CA: Arthur Clarke, 1959); Archie Binns, *Peter Skene Ogden: Fur Trader* (Portland, OR: Binford & Mort Publishing, 1967); Marjorie Wilkins Campbell, *The North West Company* (Toronto: University of Toronto Press, 1957); Gloria G. Cline, *Peter Skene Ogden and the Hudson's Bay Company* (Norman: University of Oklahoma Press, 1974); and E. S. Curtis, *The North American Indian*, 20 vols. (Cambridge, UK: Cambridge University Press, 1907).

Excellent primary sources on the Plains region include Colin G. Calloway, ed., *Our Hearts Fell to the Ground: Plains Indian Views of How the West Was Lost* (Boston: Bedford Books, 1996), and *The World Turned Upside Down: Indian Voices from Early America* (Boston: Bedford Books, 1994); Frank B. Linderman, *Pretty-Shield: Medicine Woman of the Crows* (Lincoln, NE: Bison Books, 1972), and *Plenty-coups: Chief of the Crows* (Lincoln, NE: Bison Books, 2002). Also see excellent secondary sources such as Robert H. Lowie, *Indians of the Plains* (Lincoln, NE: Bison Books, 1954), and *The Crow Indians* (Lincoln, NE: Bison Books, 1983). See also Peter Nabokov, *Two Leggings: The Making of a Crow Warrior* (Lincoln: University of Nebraska Press, 1967); George E. Hyde, *The Pawnee Indians* (Norman: University of Oklahoma Press, 1974); George F. Will and George E. Hyde, *Corn among the Indians of the Upper Missouri* (Lincoln: University of Nebraska Press, 1964); Virginia Bergman Peters, *Women of the Earth Lodges: Tribal Life on the Plains* (Norman: University of Oklahoma Press,

2000); Tracy Potter, *Sheheke: Mandan Indian Diplomat, the Story of White Coyote, Thomas Jefferson, and Lewis and Clark* (Helena, MT: Farcountry Press and Fort Mandan Press, 2003); James H. Howard, *The Ponca Tribe* (Lincoln, NE: Bison Books, 1995); Nancy Oestreich Lurie, ed., *Mountain Wolf Woman, Sister of Crashing Thunder: The Autobiography of a Winnebago Indian* (Ann Arbor: University of Michigan Press, 1966); Paul Radin, ed., *Crashing Thunder: The Autobiography of an American Indian* (Ann Arbor: University of Michigan Press, 1926); Gene Weltfish, *The Lost Universe: Pawnee Life and Culture* (Lincoln, NE: Bison Books, 1965); Alice C. Fletcher and Francis La Flesche, *The Omaha Tribe*, vols. 1 and 2 (Lincoln, NE: Bison Books, 1972); David J. Wishart, *An Unspeakable Sadness: The Dispossession of the Nebraska Indians* (Lincoln, NE: Bison Books, 1994); Hugh A. Dempsey, *The Vengeful Wife and Other Blackfoot Stories* (Norman: University of Oklahoma Press, 2003); Roy W. Meyer, *History of the Santee Sioux: United States Indian Policy on Trial*, rev. ed. (Lincoln: University of Nebraska Press, 1993); Joe Starita, *The Dull Knives of Pine Ridge: A Lakota Legacy* (New York: G. P. Putnam's Sons, 1995); Marie L. McLaughlin, *Myths and Legends of the Sioux* (Lincoln, NE: Bison Books, 1990); Joseph Epes Brown, ed., *The Sacred Pipe: Black Elk's Account of the Seven Rites of the Oglala Sioux* (Norman: University of Oklahoma Press, 1953); Raymond DeMallie, ed., *The Sixth Grandfather: Black Elk's Teachings Given to John G. Neihart* (Lincoln: University of Nebraska Press, 1984); Samuel W. Pond, *The Dakota or Sioux in Minnesota as They Were in 1834* (St. Paul: Minnesota Historical Society Press, 1986); John R. Swanton, *Source Material on the History and Ethnology of the Caddo Indians* (Norman: University of Oklahoma Press, 1996); and John Stands in Timber and Margot Liberty, *Cheyenne Memories* (Lincoln: University of Nebraska Press, 1972).

And within in the Plains and other regions claimed or traveled by the French, see the following primary documents: Reuben G. Thwaites, ed., *The Jesuit Relations and Allied Documents: Travels and Explorations of the Jesuit Missionaries in New France 1610–1791*, 73 vols. (Cleveland: Burrows Brothers, 1896–1901); or for an excellent selection of these documents, see Allan Greer, ed., *The Jesuit Relations: Natives and Missionaries in Seventeenth-Century North America* (Boston: Bedford/St. Martin's Press, 2000); and Frances B. Steck, *Joliet-Marquette Expedition, 1673*, Catholic University of America Studies in American Church History, No. 6 (Sunrise, FL: Ams Publishing, 1973). For more on this region, see Raymond W. Wood and Thomas D. Thiessen, eds., *Early Fur Trade on the Northern Plains: Canadian Traders among the Mandan and Hidatsa Indians, 1738–1818* (Norman: University of Oklahoma Press, 1985); Sylvia Van Kirk, *Many Tender Ties: Women in Fur-Trade Society, 1670–1870* (Norman: University of Oklahoma Press, 1983); Jennifer S. H. Brown, *Strangers in Blood: Fur Trade Company Families in Indian Country*

(Norman: University of Oklahoma, 1999); Richard White, *The Middle Ground: Indians, Empires, and Republics in the Great Lakes Region, 1650–1815,* Studies in North American Indian History (Cambridge, UK: Cambridge University Press, 1991); Susan Sleeper-Smith, *Indian Women and French Men: Rethinking Cultural Encounter in the Western Great Lakes,* Native Americans of the Northeast (Amherst: University of Massachusetts Press, 2001); David Thompson, John Macdonell, Charles W. McKenzie, Francois-Antoine Larocque, W. Raymond Wood, and Thomas D. Thiessen, eds. *Early Fur Trade on the Northern Plains: Canadian Traders among the Mandan and Hidatsa Indians, 1738–1818* (Norman: University of Oklahoma Press, 1999); Alfred Bowers, *Hidatsa Social and Ceremonial Organization* (Washington, D.C.: Smithsonian Institution, 1963), and *Mandan Social and Ceremonial Organization* (Chicago: University of Chicago Press, 1950); Marcel Trudel, *Introduction to the History of New France* (Montreal: Hold, Rinehart & Winston, 1968); Yves F. Zoltvany, *The Government of New France: Royal, Clerical, or Class Rule?* (Scarorough, Ontario: Prentice-Hall of Canada, 1971); and Richard White, *The Middle Ground: Indians, Empires, and Republics in the Great Lakes Region, 1650–1815,* Studies in North American Indian History (Cambridge, UK: Cambridge University Press, 1991).

Some excellent primary sources for the period include Robert M. Ballantyne, *Hudson Bay: or, Everyday Life in the Wilds of North America* (Edinburgh: W. Blackwood & Sons, 1848); Lawrence J. Burpee, *Journals and Letters of Pierre Gaultier de Varennes de la Vérendrye and His Sons: With Correspondence Between the Governors of Canada and the French Court, Touching the Search for the Western Sea* (Toronto: Champlain Society, 1927); Elliot Coues, ed., *New Light on the Early History of the Greater Northwest: The Manuscript Journals of Alexander Henry and of David Thompson, 1799–1814,* reprint ed. (Minneapolis: Ross & Haines, 1965); Gabriel Franchère, *Narrative of a Voyage to the Northwest Coast of America, 1811, 1812, 1813, and 1814, or, The First American Settlement on the Pacific* (New York: Redfield, 1854); Alexander Henry, *Travels and Adventures in Canada and the Indian Territories, 1760–1776,* ed. James Bain (Boston: Little, Brown & Company, 1901); Edna Kenton, ed., *Black Gown and Redskins: Adventures and Travels of the Early Jesuit Missionaries in North America, 1610–1791* (New York: Longmans, Green, and Company, 1956); Margaret A. MacLeod, ed., *The Letters of Letitia Hargrave* (Toronto: Champlain Society, 1947); A. S. Morton, ed., *The Journal of Duncan McGillivray of the Northwest Company at Fort George on the Saskatchewan, 1794–1795* (Toronto: Macmillan Company of Canada, 1929); Joseph Robson, *An Account of Six Years Residence in Hudson's Bay: From 1733 to 1736 & 1744 to 1747* (London: J. Payne and J. Bouquet, 1752); Alexander Ross, *Adventures of the First Settlers on the Oregon or Columbia River* (London: Smith, Elder, and Company, 1849); R. David Edmunds, *The Shawnee*

Prophet (Lincoln, NE: Bison Books, 1985); and R. David Edmunds and Joseph L. Peyser, *The Fox Wars: The Mesquakie Challenge to New France* (Norman: University of Oklahoma Press, 1993).

Atlases that will prove useful include R. Cole Harris, ed., and Geoffrey J. Matthews, cartographer, *Historical Atlas of Canada* (Toronto: University of Toronto Press, 1988), and Helen Hornbeck Tanner, *Atlas of Great Lakes Indian History* (Norman: University of Oklahoma Press, 1984).

CHAPTER FIVE

FROM THE
ALEUTIAN CHAIN TO
NORTHERN CALIFORNIA

While Spanish ships began traversing the coast of Alaska in the
16th century, the Spanish did not intend to remain a permanent
presence in the region. To meet Spain's primary interest in trade with the
Philippines, these Spanish galleons sailed from Acapulco on the western
edge of New Spain to the western Pacific Ocean. The Russians, on the
other hand, encountered Alaska not as a byway to another place, but as a
destination for economic opportunity. The Spanish could have, in fact,
laid claim to the Alaskan coastline and engaged in the extensive fur-trade
opportunities that the Russians later exploited, but the driving force behind Spanish exploration and expansion was not the economic opportunity that France and Russia would find with furs, but rather trade in the
western Pacific and mining in the Americas. Had they set aside their
quest to control the Asian trade in Europe, the Spanish could have made
their fortunes in the fur trade, but they did not expand north to claim
dominance in the northern fur trade; instead, the Russians engaged the
natives in Alaska and would forever change the future of the frigid north.

RUSSIANS ENTER THE EASTERN PACIFIC

As early as the 1720s, the Russian government and individual *promyshleniki* (Russian fur trappers and traders) had taken an interest in the fur-
bearing potential of Alaska as Siberia had a diminishing availability of furs

as a result of overhunting. Therefore, the Russian authorities sent Danish navigator Vitus Bering and Commander A. I. Chirikov to explore the northern reaches of the Pacific Ocean. His 1728 expedition, called the Kamchatka Expedition, purportedly gave Bering the right to claim the region for the czar, and Russia would maintain its hold on the region until 1867, when it sold Alaska to the United States. Bering returned to Russia with examples of the fur that could be harvested throughout the Alaskan chain and coastline. On the second Kamchatka Expedition, Bering and Chirikov made contact with southeast Alaska in the summer of 1741, thus beginning the more than century-long occupation of Alaska by Russia and marking their first encounter with the Tlingit. The length of time between voyages, however, signaled the difficulty in securing funds, support, and motivation for the officially sanctioned voyages to proceed.

In 1741, Tlingit boatmen approached the Russian ship *St. Pavel* commanded by Chirikov and, with gestures and vocal insinuations, indicated that the Russians should follow them ashore. Russian shipmates knew that just days earlier, however, about 15 men had disembarked from a different Russian vessel and vanished after reaching Tlingit shores. While some historians have suggested that Tlingit Indians had killed them all, a more likely scenario, according to Russian author Andrei Val'Terovich Grinev (*The Tlingit Indians,* 92–93), suggests that the Russian sailors who had ventured ashore seeking fresh water instead chose not to return to the Russian vessel. After all, those sailors who endured life on board a Russian vessel during these expeditions fell under very strict authority, difficult living conditions, and very stiff penalties for the slightest transgression or disobedience. Corporal punishment came swift and often, according to some reports. Therefore, Grinev argued, these Russian sailors likely instead infused themselves into Tlingit society by marrying Tlingit women. When the Russian defectors heard that more Russian ships had reached the coastline, however, they purportedly packed their wives in canoes and headed south, away from potential encounters with Russian vessels and the severe punishment they would receive for defecting.

Leaving the men behind as lost, Chirikov and Bering headed their vessels back toward Kamchatka, passing by Kodiak Island and its environs, and then passing along the Aleutian Chain. During their entire journey, the crews collected a great number of furs from a variety of animals, including sea otter (a valued commodity in China). Siberian merchants, mariners, and *promyshleniki* (see Sidebar, beginning page 238) became very interested in the potential for trade in the East, across the northern Pacific, and by 1743 Russian ships began infiltrating the Aleutian Islands, beginning with the island known as Bering Island. For the next 40 years, the Russians focused primarily on the Aleutian Island Chain (see Map 2). In the first season, Russian ships purportedly collected 1,500 sea otter pelts worth about 480,000 rubles in Russia's fur market. Alaska promised to be a profitable venture indeed, for these independent fur traders had proven the potential of the fur-bearing Aleutian Island Chain and its future in the Russian Empire.

The Aleutian Chain, consisting of dozens of islands, stretched hundreds of miles from the western end of the Bering Sea to southwestern Alaska near Kodiak Island, the island that would eventually become the Russian regional headquarters by the 1760s. Unfortunately for the Russian ship captains and pilots, navigating the waters off the chain proved a mighty challenge. The heavy fog, highly unpredictable and stormy conditions, numerous protrusions of rocky outcroppings and shoals on the peninsulas of the mountainous islands, and lack of safe harbors made the trip exceedingly dangerous. The weather was particularly difficult in the winter, but the promyshleniki only stayed in Alaska during the hunting season. Unfortunately for the Aleutians and the animals who inhabited the region, the promyshleniki had a voracious appetite for blue, brown, and white (arctic) fox; bear; beaver; wolf; mink; and sable that lived on shore and for which they could earn millions of rubles back in Russia. In the water, they also hunted whale, sea lions, and fish.

For the Russians, however, the take of furs outweighed the difficult conditions and certainly outweighed having to quell periodic uprisings from the numerous yet very small bands of islanders they encountered. To force the Aleuts to trade with the Russian vessels, they often incarcerated island women on their boats during the hunting season and demanded that the men bring back enough furs at season's end to regain the freedom of their women. As a result, the Aleuts began to resist, and by 1761, the Aleuts began to fight back with intensity. When Russians at Umnak attempted to take females hostage to force men into trapping for the season, the inhabitants chased the Russians off the island. They had achieved a small victory, and as word spread, it emboldened their neighbors as well. Within a few months, leaders at Umnak, the Fox Islands, Unalaska, and Kodiak began plotting and exacting their own revenge against the Russian oppressors. Tricking the Russians into disembarking, the Aleuts would fall upon the promyshleniki. Between 1762 and 1766, Aleuts ambushed promyshleniki, attacking and even burning Russian ships as they moored in the harbors. But the Russians refused to lose a profitable holding, so they began their reconquest, annihilating village after village, taking women captive, and massacring the remaining defenders and inhabitants. The devastation was so widespread that by the end of the 1760s, foreign visitors to the region, such as Sir George Simpson (director of the Hudson's Bay Company), commented on the immense population loss among the Aleut people. The decimation of the Aleut population was not only caused by warfare, but also by removal and impressment of Aleut men and women into Russian service. Russians recognized the Aleuts' tremendous skills in bidarkas and in the hunt, and therefore the Russians took them from their homelands and forced the Aleuts to serve the Russians by trapping on other islands, on the mainland, and even down the southeastern shores of Alaska.

Like other Europeans, the Russians obviously also brought diseases that decimated the indigenous populations. While the mortality rate was not as devastating as that of the Caribbean tribes, because the latter's warm and moist climate was a better breeding ground for disease, the devastating impact of disease on Aleut culture was still evident. The Aleut population suffered tremendously from the epidemics brought by Russians, murders of Aleuts before they rose in revolt in the 1760s, and the continued impressment of Aleut hunters and their families. To make matters worse, Tlingits, frustrated with Aleut hunters who appeared in their waters by the early 1800s, attacked and killed the Aleuts and their Russian allies in concerted strikes to reestablish their hegemony over fishing rights in Tlingit waters. The Russians continued their heavy demands on Aleuts by taking them captive and forcing them to continue working for the Russians, even as far away as southeast Alaska. Even the Tlingits took note and complained about the forced labor of the Aleuts in their Tlingit homelands in the early 1800s.

Early 19th-century illustrations of Aleuts in bidarkas, wearing rain gear from Voyages round the world: containing the whole of his discoveries, in geography, navigation, astronomy, with memoirs of his life, and particulars relative to his unfortunate death / performed by Captain James Cook, by royal authority, *1822. (Atrium Exhibit, A0867-16, Archives, Alaska and Polar Regions Collections, Rasmuson Library, University of Alaska Fairbanks)*

Grigorii I. Shelikhov, during his voyage of rediscovery in the 1780s, described the various benefits of each of the islands he encountered during the height of the Russian rampage for furs. At the Aleutian Islands, found farthest west, he discovered that Bering Island was now uninhabited, as was Copper Island, which got its name from the copper that washed ashore periodically. He described the Adrianov Islands as having many "high and stony mountains on it. . . . Vegetation is almost identical with that of Kamchatka. The berries are bear whortleberry or crowberry, but blueberries are found but occasionally." (Shelikhov, *A Voyage to America,* 72). Some islands included such attributes as hot springs, most lacked fresh water, some featured streams, others had some fish, and still others had rich edible roots. On the last island, Amlag, he described the inhabitants as:

living underground in caves where they do not make fire even in the winter. Their shirts or parkas are made from the skins of birds, murres or puffins, which they catch in snares. In rainy weather, they wear another type of garment sewn from the intestines of seals and sea lion intestines. They catch flounder with wooden rods and eat it raw. They never store anything for future use so that when the weather is stormy and they are unable to go out fishing they are obliged to eat seaweed and snails which they gather along the shore and also eat raw. . . . They do not change their clothing even in the most severe cold weather. Only when the cold is very great do they burn dry grass and warm their clothing near it. Clothing for the women and children is made from sea otter pelts in the same manner as for men. Should they have to spend the night away from their habitation, they dig a hole in the ground and lie in it to sleep, covered by a cloak or a mat woven from grasses. They never think of the future and are only concerned with the present. They have not the slightest conception of law and see no difference between decent and indecent behavior. They differ little from beasts (Shelikhov, *A Voyage to America*, 72–73).

Shelikhov assumed that eating seaweed somehow debased their culture, when in fact had he learned more about Bering and Chirikov's second Kamchatka Expedition he would have realized that seaweed helped save the shipwrecked sailors from dying of scurvy. While Shelikhov's image of the peoples that lived on Amlag seems harsh, one must remember that these peoples were among the first to feel the abuse of the Russian promyshleniki in the 1740s and 1750s, and what Shelikhov experienced were the ramifications of the devastation those island peoples had faced from those earlier years of Russian violence and the resultant near destruction of their culture. Shelikhov continued to the Fox Islands.

The Fox Islands yielded numerous varieties of food and furs. Salmon varieties abounded on some of the islands, as did berries of all sorts, including raspberries, partridge berries, cloudberries, blackberries, shiksha, and blueberries. The Fox Island inhabitants had access to sweetgrass, sarana, makarsha root, and sweetroot. The few inhabitants that remained hunted cross; black, white, and red foxes; as well as seals, sea lions, and sea otters. On some of the islands, they even hunted ground squirrels, otter, ermine, and sable. The inhabitants also headed out to sea and hunted whales and other sea animals. Shelikhov noted that the people lived in wood plank houses roofed with grass, but that inside they did not

Rugged coastal scenery in the Aleutian Islands, Adak Island, Alaska. (iStockPhoto.com)

light fires because the buildings retained warmth efficiently. In fact, he noted that the men and women normally sat in their homes naked. The people generally tattooed themselves and wore labrets (lip ornaments) and small bones in their noses. Using various types of decorations, such as beads (they particularly liked the blue glass beads the Russians brought), they traded with other islands for arrows and stones. In other words, Shelikhov learned that an extensive trade system already existed among the people who lived on the Aleutian Chain. Besides the afore-mentioned items, they also traded sea otters, clothing made from bird skins, shirts made from seal intestines (used for rain gear), skins for covering the baidaras (or bidarkas), hats made of wood, arrows, sinew thread, square buckets, large tubs (made from driftwood), and ulus (curved knives made of stone or bone), which are still used in traditional native fish camps during the salmon harvest.

But Russians were not interested in many of the items the Aleuts traditionally traded, and as they superimposed their demands for fur trapping on top of an existing system, it was no surprise that one of the systems would inevitably suffer. As island men's labor went directly to the fur trade with the Russians, the tasks that previously occupied their time (such as hunting for trade items, skins for their boats, rain gear for the hunting season, and much more) fell to the wayside, and the entire community suffered as a result. They had to focus entirely on hunting for export without consideration for their own community's needs to survive the winter and upcoming seasons. After a desperate generation of being forced to hunt only for the outsiders, they lacked the time to take care of their cultural traditions. With their wives held captive, and thus their family connections severed, they began to lose the coherence and community from which they learned their knowledge from elders. They were losing the knowledge of where the berries and roots grew, where and when seaweed should be gathered, when and how to fish the rivers and shorelines, how to prepare the catch for the long winter months, and perhaps even how to interact as a unified community. After all, the communities had changed drastically: women carried and birthed Russian-fathered babies and diseases killed those who could not survive their ravages.

ALEUTIAN LIFE CHANGES FOREVER

Siberia was an inhospitable place, and still is, but it yielded a tremendous harvest of animal pelts for those Russians who braved the elements—the promyshleniki. These hardy men headed east to the cold and windswept regions of Siberia in search of such game as sable, white or arctic fox, and sea otter. But by the early 1700s, they had depleted the fur-bearing animal populations in Siberia and began to look farther east across the Bering Sea. Alaska generated great profits for the promyshleniki, who began to appear in Alaska in greater numbers by the 1750s.

Traveling by boat to the westernmost Aleutian Islands, these fur trappers learned a valuable lesson. They could use the local populations to do their work for them while they simply waited for the furs to arrive. Granted they would have to pay the Aleutians for their efforts, but a few trinkets and cheap goods were well worth the price of not working themselves. All the promyshleniki would need was a boat with a large enough storage area to hold the furs, a cook, some food, and a small crew. So the life of a promyshleniki changed tremendously from that of trapping day by day to one of biding time while the Aleuts hunted and prepared the skins for them.

Theoretically, this was a great idea, but the Aleuts had no intentions of killing off all their fur-bearing animals and exchanging them for goods they had lived without previously, some of which were of poor quality. While some of those goods made their lives easier (metal tools, metal pots and knives, and decorative items such as beads), the freedom they gave up outweighed any gains they might have attained.

COMPETITION FOR RUSSIAN ALASKA

As the Russians continued expanding eastward, they triggered alarm among the Spanish, who in the late 1500s and again in the late 1600s had claimed everything north of the Rio Grande for the crown of Spain. Therefore, in 1774, just five years after the Spanish settled California, New Spain's infamous Viceroy Marquis A. M. Bucareli sent an expedition to the northwest coast of the Americas. At the Alexander Archipelago, the vessel *Sonoma* encountered the Tlingit. The Spanish expeditionary force investigated, noted some Tlingits hiding near a palisaded plank house, and then erected a cross, the Spanish symbol of hegemony over a conquered or claimed region.

The Spanish had no interest in remaining, but rather they simply wanted to post a claim and a warning to all future non-Indians that the Spanish had arrived first and claimed the region, therefore nullifying any future claims. The Spanish likely brought smallpox with them too, and soon, the Tlingits found their families ravaged by the disease. An Englishman, who arrived some 13 years later in 1787, described the residual evidence of the disease when he remarked that most people over 12 years old had pockmarks on their faces (a very common occurrence throughout the Americas, and a direct result of surviving a smallpox outbreak). A member of Sitka reported that the epidemic from the 1770s had had such a great impact on their people that no more than a couple of people from every family even survived the ordeal.

Another Spanish expedition arrived in 1779 to reconnoiter and secure even more lands for the Spanish crown in the far north to counter
Russian expansion to the south. On this voyage, they traded with the
Tlingit at Bucareli Bay (named for the viceroy of New Spain), then continued on as far as Prince William Sound before returning to California, which they had occupied for only 10 years. Only a dozen years
later, the Spanish would arrive again among the Tlingits, this time trading for fish, various artifacts crafted by the Indians, furs, clothing, and
metal objects (likely the highly sought after copper plates crafted by the
Tlingits that they used as giveaways at potlatch ceremonies). This was
not the first time Tlingits had acquired European goods though, for by
this time they also had English tools such as pots, clothing, axes, and
even some books and a silver spoon. Moreover, they also knew some
English words. By the time the Spanish left, Grinev wrote that it looked
as if the Tlingits had massacred a Spanish crew and stolen their uniforms. The Spanish and Yakutat often traded clothing with Yakutat, to
the point that an outside observer remarked that the Yakutat looked like
Spanish sailors. At least one Tlingit man developed an appreciation for
a Spanish sailor's jacket, and when he pilfered it, a battle nearly took
place. Relations remained tense between the Tlingit and Spanish
(Grinev, *The Tlingit Indians,* 96).

The Spanish were not the only ones who showed an interest in the
most northwestern coast of the Americas though. French, English, and
even later U.S. traders continued to show up along the coast between
Vancouver and Cook Inlet by the end of the 1700s. Perhaps most famous among them was Captain James Cook, who sailed in 1778 with
pelts from Alaska to trade with China. When reports of his successes
reached England, more voyages logically followed after 1785. Just one
short year later (yet nearly two dozen years after the French had lost their
battle with England for the north and interior of North America, and
just four years before the French Revolution), the French arrived at
Lituya Bay. The two ships, flying the French flag and navigated by Jean-
Francois de Galaup La Pérouse, engaged in trade with the Indians and
were surprised at how well versed in trading (and thievery) the Indians
were—including the Tlingit. La Pérouse claimed Lituya Bay for France
and intended for other Frenchmen to follow him to secure the bay for

the French crown (which did not happen). Lituya Bay did not turn out quite as they had hoped, however, for as the French discovered, it was a treacherous bay for vessels. The French lost a ship in the whirlpools, along with it 21 men; the Indians located at the bay also periodically suffered the same results. So, after La Pérouse collected more than 600 furs, he set off for Asia. Another French ship did not arrive for several more years. In fact, only four French ships actually engaged with the Indians of the far Northwest coast according to one Russian historian. La Pérouse's claim for a northern fur trade frontier had turned out to be a failure, perhaps due as much to timing as anything else.

The English, however, would return with regularity between 1785 and 1794, and more than 35 ships operated in the region during those years. The English had just signed the Treaty of 1783 in which they relinquished their sovereignty over the East Coast colonies, thereby losing their foothold south of the Saint Lawrence River. Fewer U.S. ships arrived, however, and certainly not until the late 1780s (not surprising, as they had only just become a nation and had no holdings on the Pacific side of the Americas). A mere 15 ships would appear before 1795. None of the French, English, or U.S. ships would reach as far as Cook Inlet (up to this point, anyway), according to available records. Therefore, Alaska seemed to fall more completely into the control of the Russians, who had begun to move ever eastward in their quest for furs and trade. The periodic availability of other foreign powers with whom the Indians could trade, however, would confound the Russians until they established complete sovereignty over their Alaskan claims.

As the Russians exhausted the supply of furs on the westernmost Aleutian Islands, Russian exploitation of the fur trade shifted from individual promyshleniki to companies that operated along the coastline of Alaska. Exploitation of furs escalated as the companies became more successful at navigating and more systematic in their methods of trade, barter, and control. By the late 1700s, ships and crews were larger, causing more capital to be invested, and therefore the larger companies edged out the independent promyshleniki, who now found employment on board ships or at the redoubts that had begun to pop up along the Alaskan coastline, with the more than 40 companies that operated throughout Russian Alaska.

Because of their treatment by the Russians and early trade policies, Aleut and Kodiak cultural survival had become more precarious. They consolidated (either by force or because they had no other choice for survival), but still found themselves dependent on the Russians as a result of the lack of traditional food sources on their previously bountiful islands. By the time the Russians had moved to Kodiak Island, the natives had tired of the poor quality of Russian trade goods, demanding higher-quality items. Dentalie (shells), blue glass beads, small reflecting glasses, and various forms of metal wires (for jewelry), no longer satisfied them. They sought instead metal tools that they had seen the Russians use on their ships, at the ports, and at the redoubts or forts. They desired metal knives and hatchets as well as guns, which the Russians had trained on them before in periods of conflict. As the French, English, and Americans entered the southeastern Alaskan realms, the natives began desiring the better-quality goods that the other European powers supplied, such as woolen Hudson Bay blankets and other textiles, as well as guns and other metal tools. Their desire for Western European trade goods would not go unnoticed by the Russian colonial authorities, or at times, unpunished.

By the 1770s, Shelikhov had begun his extensive forays into Alaska from Siberia and Kamchatka. He hoped to acquire control over the fur trade throughout Russian Alaska and, therefore, at times acted as if he had the right to dominate the lives of the Alaska Natives as well. After all, he would argue, he had established a well-devised system for the effective exploitation of the fur and human resources with Kodiak Island serving as the headquarters for the fur trade at Three Saints Bay. He brought with him more than 200 men from Okhotsk in eastern Russia who settled at the new post.

In 1788, Governor-General I. V. Yakobi of Irkutsk sent out Dmitrii I. Bocharov and Gerasim G. Izmailov on the *Tri Sviatitelia* (Three Saints) to continue exploring the Alaskan coastline and its environs to the east. He supported Shelikhov's vision of a united effort to consolidate trade in Russian Alaska. During that expedition, which skirted the Alaskan coastline all the way from Prince William Sound to Lituya Bay, the two leaders navigated the *Three Saints* along the shorelines with an order to discover new islands and shores, as well as to bring all the Indians they encountered under Russian control. They also intended to affirm Russian control over

Eighteenth-century engraving of Three Saints Bay, Alaska. (Alaska State Library, James Wickersham State Historic Sites Photograph Collection, Luka Voronin, P277-008-004)

the region by "marking the land with signs appropriate and natural to the Might and Name of Russia" (Shelikhov, *A Voyage to Alaska,* 83).

Bocharov and Izmailov took 40 Russians, 2 Fox Island interpreters, 4 Koniags, trade goods to suffice the journey, and copper crests or coats of arms that they would then distribute to the native peoples. By accepting these copper gifts, the Russians argued that the native peoples had acquiesced to placing themselves under the sovereignty of Russia. Without realizing the significance of such a gesture, the Tlingit and others accepted the copper plates, an honored gift already at the potlatches. Had the Russians understood the significance of the Tlingit abject rejection of the sovereignty of another entity over them, perhaps they would have understood why the Tlingit would become one of the fiercest, most determined, and most capable adversaries they would face in the Americas.

To the Tlingit, placing oneself or one's community into a position of submission to another, in fact, denoted slavery—something that already existed in their society. Slaves had no rights and, on occasion, found themselves sacrificed at potlatches. No tribe would willingly submit to another authority in this fashion. In fact, when the Tlingit had accepted the copper gifts from the Russians, they assumed they were a form of clan totem of the Russian bearer or something of great value. In return, the Tlingits offered such things as amulets shaped as the head of *Yel,* the Raven (part of their spiritual and religious belief system), and other items representative of their spiritual, magical, or economic powers. Within a few years, this key misunderstanding would erupt into warfare that would continue until the last days of Russia's hold on Alaska.

When Bocharov and Izmailov returned, the newly confident Russians established a base of operations at Kenai and Chugach bays by 1792. Unfortunately for the new community, the Tlingit shuddered at the thought of outsiders locating so close to their homeland, and so in that same year, they attacked the Russian camp in the middle of the night. Surrounding the Russians and their 300 Kodiak allies on all sides, the Tlingits closed in—their thick wooden armor holding up well against the Russian weapons. Alexandr Baranov (later the first governor of the Russian-American Company), nearly killed at the outset of the hostilities, had only steel mail to protect him. The attacks continued until sunrise when Izmailov's ship arrived as reinforcement and forced the Tlingit to disperse. It was a rude awakening indeed; the Russians had lost a dozen men and 15 men were injured in what they reported as an unprovoked attack. The Russians recognized the Tlingit as a serious opponent, and one that needed to submit to Russian authority. The Tlingit continued to engage the Russians for years. In the meantime, the Russians continued to expand southward, and by 1793, Baranov had established Russian authority down the coast as far as Vancouver Island (Grinev, *The Tlingit Indians,* 101–104).

THE RUSSIAN-AMERICAN COMPANY

By 1794, the establishment of control by the Shelikhov-Golikhov Company, later known as the Russian-American Company, had effectively ended the first contact era in Alaska. After the Russians had finally subdued the Aleuts and occupied and subdued Kodiak Island, Russian control expanded all the way south along the Alaskan coast to Vancouver. They established a strong fur trade with the numerous coastal tribes they encountered, and effectively ended any other nation's potential for claim in Alaska (see Map 10).

Because Shelikhov had been so diligent in his reporting about the potential for each island in the chain and throughout Alaska, and because he formally established a permanent Russian foothold at Kodiak and later Sitka in Tlingit territory in Southeast Alaska, he began to attempt to convince the Russian czarina to allow him a complete monopoly over Alaska. He even traveled literally halfway around the world from Kodiak back to St. Petersburg to plead his case to the Russian authorities for his monopoly. Shelikhov found himself answering to the charges of brutality against the Alaska Natives while in St. Petersburg, and of forcing the sailors and promyshleniki to labor in grueling working conditions. Stunned by the reports of forced imprisonment, rape, and violent responses to uprisings, the authorities refused to grant him a monopoly. To appease the authorities, Shelikhov immediately ordered several of the abusers rounded up and summarily punished. He also began negotiations with the Russian Orthodox Church, arguing that it was critical that the church set up missions throughout Alaska to convert the native peoples. He hoped that by promising that his monopoly would work tirelessly to further the conversion of the native populations, St. Petersburg would grant his Russian-American Company full monopoly over Alaskan missions and Russian Alaska.

Shelikhov argued that if one company were not allowed to control all of Alaska, information could not be gathered effectively and systematically about the potential infiltration by the French, English, and U.S. traders and merchants into Russian territories. Therefore, her Russian excellency would not suffer the financial loss that he could thwart by imposing such a monopoly. If she would give him the monopoly, he argued, all information would be channeled through his company, and the Russians could react much more quickly to foreign incursions on Russian Alaska's soil. More importantly, resources would not be wasted, processing could be streamlined, and the shipments back to Russia could be regularized. To set the monopoly into motion, he argued, he had worked hard to assimilate numerous competing fur companies throughout Russian Alaska, more than 40 in all by 1790. Unfortunately, Shelikhov would never witness the reality of his vision, for he died suddenly, possibly of a medication overdose (but also, some have speculated, potentially a poi-soning by his wife or her family). His wife Natali'a, of the famous and well-established Rezanov trading family, had been brought up in the fur industry, so she carried forward her late husband's plan for consolidation under a monopoly of the Russian-American Company and continued to petition the Russian authorities. When Pavel became czar in 1799, he granted Natali'a's request. Fortuitously, before he died, Shelikhov had ap-pointed Alexandr Baranov as governor of the Russian Alaska Company, the first functional and approved Russian monopoly in Alaska. A well-organized, albeit heavy-handed, leader, Baranov had experience in the fur industry in northern Russia, and adjusted well to his new task of consol-idation. For the next 68 years, the Russian-American Company would operate redoubts (posts) across Alaska for the organized, orderly, and de-pendable collection and processing of furs for shipment to Russia. More importantly, perhaps part of Natali'a's success in acquiring the monopoly involved her promise to bring Russian Orthodox missionaries and priests to Alaska to proselytize the natives. At many of the redoubts, these mis-sionaries set up missions to begin the conversion of the Alaska Natives.

IVAN YEVSEYEVICH VENIAMINOV

Venerated as the single-most influential Russian missionary in Alaska, Ivan Yevseyevich Veniaminov (Veneaminoff), also known as Saint, Metropolitan of Moscow and Lolomn Innokentii (Inneokenty Veniaminov), was a Russian ethnographer and priest who has since been canonized as a saint in the Russian Orthodox Church. Veniaminov was not the first to bring the ideas of the Russian faith to the Alaska Natives. In fact, according to oral tradition, the Aleuts were intrigued by the fact that the earliest Russian fishers and whalers would pray on the beaches before embarking on their hunting expeditions, very similar to what the Aleuts themselves had done.

Veniaminov arrived from Siberia to convert the Alaska Natives, but he was also skilled in mechanics and was a clock and instrument maker. After learning the Aleut language, he traveled to Unalaska in 1823 and stayed for 10 years. While

Ivan Veniaminov, Saint Innokentii (1797–1879). (Alaska State Library, Portrait Photograph Collection, P01-1983)

there, he engaged daily with the Aleuts, teaching them skills needed to build the church and school (carpentry, brick making, and stone masonry). He also transferred their oral language into a written one, and then translated parts of the Bible and the Russian Orthodox catechism into Aleut. His attempts to convert the Aleuts had some success because he respected them as a people. He referred to them as intelligent and industrious, and he even found that once they learned chess, they could beat the Russians at their own game. When

he returned to Sitka in 1834, he wrote the definitive
ethnographic work on the Aleuts.

In 1838, Veniaminov journeyed to St. Petersburg to report
on his activities and request an expansion of the Russian
Orthodox Church's activities in western Siberia and Russian
America. In 1840, as a new eparchy was created in
Kamchatka, Veniaminov took vows as a monk and chose the
name Innokentii in honor of Bishop Innokentii of Irkutsk. Over
the next 27 years, he served as the bishop of Kamchatka and
Kuril Islands in Russia and the Aleutian Islands in Russian
America, becoming an archbishop in 1850. He took frequent
trips throughout his enlarged diocese and devoted much
energy to translating the scriptures and service books into local
languages and studying Aleut culture. In 1867, he was
appointed the metropolitan of Moscow and Kolomna,
replacing his friend and mentor, Filaret, who had died.

The late Shelikhov's arguments had been corroborated clearly by
evidence, for by 1792, almost two dozen non-Russian trading ships appeared in the Pacific, threatening Russian hegemony. While Alaska Natives benefited from the superior trade goods from British and U.S.
traders, these infiltrations certainly had worked to convince the Russian
authorities that Shelikhov's monopoly would allow the Russians to gain
complete control over the Alaska fur industry. Shelikhov had understood
the ramifications of non-Russians in the region and moved to streamline
Russian interaction with Alaska Natives, recognizing that it was imperative to their success in controlling trade.

One of Baranov's first tasks was to force entire villages of Aleuts to relocate to Kodiak, stripping them of their homes, their livelihoods, their
sacred places, and the graves of their ancestors. He forced all of them to
work for the company, whether hunting on their boats or processing the
pelts at the post. More than 1,500 Aleut men were thus forced into hunting in their bidarkas under the watchful eye of overseers, or foremen. Because of the large number of Aleuts relocated to Kodiak and the fact that
resupplying the community from Russia was impossible, feeding the
community was a perpetual problem. Baranov had a crew of men that
fished and collected other sea mammals, while the women prepared the
food and processed the hides for the clothing and boots workers needed.

Women labored to split and dry sea mammal intestines, and out of those materials they created protective spray skirts (to keep the water out of the boats) for the bidarkas and umiaks, as well as waterproof jackets or coverings for the men. Besides preparing the meat, women also dug for roots, collected berries in season, cured and dried fish, and made all of the clothing necessary to survive the seasonal variations in climate.

As Baranov expanded the Russian-American Company's operation to the south, he encountered a group of Tlingit Indians at Yakutat Bay. They did not appreciate his authoritative style, his demands on their people and their labor, or his control over the Aleuts. They refused to participate in the fur trade and showed contempt for his trade goods. After all, they had already acquired similar trade goods, but of better quality and at a more reasonable price, from the British and U.S. traders who had found their way up the Alaskan Inside Passage along the west coast of Canada and Alaska.

The Tlingit had already proven problematic to Baranov's predecessors, the promyshleniki, and they seemed emboldened by their past successes. But the Tlingit region had fur-bearing animals, and Baranov would not allow the region to fall into the hands of another foreign power, so he brought Aleuts and their bidarkas to the Tlingit homeland and waters to hunt instead of impressing the Tlingit into service. Tlingits objected strongly and demanded compensation for any animals taken by the Russians and their allies in the hunt. After negotiating with the Tlingits, who justifiably demanded that the Russians respect their waters, lands, and resources, Baranov offered an exchange of goods. The Tlingits monitored the activities of the Russians to make certain that the Russians lived up to their end of the bargain, and to make certain that they took no more than they had negotiated. Baranov had learned quickly and personally that the Tlingits could be powerful adversaries. The Tlingits would continue to defend their homeland and its resources throughout the 19th century as well, becoming a continual thorn in the side of Russian expansion of the fur industry throughout southeast Alaska.

Even as he found the Tlingits aggressive in their defense of their homeland and their resources, Baranov knew that his responsibilities included converting natives to the Russian Orthodox faith, protecting them from their adversaries, and treating them humanely. On the last point, the Russians did not yet have a good track record. Regarding protection against adversaries, the Russians had so disrupted the balance of power, populations, and even the very existence of villages in the chain that in the past, this had not been much of an issue. In the southeastern region, however, the story was quite different. The balance of power was complicated because of the many islands throughout the archipelago and the fact that the Tlingit community operated not as a single unit, but rather in an elaborate interrelationship of toions and kwa'ans. This involved a delicate balance of protecting resources, sharing potlatches, trading, asserting power, and demanding respect if not given.

At first the Russians did not understand the collaboration and periodic controversies that erupted between the toions and kwa'ans, or even within the larger communities of Tlingits. With the assistance of allies within the Tlingit community, however, the Russians began to understand and document who to approach and who should be given gifts when they arrived for trade or negotiation. The Russians also began to comprehend the complex system of respect, status, and clan upon which Tlingit cultural interaction occurred. Only after the Russians understood these connections could they truly begin to interact positively with and potentially help to protect the Tlingit and related tribes against their enemies.

To support the Russian-American Company's commitment to converting the native peoples, the Russian Orthodox Church began to send missionaries among the various tribes, from the Aleutian Chain along the coast to Southeast Alaska around the Tlingit community. Baranov had already had some success in that area, however, as the chief toion, Fedor, of the one of the strongest and most powerful Tlingit groups in the Yakutat area, had approached the Russians and converted to orthodoxy with great celebration as early as the late 1790s.

THE TLINGIT SOCIAL STRUCTURE

Tlingit culture rested on a very stratified system of lineage and status, and the "chief" of the tribe was recognized for his status, rank, and wealth. This rank gave him the privilege of collecting various tangibles that could provide (or consisted of) economic wealth, such as fish camps, robes, copper plates, or other items. He also had the sole right to use ceremonial or spiritual songs and dances, as well as names and other intangibles. With the privilege of leading and overseeing his people, he had responsibilities to accumulate wealth and give it away at potlatches. While his comportment and lineage were also important, they did not form his only claim to power.

Beneath the chief of a settlement, a káau, were the heads of lineages. Also known as the "man of the village," historians have sometimes misunderstood that to mean the head of a lineage. Sublineages also had a leader, called everything from the "guardian of the house" (as each sublineage had their own plank houses), or "master of the house." Below the heads fell the elites. Still of noble lineage, these individuals held a relatively high social status within the community. Under them fell the commoners, who did much of the menial labor around the villages. Below them were the "people of low status," sometimes translated as "nonentity," or one of illegitimate birth. These folks lived in front of the houses, and often came to this position through birth or being released from slave status for various reasons; they were poor or often descended from slaves. Finally came the slaves themselves. Although slaves sometimes came from within the community, they were mostly obtained from outlying communities that had either engaged the Tlingit kwa'ans in warfare, or perhaps had found themselves occupying a region into which the Tlingits chose to expand.

In return for the Russian-American Company's commitments, the natives had an obligation by the charter to provide services and pelts to the company. Like many agreements involving the labor, tribute, or material goods demanded of American Indians, this contractual agreement occurred between outsiders (in this case the Russians) without any input or ability for dissent by those that it affected, the Alaska Natives. Bound by an agreement they were not party to creating, the Alaska Natives at least had some protection against the hands of the foremen, those promyschleniki who had brutalized them in the past. Similar to the Spanish *repartimiento*, they had a service contract that involved a three-year commitment to the company, and all men between the ages of 18 and 50 had to hunt to fulfill their obligation. Tribes whose homelands lay beyond the immediate control and oversight of the Russian-American Company's authority, such as those residing east of the Tlingit in the interior beyond the mountains, were to send tribute yearly in the form of furs. Those not meeting the obligation faced reprisals from the Russian enforcers.

The Russian-American Company certainly benefited greatly from the labor of the numerous Alaskan Natives who provided services for the Russians through hunting and preparing pelts. Between 1799 and 1867, the Russians collected nearly 4 million pelts. But along with the increased pressures on the natural resources and the environment, the company faced the increased frustrations of the Tlingits. Continued skirmishes and outright uprisings taxed the Russian-American Company until it relinquished control over Alaska in the 1860s.

RESISTANCE TO RUSSIAN AUTHORITY

As previously mentioned, the Tlingit people were protective of their homeland and resources, and they did not appreciate the cheap quality yet expensive goods the Russians tried to pawn off on them. As a result, most of the Tlingit refused to participate in the fur trade. They had acquired guns from the English and U.S. traders and skillfully used them in their defense of homeland. Several actions by the Russians caused the Tlingits to resort to violence. In the 1790s, Baranov had sent hunting expeditions into the heart of Tlingit territory, and worse, with Aleut and Koniag Indians at their side. The Tlingit saw this as a direct threat to their hegemony over the region and caused some of the first major outbreaks of reciprocal violence between the Russians and Tlingit. Second, Baranov relocated the Russian-American Company's permanent headquarters to New Archangel, or Sitka (with Yakutat serving merely as a resupply base). From this post, they intruded even more deeply into Tlingit hunting grounds. Tlingits worried that their resources would be so depleted by the fur-hungry Russians that they would have nothing left to eat or trade for goods to the British or U.S. traders who arrived periodically from the south and west. Finally, some Russian men took Tlingit women and forced them into being their common-law wives. Baranov himself took an 18-year-old girl, who bore several of his children.

Boats in Sitka Harbor, Alaska, in 1869. (National Oceanic and Atmospheric Administration)

Frustrated by the continuous incursions and lack of deference to the Tlingit, they rose up in 1802 and bushwhacked Russian-directed trading and hunting parties. They swept into New Archangel and burned all of the buildings, killed 150 Russians and Aleuts, and took back 4,000 sea otter pelts that they claimed had been wrongfully taken by the Russian and Aleut hunters. Baranov could not allow such a violation in his system, and he returned in 1804 with an armada of war ships with cannons. From their ships they attacked the Tlingits who had occupied New Archangel. The Russians succeeded in routing the Tlingits, who suffered many losses during the bombardment.

A year later, the Tlingits returned the favor at Yakutat, attacking the village and killing or capturing almost two dozen Russians. In 1806, the Tlingit once again amassed a large force with the intention of renewing their war with another assault at Sitka, but young Tlingit girls at the post warned the Russians who immediately realized that they could not withstand an attack from more than 2,000 natives lying in wait for the perfect opportunity to strike. Instead, they offered the Tlingits a celebration and feast at the post, with extravagant displays of food and entertainment; thus, they diffused what could have been a bloody incident and the likely second loss of New Archangel in less than five years. But native frustrations could not always be bought off so easily, as the Russian fur trade continued to expand, and the pressures on the natural environment and native communities mounted.

The periodic raids continued after Baranov's move from Kodiak to Sitka, but he refused to relinquish control because Sitka had a more manageable climate and would provide an excellent base for upcoming forays into northern California and the establishment of Fort Ross as an agricultural outpost and southern fur-trading center. Native and Russian inhabitants of the company redoubts and headquarters faced the threat of daily raids from their neighbors. Serious attacks in 1809 and 1813 forced the Russians and Aleuts to fight together to defend the mixed community of Sitka. Baranov called in the navy, and by 1818, a Russian naval ship regularly patrolled the harbor at Sitka. The Tlingits were a credible and awesome threat. All of the expense of protecting Alaska, however, began to wear on the Russian crown (similar to the situation in New France in the 1700s).

In an attempt to appease and perhaps establish a more positive permanent relationship with the Tlingits, Baranov held councils periodically with the various kwa'ans throughout southeast Alaska hoping to convince them to forgo their trading partnerships with the British and U.S. traders, and that the Russians had the better prices and goods. The board of directors of the Russian-American Company had grown weary of the reports of incursions by other nations. After all, one of the initial promises of the company was to be present to curb that very sort of incursion. But the Tlingit response was always the same. If the Russians could provide the same excellent quality goods that their other trade partners provided, they might consider it. Moreover, they also expected knives, hatchets, and guns, besides the typical fine-quality textiles (blankets, cotton, and linen) for which they traded with England, France, and the United States. When the Tlingits realized that the Russians simply did not have the capacity to deliver those goods and at that quality, the talks broke down. The Russians charged that the Tlingit had received special gifts from the British and U.S. traders, perhaps as a bribe to keep them from trading with the Russians.

In an attempt to force the Tlingit into an exclusive trade relationship, Baranov suggested that the Tlingit deliver hostages, of sorts, to the Russians so they could learn about Russian ways and convert to Russian Orthodoxy. The Tlingit agreed, but only after the Russians handed over two mestizos, hostages of their own. This custom of hostage exchange became a common occurrence until the end of the Russian period, and the practice led to a growing understanding and bridging of the two cultures, which in turn provided a stronger base of respect, a sort of foundation for cultural interchange. And as hostilities actually quieted for a while, the Tlingits indeed began to trade with their new Russian partners. But the constant fear of violent outbreaks caused great angst for members of the New Archangel community throughout the end of the Russian empire in the Americas. Even as late as the 1850s, Russians complained about hundreds of armed and threatening Tlingits living right outside of the community palisades.

EXPANSION OF THE RUSSIAN-AMERICAN COMPANY

The Russians' occupation, regardless of their ability to control or subdue the Tlingit, continued—as did their interest in continued expansion of the empire to the south to California, where they met an entirely different group of Indians. Northern California was an important acquisition for the Russians, as resupplying the Russian frontier with reliable and quality food continued to be a challenge. The Russians had already learned that grains did not mature above 60 degrees north latitude. The northern valleys of California, in the southernmost regions of Russian-held territory, provided fertile grounds, as well as access to even more fur-bearing animals (seals and sea lions) and sea-bird eggs for consumption.

After establishing their post at Fort Ross at Bodega Bay, the Russian and Aleut transplants planted vineyards, orchards, and fields with grains to feed the northern inhabitants. Russians forced the Pomos, the local Indians, to work for them. Because they were not an agricultural people, however, the Pomos quickly became disenchanted by the increasing Russian demands, expecting them to change the way they lived their lives. When the Russians put more land under agricultural use, the demand for Indian labor logically increased. But the Pomos grew weary of toiling in fields, as their traditional lifestyle involved a seminomadic existence of following migrations and collecting plants, roots, seeds, grains, and shellfish. They fled south to the Spanish missions. Regardless, the Russians continued to demand the labor of the remaining Pomos and imposed a system similar to the Spanish repartimiento: forced labor of 100 men per year to work the fields. This number was increased to more than 200 by the 1830s, however.

Much like the Aleuts and Tlingits, the Pomos hit their breaking point and refused to participate in forced labor for outsiders who did not respect their culture or their people. To protest, the Pomos burned the crops in the fields, killed the cattle, and then hid from the Russians who sent men to find and round them up. If the Russians did find them, "sometimes as many as 150 are driven together by force and are put to hard work in the fields. [They are fed] only flour for thin gruel. As a result of this scanty food and the hard labor . . . the Indians reach in the end a state of complete exhaustion" (Okum, *The Russian-American Company*, 143). Demands on Indian labor would continue because few Russians had any interest in working the land either, as they thought they could earn far more in fur trade activities.

Not far behind the explorers and the Russian-American Company in the interior followed the Russian Orthodox missionaries, who hoped to convert as many of the Alaska Natives as they could.

THE RUSSIAN ORTHODOX CHURCH

Baranov had not forgotten that part of his responsibilities involved converting the natives to the Russian Orthodox faith. While support for the missions was shipped from Okhotsk the same year as the Russian-American Company received its monopoly, the first Russian Orthodox missionaries arrived in Kodiak in 1794. It had taken more than a year to cross Siberia and arrive in the Alaskan frontier, "the longest missionary journey in Christian history" according to the Russian Orthodox Diocese in Alaska. Even though Baranov had pledged the support and financial means to begin the missionization process in Alaska, underscoring Shelikhov's arguments that it was imperative that the Russian Orthodox Church acquire a foothold in the New World, 1809 saw only one missionary in the entire province. By the 1830s, however, they stepped up their efforts and established a series of missions, including one founded at Nushagak in 1837, up the Nushagak River from Bristol Bay (marked today by a huge white cross put up by local Dillingham resident Gusty Wahl).

View of Unalaska and its church, Church of the Holy Ascension, originally built in 1825. (Library of Congress)

The location was a logical place for a mission, for in 1818, the Russians had established the Alexandrovskii Redoubt nearby to trade with the region's inhabitants, the Eskimos and Athabaskans. By the 1840s, Russians claimed success to the southeast and even more Tlingits were converting to Orthodoxy. By 1848, the first diocese was established in Sitka. The goal of the Russian Orthodox Church, similar to that of the Roman Catholic Church under Spain, was to encourage the pacification and not the outright conquest of the natives and force the Alaska Natives to pledge their allegiance to the authorities, both religious and temporal.

Unfortunately, the Russian Orthodox Church did not have the success it had hoped for and did not persuade large numbers of the population to convert. By 1855, between 6 and 65 Tlingits a year converted to the Russian Orthodox Church; perhaps only as much as 20 to 30 percent of the entire Tlingit population had converted. In the end, fewer than 500 Tlingit in total had converted to Orthodoxy. The lasting impact of the Russian Orthodox Church in Alaska, however, might suggest a different story and may very well be a result of the attitude, personality, and genuine efforts of Ivan Veniaminov in the 1820s and throughout the end of the Russian era until his death.

Russian historian Grinev describes the basic reasons why the Tlingit in particular did not accept conversion. Because they prided themselves on their independence, they saw conversion as submission—which in their culture was tantamount to slavery. Also, because their relationship with the Russians continued to remain unstable, and because shamans held the real authority in Tlingit communities, they listened to their shamans rather than to the Orthodox clergy. They feared that the stratification Christianity imposed on cultures would undermine their traditional cultural systems of the kwa'an, clan, and toion. Christianity would also undermine traditional methods of conveying and retaining property and rank, a major foundation for the Tlingit culture. Another issue that arose among the Tlingit and the Russian Orthodox missionaries was that the missionaries believed the traditional Tlingit culture did not necessarily fit in the "'Christian virture': gentleness, humility, and charity" (Grinev, *The Tlingit Indians,* 266). Finally, because the Tlingit were completely economically independent, unlike some of the other tribes in the surrounding areas, they did not feel a need to reach out to other religions for spiritual assistance to deal with their environment (perhaps like the Aleuts, or other inland or more northern coast tribes). But the Russian Orthodox Church did have some major successes in other locations in Alaska.

Most of the praise for the success of the missions should in fact go to the well-revered and -remembered Ivan Veniaminov. After his success at converting the Aleuts in the 1820s along the Aleutian Chain, at the request of the authorities, he moved to Sitka to convert the Tlingits so that they could be subdued more easily. While his success was minimal with the Tlingits, he nevertheless managed to convert just over 100 and build a mission and school.

Those missionaries who struggled to and actually did learn Indian languages obviously had greater success in their proselytizing efforts. They transformed the indigenous languages into written form and used those languages to prepare texts for the children in the schools. Veniaminov then moved to the interior of Alaska, a region only minimally touched by the Alaskan promyshleniki. He built missions along the Bering Sea, along the lower Yukon and Kuskokwim river basins. Some of the youths who had attended his schools in Alaska continued their educations, expenses completely paid by the Russian-American Company, in St. Petersburg.

Much like Bartolomé de las Casas, Veniaminov was an outspoken critic of the cruel treatment of the Indians by the Russian-American Company. His reports to St. Petersburg highlighted the Russian oppression of the Indians along with Veniaminov's own suggestions for improvements. While the court sent investigators, unfortunately little improved for his charges. Nevertheless, his complaints provided another key description of Russian Alaska from the perspective of the native peoples that would provide research sources for future historians.

Russian Alaska was never highly populated by Russians, even with the advent of permanent communities at Kodiak and New Archangel. In fact, by 1860, no more than about 1,000 Russians actually lived in Russian Alaska. They intermixed with local populations, for as with New France, it was mostly men who took the journey to Alaska to find their wealth in the fur industry. Their mixed-blood children had no obligation to the Russian-American Company or its forced labor conscriptions. If, however, they had been educated in one of the schools set up by the company, the company required them to work off that "debt" for a period of perhaps as many as 10 or more years. Those who took advantage of schooling were not prohibited from serving the Russian-American Company, however, and some of them even rose to great prominence within the company, such as Adolph Etolin (1840–1845) who become the governor-general of the Russian-American Company. Those men were not caught between two cultures, like the *genízaros* of New Spain or the *métis* of New France. Their integration into non-indegenous cultures was complete.

MISCEGENATION: MÉTIS AND MESTIZOS

An important result of the early colonization period is the intermixing of peoples that occurred when non-Indians encountered traditional cultures. In the Southwest, the first region of the West to encounter outsiders on a long-term basis, the offspring of Spaniard and Indian were termed mestizos.

Some of those encounters were rape (or what some people term an unfortunate consequence of war or conflict). Other encounters occurred as a way of sealing a political or economic relationship, a way to escape Russian punishments, or perhaps out of affection, although this was not nearly as common.

The Spanish had a very detailed classification system of miscegenation with 64 specifically named categories of racial intermixing. Offspring of Indian and Spaniard were called mestizos, and the children of African descendants and Spaniards were called mulattos. By the time the Spanish established a permanent foothold in their northern frontier, they had intermixed with indigenous blood for more than 100 years.

Offspring of the French and Indian were termed métis, and they developed a very distinct culture within the French empire. Perhaps the most recognizable example of this union is Toussaint Charbonneau, a French trapper who was the husband to Sacagawea, the guide of the famous Meriwether Lewis and William Clark Expedition. Most unions in the West between French and Indians occurred as a result of the fur trade, established in the West by the French.

In the Russian zone, depending on the historian, the offspring were designated as mestizos or creoles. Perhaps the least flexible of all when it came to intermixing races were the English, who made it impossible for a white woman released from captivity among American Indians to return to a normal life, for according to white custom she had been tainted.

INTERIOR ALASKA

While expansion in Russian Alaska continued along the coastlines to the east and south, it also continued along the northern side of the Aleutian Chain into Bristol Bay, along the southwestern and western portions of Alaska. When the headquarters of Russian Alaska transferred from Kodiak to Sitka, little was known about the northern coastal or interior regions. Heavy trapping throughout the already exploited areas of Russian Alaska had led to a drop in fur-bearing animals, and new regions needed to be opened for the venture to continue to be profitable.

Therefore, in 1818 and 1819, major expeditions led by Pëtr Korsakovskiy headed toward the Bristol Bay area, with the hopes of establishing a redoubt at the mouth of the Nushagak River. This redoubt would serve as a stepping-stone to interior, southwestern, and western Alaska. The first post constructed in 1819 was the Aleksandrovskii Redoubt on the Nushagak River. The trader left to oversee this venture was Fëdor Kolmakov, a man of mixed blood who quickly established trade relations with the various villages in the region who seemed pleasant and eager to trade. Beaver, plentiful in the area, was the main trade item. The location of the Aleksandrovskii Redoubt turned out to be wise, as the Nushagak River connected with many rivers that flowed from the interior, including the Mulchatna River (which flowed from the east as far as today's Lake Clark National Park and Preserve) and the Wood River (which flowed from what is today's Wood-Tikchik State Park to the north and west). Bristol Bay and the Nushagak River today remain a major salmon fishing region.

It took a few more years for the surveys of the southwestern coast of Alaska to occur, but by 1821, the expedition began under the command of Vasilii Stepanovich Khromchenko and Adolph K. Etolin. They surveyed as far as Cape Newenham and Norton Bay (just south of the Bering Peninsula), and the contacts they made along the way provided an opportunity for future trade. The Kuskokwim River, a much longer river that reached far into the interior of Alaska, would soon have its own post, the Mikhailovskii Redoubt, founded in 1833. From this location, the Russian-American Company had firm footing to begin explorations into the Yukon River Valley in subsequent years. The fur trade once again expanded, and by the middle of the 19th century, most of southwestern Alaska had been rudimentarily mapped. The Alaska Natives within southwestern Alaska and some of the interior became part of the Russian-American Company's sphere of influence and began trading exclusively with their Russian partners, for U.S. and English ships never ventured that far.

As Russia expanded into the southwestern portion of Alaska, other European powers expressed interest in more than just the southeast coastal reaches of Alaska, as the Russians had experienced with British,

Aleut in a kayak off the coast of St. Paul in the Pribilov Islands. (Alaska State Library, Louis Choris Collection, P139-048)

French, and U.S. traders by the late 1700s. Captain James Cook had explored Alaskan coastlines at the end of the 1770s, including Bristol Bay; Captain George Vancouver had also explored Alaska in the 1790s. For these reasons, whether they intended a permanent establishment of a redoubt or not, the Russians beefed up their efforts to explore the western and northern coasts to assert their claims to Alaska. Therefore, Captain Otto von Kotzebue explored the sound named for him, located just north of the Bering Peninsula. By 1838, a Russian party succeeded in doing what no other European had done—under the leadership of Aleksandr Kashevarov, the Russian expeditionary force in skin boats arrived 30 miles east of Point Barrow.

The year was propitious for another reason: a major smallpox epidemic hit, and in the interior, where the native peoples had not yet been exposed to the disease, the Athabascans died in significant numbers. In the interior, the Russians constructed the Kolmakovskii Redoubt on the

Kuskokwim River and had a post at Old Iliamna (likely established in the early 1790s). In fact, the interior near Lake Iliamna had the best of three worlds. Inland tribes (Nushagak, Kodiak, or Kenai, and Tyonek) could play Russian trading posts off each other to get the best trades. Nevertheless, within 30 years, most of the Southwest had been brought into the fur trade.

As a result of the limited Russian population and lack of military force, however, the fur trade proceeded far differently than it had along the Aleutian Chain. Instead of forcing the Alaska Natives to trade by taking captives, they engaged with the leaders of the various villages, first establishing their leadership and appointing a toion, as they had done among the Tlingits. Russians carefully recorded the distribution of the toion medals, as well as the life span of its owner, so that upon his death they could come back and collect the medal to redistribute it to another toion. The toion, mostly chosen by his community, was a well-respected leader who engaged the Russians in a friendly manner. The toion was to encourage his villagers to bring their pelts to the redoubt, or to a Russian representative of the redoubt for trade when he arrived. Ideally, this arrangement would encourage the Alaska Natives to engage in trapping more than they normally would at the request of the toion.

Just like in other areas of Russian Alaska, Alaska Natives were encouraged to buy on credit so that they would become indebted to the Russian-American Company, and therefore continue to increase the amount of furs that they brought in. Once indebted, the Russians could reduce the amount they paid for furs—which is why those in the Iliamna area had slightly more control over their relationship with the Russian traders.

In the end, however, the United States acquired Russia in 1867 in something termed "Seward's Folly" by those U.S. senators who believed the $7 million paid to Russia was a waste. The region was also known as the "polar bear garden" and "Seward's ice box." Secretary of State William H. Seward would be vindicated in a generation when gold was discovered at Dawson in 1897, and the rush was on. Interest in Alaska would grow, but not until the threat of Japanese incursions into Alaska did the real population explosion of non-Alaska Natives occur, and the Alaska Natives would find out about U.S. policy toward native peoples and how it truly functioned.

Tsimshian village with totem poles in Port Simpson, British Columbia, in 1869. (National Oceanic and Atmospheric Administration)

At the end of the colonial period in the American West, Spain, France, and Russia all ultimately lost territory to the United States. Each country had seen the United States (or its former colonial power England) as land hungry, expansionist, and hostile to native populations. Evidence of this was found in the takeover of their lands, the removal of their people (such as the Cherokee, Choctaw, Chickasaw, Creek, and Seminole in the Southeast, as well as the many Ohio Valley tribes)—all of whom ended up in an ever-shrinking Indian Territory west of the Mississippi River. Even though these western tribes found their lands swallowed up by the ever-expanding United States, they had long traditions of trade, exchange, intermarriage, war, and friendship with their former colonial powers. Many of the Indians the United States would encounter in the West had been exposed to Christianity for more than 200 years, while others in more interior or mountainous regions had had very little interaction with any European peoples. Regardless, they would fall under a new regime that had its own set of laws and expectations. This would provide the western tribes with new challenges on how to maintain their culture, their language, and their traditions in the face of an increasingly aggressive policy to eliminate American Indian peoples and their tribal affiliations.

BIBLIOGRAPHIC ESSAY

For excellent resources on Russian Alaska and Alaska Natives, see Claus-M. Naske and Herman E. Slotnik, *Alaska: A History of the 49th State* (Norman: University of Oklahoma Press, 1979); Steven J. Langdon, *The Native People of Alaska,* 3rd ed. (Anchorage: Greatland Graphics, 1998); Wendell H. Oswalt, *Bashful No Longer: An Alaskan Eskimo Ethnohistory, 1778–1988* (Norman: University of Oklahoma Press, 1990); Harry Ritter, *Alaska's History: The People, Land, and Events of the North Country* (Anchorage: Alaska Northwest Books, 1993); and Jan Halliday, *Native Peoples of Alaska* (Seattle: Sasquatch Books, 1998). For a wonderful oral tradition regarding life in the subarctic before interference by nonindigenous peoples, see Velma Wallis, *Two Old Women: An Alaskan Legend of Betrayal, Courage and Survival* (New York: Perennial, 1993), and *Bird Girl and the Man Who Followed the Sun: An Athabaskan Indian Legend from Alaska* (New York: Harper Perennial, 1997); and John Branson and Tim Troll, eds., *Our Story: Readings from Southwest Alaska, An Anthology* (Anchorage: Alaska Natural History Association, 2006).

The segment on the Russians drew from numerous sources, including David Damas, ed., *Arctic,* vol. 5, *Handbook of North American Indians* (Washington, D.C.: Smithsonian Institution, 1984), as well as Arrell Morgan Gibson, *The American Indian: Past and Present* (Lexington, MA: D.C. Heath and Company, 1980) and the most inclusive and comprehensive book yet on the Russian experience with Alaska Natives, Andrei Val'terovich Grinev, *The Tlingit Indians in Russian America, 1741–1867,* Richard L. Bland and Katerina G. Solovjova, trans. (Lincoln: University of Nebraska Press, 2005).

Other useful sources on the Russian and native experiences include Semen Bentsionovich Okum, *The Russian-American Company* (Cambridge, MA: Harvard University Press, 1951); Hector Chevigny, *Lord of Alaska: Baranov and the Russian Adventure* (New York: Robert Hale Limited, 1942) and his *Russian America: The Great Alaskan Adventure, 1741–1867* (New York: Ballantine Books, 1965); William R. Hunt, *Arctic Passage: The Turbulent History of the Land and People of the Bering Sea, 1697–1975* (New York: Scribners, 1975); Mary Childers Mangusso and Stephen W. Haycox, eds., *Interpreting Alaska's History: An Anthology* (Seattle: University of Washington Press, 1995); Corey Ford, *Where the Sea Breaks Its Back: The Epic Story of Early Naturalist Georg Steller and the Russian Exploration of Alaska* (Anchorage: Alaska Northwest Books, 1966); F. A. Golder, *Russian Expansion in the Pacific* (Cleveland: Arthur Clark Company, 1914), and *Bering's Voyages,* 2 vols. (New York: National Geographic Society, 1925); Peter Lauridsen, *Vitus Bering, The Discoverer of Bering Strait* (Chicago: S. C. Griggs & Company, 1889); and Robert Murphy, *The Haunted Voyage* (New York: Doubleday & Company, 1961).

Other excellent primary sources include Grigorii I. Shelikhov, *A Voyage to America, 1783–1786* (Kingston, Ontario: Limestone Press, 1981); and works by

Kiril Timofeevich Khlebnikov, including *Baranov: Chief Manager of the Russian Colonies in America* (Kingston, Ontario: Limestone Press, 1973), *Notes on Russian America, Part I: Novo-Arkhangel'Sk* (Fairbanks: University of Alaska Press, 1995), and *Notes on Russian America, Parts II–V: Kad'Iak, Unalashka, Atkha, the Pribylov* (Kingston, Ontario: Limestone Press, 1995). See also A. I. Alekseev, *The Destiny of Russian America, 1741–1867,* trans. Marina Ramsay, ed. Richard A. Pierce (Kingston, Ontario: Limestone Press, 1991). See also books by Aleksandr I. Andreyev, including *Russian Discoveries in the Pacific and North America in the Eighteenth and Nineteenth Centuries,* trans. Carl Ginsburg (Ann Arbor: University of Michigan Press, 1952), and *The Destiny of Russian America, 1741–1867* (Kingston, Ontario: Limestone Press, 1991). Other excellent translated Russian sources include Svetlana G. Fedorova, Richard A. Pierce, and Alton S. Donnelly, eds., *The Russian Population in Alaska and California* (Kingston, Ontario: Limestone Press, 1973); P. A. Tikhmenev, *History of the Russian-American Company* (Kingston, Ontario: Limestone Press, 1978); and Ivan E. Veniaminov, *Notes on the Islands of the Unalashka District,* with L. T. Black and R. H. Geoghegan, trans., and Richard. A. Pierce, ed. (Kingston, Ontario: The Limestone Press, 1984).

See the several volumes by Richard A. Pierce: *Russian America: A Biographical Dictionary* (Kingston, Ontario: Limestone Press, 1990); Richard A. Pierce, ed., *Russia in North America* (Kingston, Ontario: Limestone Press, 1990); Richard A. Pierce, ed., *Russia's Hawaiian Adventure, 1815–1817* (Kingston, Ontario: Limestone Press, 1976); Richard A. Pierce, trans. *The Russian-American Company: Correspondence of the Governors, Communications Sent, 1818* (Kingston, Ontario: Limestone Press, 1984); A. S. Donelly, trans., *Russians on the Pacific, 1743–1799* (Kingston, Ontario: Limestone Press 1975); and George V. Lantzeff, *Eastward to Empire: Exploration and Conquest on the Russian Open Frontier to 1750* (Kingston, Ontario: McGill-Queen's University Press, 1973). See also L. T. Black, *Russians in Alaska, 1732–1867* (Fairbanks: University of Alaska Press, 2004); R. F. Fortuine, *Chills and Fever: Health and Disease in the Early History of Alaska* (Fairbanks: University of Alaska Press, 1992); J. R. Gibson, *Imperial Russia in Frontier America: The Changing Geography of Supply of Russian America, 1784–1867,* The Andrew H. Clark Series in the Historical Geography of North America (Oxford: Oxford University Press, 1976); James B. Townsend, "Ethnoarchaeology in Nineteenth Century Southern and Western Alaska: An Interpretive Model," *Ethnohistory,* vol. 20, no. 4 (1973): 393–412; James B. Townsend and S. J. Townsend, "Additional Artifacts from Iliamna Lake, Alaska," Anthropological Papers of the University of Alaska, vol. 12, no. 1 (1964); James W. VanStone, *Eskimos of the Nushagak River: An Ethnographic History* (Seattle: University of Washington Press, 1967); and, J. W. VanStone, ed., *Russian Exploration in Southwest Alaska: The Travel Journals of Petr Korsakovskiy (1818) and Ivan Ya. Vasilev (1829),* trans. David H. Kraus (Fairbanks: University of Alaska Press, 1988); Ernest S. Burch, Jr., *The Iñupiaq Eskimo Nations of Northwest Alaska* (Fairbanks: University of Alaska Press, 1998).

Other valuable sources include Hubert H. Bancroft, *History of Alaska 1730–1885* (1886, reprint, New York: Antiquarian Press, 1959); Glynn Barratt, *Russia in Pacific Waters, 1715–1825: A Survey of the Origins of Russia's Naval Presence in the North and South Pacific* (Vancouver: University of British Columbia Press, 1981); Vasilii Nikolaevich Berkh, *The Chronological History of the Discovery of the Aleutian Islands; or, The Exploits of the Russian Merchants: With the Supplement of Historical Data on Fur Trade,* trans. Dmitri Krenov and Richard A. Pierce (Kingston, Ontario: Limestone Press, 1974); Vasilii Afanasevich Divin, *The Great Russian Navigator, A.I. Chirikov,* trans. Raymond Henry Fisher (Fairbanks: University of Alaska Press, 1993); Svetlana G. Fedorova, *The Russian Population in Alaska and California: Late 18th Century to 1867,* trans. Richard A. Pierce and A. S. Donnelly (Kingston, Ontario: Limestone Press, 1973); O. W. Frost, ed., *Bering and Chirikov: The American Voyages and Their Impact* (Anchorage: Alaska Historical Society, 1992); James R. Gibson, *Feeding the Russian Fur Trade: Provisionment of the Okhotsk Seaboard and the Kamchatka Peninsula, 1639–1856* (Madison: University of Wisconsin Press, 1969); James R. Gibson, *Imperial Russia in Frontier America* (New York: Oxford University Press, 1976); Frank Alfred Golder, *Russian Expansion in the Pacific, 1641–1850: An Account of the Earliest and Later Expeditions Made by the Russians along the Pacific Coast of Asia and North America; Including Some Related Expeditions to the Arctic Regions* (1914, reprint, New York: Paragon Book, 1971); Frank A. Golder, ed., *Bering's Voyages: An Account of the Efforts of the Russians to Determine the Relation of Asia and America,* American Geographical Society, Research series, Nos. 1–2 (New York: American Geographical Society, 1922); W. Bruce Lincoln, *The Conquest of a Continent: Siberia and the Russians* (New York: Cornell University Press 1993); Richard Vaughan, *The Arctic: A History* (Dover, NH: Alan Sutton Publishing Inc., 1994); and Kenneth M. Ames and Herbert D. G. Maschner, *Peoples of the Northwest Coast: Their Archaeology and Prehistory* (London: Thames and Hudson, 1999).

For the Russians, Pavel Nikolaevich Golovin, *End of Russian America: Captain P. N. Golovin's Last Report, 1862* (Seattle: University of Washington Press, 1982), is an excellent overview of the end of the Russian Alaska era. And finally, Robin Fisher and J. M. Bumsted, *An Account of a Voyage to the Northwest Coast of America in 1785 and 1786 by Alexander Walker* (Seattle: University of Washington Press, 1982); Louise Phelps Kellogg, ed., *Early Narratives of the Northwest, 1634–1699* (New York: Scribner's, 1917); W. Kaye Lamb, ed., *George Vancouver: A Voyage of Discovery to the North Pacific Ocean and Round the World, 1791–1795,* 4 vols. (London: Hakluyt Society, 1984), and *The Journals and Letters of Sir Alexander Mackenzie* (Cambridge: Cambridge University Press for the Hakluyt Society, 1970); Mary Malloy, ed., *"A Most Remarkable Enterprise" Lec-*

tures on the Northwest Coast Trade and Northwest Coast Indian Life by Captain William Sturgis (Marstons Mills, MA: Parnassus Imprints, 2000). See also Iris Higbie Wilson, trans. and ed., *Noticias de Nutka: An Account of Nootka Sound in 1792 by José Mariano Moziño* (Seattle: University of Washington Press, 1970); Robert H. Ruby and John A. Brown, *The Chinook Indians: Traders of the Lower Columbia River* (Norman: University of Oklahoma Press, 1976); Hermann Haeberlin and Erna Gunther, *The Indians of Puget Sound,* University of Washington Publications in Anthropology, vol. 4, no. 1 (September 1930): 1–84 (Seattle: University of Washington, 1952 reprint).

CHAPTER Six

HISTORIOGRAPHY
AND MAJOR ISSUES IN
THE STUDY OF AMERICAN
INDIAN HISTORY

U nderstanding the very long story of American Indians in the early West is a key to comprehending their later interactions with the United States in the 19th century. Knowing whether American Indians engaged other European nations as partners in trade or family relations, or lived side by side or fought tooth and nail, or never encountered a permanent European settlement helps readers of U.S. history understand the reactions of native peoples to the demands of U.S. Indian policy.

The American Indians lived in and developed fascinating cultures, religious and political structures, agricultural advancements, beautiful artwork, and unique housing structures (to name but a few) thousands of years before the arrival of the English at Jamestown. They had massive apartment building complexes, the likes of which would not be seen in the United States until the late 19th century. They had very detailed, stratified, and ritualistic religions that involved everything from regional ceremonial centers with multilayered Roman-type roads leading out toward spiritual sites or communities to mounds and pyramids. They had burial rituals, beliefs in the afterworld, and an understanding of the interconnectedness between their world and their lives and of celestial beings as well. They understood seasons, could predict the location and movement of the moon, and understood the motion of the tides. They worked with metals, created beautiful jewelry from quarried and mined

Cliff dwelling at Gila National Monument in New Mexico. (Sandra K. Mathews)

materials, and perfected hunting methods that later non-Indians would marvel at and attempt to copy. They lived with an understanding of how they fit in their world, affected the natural world by selective burning, built cisterns for water and large irrigation systems for irrigation, and even constructed defensive structures to protect themselves against the creatures and other humans in their environs. While they may not have invented some of the technologies that some Europeans had at the point of contact, they did not have the need for them, for their tools and methods of trapping, hunting, preparing pelts, cooking, and much else in their lives more than sufficed.

Because the scope of this work covers many thousands of years, it would be impractical to include a complete historiographical study in the space allotted. Instead, I have incorporated the major historiographical pieces through the bibliographies at the ends of the chapters about the origins and historical development of American Indians in the early West. Therefore, this segment is limited to some of the major issues and a highly selective bibliography that encompasses or addresses those broader issues.

TRADITIONAL HISTORICAL VIEWS
CHANGE AFTER 1960S

The study of American Indians has undergone a major shift over the past few generations of scholarly study. Before the 1960s, most of the histories written involved a primarily military focus, were highly biased toward the male gender, and had very little to do with anything other than the development of great civilizations, such as Cahokia or the Iroquois Confederacy, for example, and even those were limited. As a result of two major shifts, much of this historical bias and shortsightedness in historical research would soon change. The first involved the shifts in affiliation and organizational capabilities of tribes resulting from the Termination and Relocation era during the 1940s, 1950s, and 1960s in U.S. history, during which time the U.S. government attempted to break down tribal coherence and terminate its federal relationship with tribes. As the U.S. government bussed American Indians off the reservations and forced them into urban settings away from the stability, security, and comfort of family, home, and traditional homelands, these displaced tribal people began to engage with other American Indians from tribes all over the region broadly defined. Some of those centers included Minneapolis; Oakland, California; Phoenix; Seattle; and other major cities across the West.

As a result American Indians began to talk with each other and realized the similarities in their historical pasts. Coupled with the Civil Rights movement and the political awakening of minority rights, they began to speak out. Various key organizations formed, including the National Congress of American Indians (NCAI), the American Indian Movement (AIM), and United Indians of All Tribes (these were some of the most famous, but others existed as well). They began to organize, as in the case of the NCAI, which was founded in 1944, and put together statements around which the Indian people could rally, organize, and effect change. In their mission statement, they "stressed the need for unity and cooperation among tribal governments for the protection of their treaty and sovereign rights." (For more information, see their official Web site at www.ncai.org.) They continue to monitor the federal government for the purpose of protecting their rights. AIM officially began in the Minneapolis area to protect American Indians against the brutality of the police force, but the group would argue that it had existed for more than 500 years without a name. They continued to demand that their rights be recognized by state and federal governments during their Trail of Broken Treaties march on Washington, D.C., and occupation of the Bureau of Indian Affairs building; by helping the Lakota in 1973 at Wounded Knee; and by occupying Alcatraz in 1969 (organized by Indians of All Nations). They were indeed a harbinger for change. (For more information, see their official Web site at www.aimovement.org.)

Another key piece to this puzzle was the advent of American Indian studies centers, such as at the University of California at Los Angeles that started in 1969, as well as Berkeley, in response to a call from the community for universities to take a more critical and accurate look at American Indian issues, history, and culture. As a result of the demands by American Indians that outsiders and the government respect them as a people, more realistic and accurate portrayals have begun to appear in monograph, anthology, encyclopedic, and other media forms. Historians began to use resources other than just military and one-sided western journalistic reports written by the dominant white culture to paint a more accurate image of the Indian experience; they also incorporated archaeology, ethnohistory, oral history, musicology, religious and spiritual information, population studies, and a wide variety of other sources to inform their research. Perhaps more importantly, the American Indian studies and ethnic studies centers began to produce American Indian scholars who could provide the perspective that has so long been left out in Indian history—their own.

Another result of this bourgeoning community of Indian scholars has been the beginning of a fascinating interchange between non-Indian and Indian scholarship. With that, however, has come some harsh criticism, rightfully leveled at the previous scholarship that ignored the sovereignty of the tribes and their cultural and traditional histories, as well as the previous studies that included an incorrect and frankly biased assessment of their historical development. Currently, that debate is still raging and some non-Indian scholars have been told (or know someone who has been told) that they have no right researching or writing Indian history. Decolonization of Indian history is indeed an important conversation. Enough Indian scholars have contributed to the published field of history that a variety of scholarship is available, and formerly recognized and respected one-sided histories of the West and American Indian issues can be replaced by histories that are more inclusive, representative, and respectful of American Indian history.

More importantly, U.S. Indian policy has also shifted, mostly as a result of Indian activism, leading to a shift in non-Indian scholarship. Many non-Indians have listened with a sympathetic ear and attempted to continue (or begin) writing American Indian histories that have a more accurate historical picture that is more representative of the Indians' varied experiences from their perspective. But as these non-Indian scholars are either non-Indians or were not raised culturally in their tribal culture, it is impossible for them to be able to understand all of the nuances of American Indian history from the outside. That is why Native scholarship adds such a crucial element in the telling of the story.

Because of this flowering of interest in an accurate portrayal of American Indian history from something other than a military perspective of warfare and military engagement, great works have appeared in the past 20 to 30 years. This is not to say that very useful sources did not exist before. Perhaps one of the first was by Alvin M. Josephy, Jr., a former journalist who became a student of American Indian history and published several books, some of which highlighted mostly the military perspective, but he also began to look into traditional culture as well, including *The Nez Perce Indians and the Opening of the Northwest* (New York: Houghton-Mifflin, 1965) and *The Patriot Chiefs: A Chronicle of American Indian Leadership* (New York: Penguin, 1963). His *The Indian Heritage of America* (New York: Alfred A. Knopf, 1968) was an attempt to look well into the Native past to provide an understanding of what archaeologists and anthropologists could tell historians about traditional Native cultures before the arrival of the European interlopers.

BROADENING HISTORICAL UNDERSTANDINGS

To understand the historiography of American Indian history, one must reach far back into and beyond the colonial past to hear what history can tell the United States about the people who inhabited the Americas long before the Europeans dreamed of the existence of another continent, and even before great monarchies existed. This history delves into archaeology, the realm of petroglyphs, pictographs, and excavations—whose very discovery and excavation (and sometimes theft) at times caused incredible harm to Indian peoples. Even today, they still fight to reclaim the bones of their ancestors and other funerary objects that were stolen by archaeologist-profiteers, grave robbers, and even early archaeological researchers who did not understand the gravity of their actions—shipping human remains off to such museums as the Smithsonian in Washington, D.C. Luckily U.S. Indian policies now protect these sacred remains and sacred funerary and other associated objects belonging to their ancestors, but only fairly recently with the passage of the Native American Graves Protection and Repatriation Act (NAGPRA) of 1990. NAGPRA created a process by which American Indian communities can request the return of "human remains, funerary objects, sacred objects, and objects of cultural patrimony" from federal agencies and museums, but they can be released only to "lineal descendants, culturally affiliated Indian tribes, and Native Hawaiian organizations." (For more information, see the U.S. government's official Web site at www.cr.nps.gov/nagpra.) As a result of this major change in policies, archaeologists had to proceed with far more caution, oversight, and respect, but it certainly did not stop the important continued discoveries that the field of archaeology continues to contribute to the historical understanding of precontact cultures.

While much of the moviegoing public conjures up images of the 19th-century horse-riding and warrior culture of the Plains tribes when the term "Indian" is mentioned, American Indian culture is actually a living entity. Truthfully, the traditions of each of the more than 500 individual indigenous cultures that existed in the United States can only be completely understood by those who lived within it. But that does not mean others should not try to understand and appreciate the many indigenous cultures that exist in the United States. In fact, if not for the changes in American Indian scholarship, activism, and yes, even militant action, U.S. policy would not have shifted to the self-determination policies that emerged after President Richard M. Nixon signed into law the Indian Self-Determination Act of the 1970s (and others that succeeded it in fairly rapid succession involving laws regulating the adoption of Indian children, health care, and others that were intended to improve life on the reservation without undermining traditional tribal authority). But not all historical scholarship can claim the positive benefits of the past 30 years. For those who have studied American Indian history, one thing becomes quickly apparent: some of the earlier researchers did not believe American Indian history belonged only to the Indian people, and they took from those communities the sacred stories about their traditional culture, their spiritual secrets, and their lifeways and shared them with the outside world through published sources without tribal permission. Much of this unauthorized sharing of sacred knowledge began to occur as early as the late 19th century in U.S. history, beginning with those who feared American Indians would vanish from the face of the earth. They headed west to research their cultures, write as much as they could, and collect artifacts (and even dug up burial sites) to save what they could of this purportedly vanishing race. In the late 19th century and early 20th century, easterners wanted to see the remaining Indians in their "natural setting," and hoped to buy their handmade pots, blankets, jewelry, and anything else the Indians would sell. Other collectors also headed west and began purchasing the massive family black kettles that families had traditionally used for generations over the fires. More importantly, with them came the researchers and recorders of cultural history who would forever cause a rift between many American Indian communities and the academic community. Especially by the 1920s and 1930s, anthropologists and other researchers began circulating among tribes in the West to record for posterity the lives of western tribes, for U.S. policies against American Indian cultures were tantamount to cultural genocide before the mid-1930s. Trusting and sharing with these interested outsiders, some Indian people described their most intimate and sacred information, not realizing that these men and women intended to record these "facts" and publish them as part of books, journal articles, or even the Smithsonian Institution's Annual Bureau of American Ethnology Reports.

Some of these early researchers came from the newly formed Bureau of American Ethnology (BAE). The BAE was established by Congress within the Smithsonian Institution in 1879. Its purpose was to conduct anthropological research among the North American Indians during a time of rapid change in the various indigenous communities as a result of U.S. policies (particular as a result of the Dawes Act, or the General

Allotment Act). The Smithsonian Institution accurately argues that for the next 100 years, the research and the reports themselves "played a defining role in the development of American anthropology as a discipline." (For the complete Table of Contents of the reports, see www.sil .si.edu/DigitalCollections/BAE/baeintro.htm.) The BAE published 200 annual reports (1879–1931) covering a wide variety of topics, including archaeology, anthropology, musicology, cultural studies, ceremonials, accoutrements, clothing styles, food, housing or shelter, use of horse and other animals, dictionaries and syllabary, physiology, medical information (healing techniques, healing herbs and practices, for example), myths or stories (such as creation stories or stories teaching behavioral or other lessons), population studies, ethnobotony, ethnozoology, antiquities (found at various sites), sacred bundles, burials and ceremonies, history, customs, and so much more. A veritable encyclopedia of precontact information, the Bureau of Ethnology Reports to the Smithsonian Institution, first directed by John Wesley Powell, are a valuable source of information for American Indian studies.

BROADENING INTEREST IN THE "CENTURY OF DISHONOR"

Also at the end of the 19th century, Eastern philanthropists, the "Friends of the Indians," evolved out of a frustration at U.S. policy toward the destruction of the Indian people and their cultural heritage. They feared that Indians were going to disappear as a cultural group. They saw their mission as one of saving Indian cultures, and they garnered support throughout the United States for a change in Indian policies that they hoped would save the Indian people. A wonderful example is Helen Hunt Jackson, who wrote *A Century of Dishonor: A Sketch of the United States Government's Dealings with Some of the Indian Tribes* (Norman: University of Oklahoma Press, 1995). In the book, which was published originally in 1881, Jackson hoped to illustrate to Congress the error of its ways to effect a positive change for the American Indians. Unfortunately, the policies that the Friends of the Indians espoused, in fact, would do more damage and work against tribal coherence more than almost any other U.S. policy to date. To learn more about this attitude of a "vanishing" In-

INDIAN LAND FOR SALE

GET A HOME
OF
YOUR OWN
✻
EASY PAYMENTS

PERFECT TITLE
✻
POSSESSION
WITHIN
THIRTY DAYS

FINE LANDS IN THE WEST

IRRIGATED
IRRIGABLE
GRAZING
AGRICULTURAL
DRY FARMING

In 1910 the Department of the Interior Sold Under Sealed Bids Allotted Indian Land as Follows:

Location.	Acres.	Average Price per Acre.	Location.	Acres.	Average Price per Acre.
Colorado	5,211.21	$7.27	Oklahoma	34,664.00	$19.14
Idaho	17,013.00	24.85	Oregon	1,020.00	15.43
Kansas	1,684.50	33.45	South Dakota	120,445.00	16.53
Montana	11,034.00	9.86	Washington	4,879.00	41.37
Nebraska	5,641.00	36.65	Wisconsin	1,069.00	17.00
North Dakota	22,610.70	9.93	Wyoming	865.00	20.64

FOR THE YEAR 1911 IT IS ESTIMATED THAT **350,000** ACRES WILL BE OFFERED FOR SALE

For information as to the character of the land write for booklet, "INDIAN LANDS FOR SALE," to the Superintendent U. S. Indian School at any one of the following places:

CALIFORNIA:
  Hoopa.
COLORADO:
  Ignacio.
IDAHO:
  Lapwai.
KANSAS:
  Horton.
  Nadeau.

MINNESOTA:
  Onigum.
MONTANA:
  Crow Agency.
NEBRASKA:
  Macy.
  Santee.
  Winnebago.

NORTH DAKOTA:
  Fort Totten.
  Fort Yates.
OKLAHOMA:
  Anadarko.
  Cantonment.
  Colony.
  Darlington.
  Muskogee,
  Pawnee.

OKLAHOMA—Con.
  Sac and Fox Agency.
  Shawnee.
  Wyandotte.
OREGON:
  Klamath Agency.
  Pendleton.
  Roseburg.
  Siletz.

SOUTH DAKOTA:
  Cheyenne Agency.
  Crow Creek.
  Greenwood.
  Lower Brule.
  Pine Ridge.
  Rosebud.
  Sisseton.

WASHINGTON:
  Fort Simcoe.
  Fort Spokane.
  Tekoa.
  Tulalip.
WISCONSIN:
  Oneida.

WALTER L. FISHER,
Secretary of the Interior.

ROBERT G. VALENTINE,
Commissioner of Indian Affairs.

Not Afraid of Pawnee, a Yankton Sioux, on an advertisement by the U.S. Department of the Interior offering surplus lands for sale in 1910–1911. (Library of Congress)

dian, see Brian Dippie, *The Vanishing American: White Attitudes and U.S. Indian Policy* (Lawrence: University Press of Kansas, 1991). Largely as a result of these activists, as well as people within the U.S. government who made policy, the Dawes Act passed, which determined to remove the communal element from the reservation itself. As a result, a massive land grab occurred where nearly two-thirds of tribes lost two-thirds of all their land, forcing tribal members to claim a plot of farmland from the former reservation and live separately as farmers. This caused major devastation among tribes and significantly diminished their ability to respond as a unit to U.S. governmental policies or laws.

While the political atmosphere cooled a little for American Indians between 1934 and 1945 with the advent of Commissioner of Indian Affairs John Collier's Indian New Deal and the revival of Indian culture (albeit on paternalistic terms, some would argue), the United States would again accelerate efforts to terminate Indian tribal relations with the U.S. government and effectively attempted to cause tribes to cease existence by the 1940s and 1950s. As a result of U.S. policies, Indian boarding schools, and the suppression of native cultures by often devastating means by the U.S. government, many of the stories and traditional knowledge and even languages of Indian tribes have slipped into the realm of the unknown. But they had not died, as Daryl Baldwin of the Miami tribe would argue (learn more at their Web site, www.myaamiaproject.com). Laboring to keep alive traditional languages, in his case the Miami language in particular, he instead argues that the languages did not die, they just went out of use. Luckily for the Miami tribe, the Jesuits of New France had an interest in learning the languages and cultures of the tribes they encountered. Learning what they could, the Jesuit fathers recorded the information in detailed reports, *The Jesuit Relations,* and in dictionaries that could be found hundreds of years later, buried in boxes in archives. From those boxes, native culture and languages could be brought back, taught to their descendants, and revived. But not all cultures had outsiders who handwrote extensive records of daily life, language, religion, and foodways. In fact, most of those who recorded the information were religious and military men who found greater interest in the Indian men's lives than in the women's daily chores and choices. Therefore, the recorded history is often skewed toward the views of biased male outsiders who had their own cultural predispositions, cultural baggage, and prejudices (and sometimes ulterior motives such as potential for conversion or potential for military action against the people). Therefore, American Indian scholarship reflected these biases and was based almost entirely upon a U.S. Indian policy perspective, using mostly U.S. military and government documents. Finally, some tribes kept some information private, never intending to share it with outsiders. When the elders died without having an opportunity to share the stories with the next generations, some of those stories were lost. As a result, the stories of tribes will almost always be incomplete. Even though that may be the case, it is still imperative that researchers attempt to eliminate the potential for prejudice that comes primarily with lack of knowledge or respect for others.

RECENT SCHOLARSHIP

Thankfully, scholarship has shifted, and more recently the Smithsonian Institute has published an excellent series of volumes about American Indians: the *Handbook of North American Indians.* The series editor, William Sturtevant, had great foresight to have published a wide collection of materials that spanned the Bureau of Ethnology Annual Reports, but with much more up-to-date historical, ethnohistorical, and scientific research incorporated throughout. Still available through a variety of sources, this 17-volume set is a veritable cornucopia of information about American Indian culture. Each volume covers a particular region of the United States, and each volume is edited by an expert in that particular region's cultures. The segments related to the American West include the following: David Damas, ed., *Arctic,* vol. 5 (1984); June Helm, ed., *Subarctic,* vol. 6 (1981); Wayne Suttles, ed., *Northwest Coast,* vol. 7 (1990); Robert F. Heizer, ed., *California,* vol. 8 (1978); Alfonzo Ortiz, ed., *Southwest,* vol. 9 and vol. 10 (1979); Warren L. D'Azevedo, ed., *Great Basin,* vol. 11 (1986); DeWard E. Walker, ed., *Plateau,* vol. 12 (1998); Raymond J. DeMallie, ed., *Plains,* vol. 13, parts 1 and 2 (2001); Bruce G. Trigger, ed., *Northeast,* vol. 15 (1978); and Ives Goddard, ed., *Languages,* vol. 17 (1996).

Therefore, in an attempt to provide a much more balanced view of American Indian history, in more recent years, historians have taken a

closer look at the work of anthropology, archaeology, oral history, population studies, environmental history, ethnohistory, and much more and
have created amazing resources for those who want to learn more about
American Indian history, such as are included in the *Handbook of North
American Indians*. Some of the most recent and useful resources for American Indian history include Barry M. Pritzker's *A Native American Encyclopedia: History, Culture, and Peoples* (Oxford: Oxford University Press,
2000), and even his more recent work co-edited with Bruce E. Johansen,
Encyclopedia of American Indian History (Santa Barbara, CA: ABC-CLIO,
2007). Organized similarly to Alvin M. Josephy, Jr.'s, older, but still useful
The Indian Heritage of America (New York: Alfred A. Knopf, 1969), it follows regional variations. Unlike Josephy, however, within those regional
variations, Pritzker organized each section alphabetically by tribe, including their name, location, population, language, and history (including religion, government, customs, dwellings, diet, technology, trade, notable
arts, transportation, dress, war, and weapons). He also included contemporary information such as economy, legal status, daily life, and reservation or government information. Those who would like to know more
about contemporary Indian issues should consult Veronica Velarde Tiller,
Tiller's Guide to Indian Country, 2nd ed. (Albuquerque: BowArrow Publishing, 2006). Another excellent resource for American Indian prehistory
and historical culture is Frederick E. Hoxie, *The Encyclopedia of North
American Indians: Native American History, Culture, and Life From Paleo-
Indians to the Present* (New York: Houghton Mifflin Publishing, 1996). A
wonderful narrative and one of the only American Indian history texts
currently available on just tribes in the American West, and an excellent
and accessible narrative history is Colin Calloway's magnum opus, *One
Vast Winter Count: The Native American West before Lewis and Clark* (Lincoln, NE: Bison Books, 2006), a tome of more than 600 pages. Infusing
the Native American cultural perspective throughout the traditional history of religious, political, and military conflict, he has indeed provided an
amazing resource. Before Calloway's work appeared, however, most consulted a variety of Indian histories that attempted to get away from the
purely political and military perspective that appeared before the 1970s.
Works such as Angie Debo's *A History of the Indians of the United States*
(Norman: University of Oklahoma Press, 1984) was and continues to be

a standard resource. Other classic sources, to name just a few, include Francis Jennings, *The Founders of America: From the Earliest Migrations to the Present* (New York: W. W. Norton, 1993), as well as his *The Invasion of America: Indians, Colonialism, and the Cant of Conquest* (Chapel Hill: University of North Carolina Press for the Institute of Early American History and Culture, 1975); James Axtell's *The European and the Indian: Essays in the Ethnohistory of Colonial North America* (New York: Oxford University Press, 1981), as well as his *Natives and Newcomers: The Cultural Origins of North America* (New York: Oxford University Press, 2001); and Robert F. Berkhofer's *The White Man's Indian: Images of the American Indian from Columbus to the Present* (New York: Knopf, 1978).

Scholars have also gone back to reconsider the Paleo-Indian and Archaic periods. For a more thorough bibliography, see the bibliographic essay at the end of Chapter 1 on origins. Perhaps two of the most well-known sources that began to challenge colonialism for historians are Kirkpatrick Sale's *The Conquest of Paradise: Christopher Columbus and the Columbian Legacy* (New York: Penguin, 1990), and Alfred Crosby's *Columbian Exchange: Biological and Cultural Consequences of 1492* (New York: Praeger Paperback, [1973] reprint 2003). See also Alvin M. Josephy, Jr., ed., *America in 1492: The World of Indian Peoples before the Arrival of Columbus* (New York: Vintage, 1993), and Charles C. Mann, *1491: New Revelations of the Americas before Columbus* (New York: Vintage, 2006).

For those teaching American Indian history, some excellent and recent texts include R. David Edmunds, Frederick E. Hoxie, and Neal Salisbury, *The People: A History of Native America* (New York: Houghton Mifflin Company, 2007). All three of these men have spent their careers studying American Indian history, and therefore provide an amazing breadth of resources, knowledge, and context for American Indian history and issues. Other wonderful sources for teachers include Clifford E. Trafzer's *"As Long as the Grass Shall Grow and the Rivers Flow:" A History of Native Americans* (New York: Thomson Learning, Inc., 2000); Philip Weeks, ed., *"They Made Us Many Promises": The American Indian Experience, 1524 to the Present*, 2nd ed. (Wheeling, IL: Harlan Davidson, 2002); and the following by Colin Calloway: *First Peoples: A Documentary Survey of American Indian History* (New York: Bedford/St. Martins,

1999, 2004) and *New Worlds for All: Indians, Europeans, and the Remaking of Early America* (Baltimore: Johns Hopkins University Press, 1997). See also Robert W. Venables, *American Indian History: Five Centuries of Conflict & Coexistence: Conquest of a Continent, 1492–1783* (Santa Fe, NM: Clear Light Books, 2004). And while most of his 1,300-plus-page tome deals with the U.S. period and not only the West from a U.S. Indian policy perspectivce, Francis Paul Prucha's *The Great Father: The United States Government and the American Indians* (Lincoln: University of Nebraska Press, 1995) is an excellent source for students of American Indian history. Finally, perhaps the best new (three-volume set) on U.S.-Indian relations will be Donald Fixico, ed., *Treaties with American Indians: An Encyclopedia of Rights, Conflicts, and Sovereignty* (Santa Barbara, CA: ABC-CLIO, 2008).

To better comprehend the perspective of the American Indian when writing or reading American Indian history, there are several sources that should be consulted, including Donald L. Fixico, *The American Indian Mind in a Linear World: American Indian Studies and Traditional Knowledge* (New York: Routledge, 2003). To further one's understanding about Native perspectives on writing history (by outsiders and otherwise), the best source for full and unabashed disclosure from a native perspective comes from Devon Abbott Mihesuah, *So You Want to Write about American Indians? A Guide for Writers, Students, and Scholars* (Lincoln: University of Nebraska Press, 2005); Devon Abbott Mihesuah, ed., *Natives and Academics: Researching and Writing about American Indians* (Lincoln: University of Nebraska Press, 1998); and Devon Abbott Mihesuah and Angela Cavender Wilson, eds., *Indigenizing the Academy: Transforming Scholarship and Empowering Communities* (Lincoln: University of Nebraska Press, 2004). Laurence M. Hauptman also has a very useful book entitled *Tribes & Tribulations: Misconceptions about American Indians and Their Histories* (Albuquerque: University of New Mexico Press, 1995). To provide some direction for future researchers, Colin Calloway wrote *New Directions in American Indian History* (Norman: University of Oklahoma Press, 1988), hoping to give some new ideas and direction to a new generation of scholars. Donald L. Fixico, ed., *Rethinking American Indian History* (Albuquerque: University of New Mexico Press, 1997), offers an excellent anthology from major scholars in the field addressing issues about historiography, analysis, and methodology. And finally, perhaps one of the best overarching nonlinear historical studies of American Indian history is the anthology by Philip J. Deloria and Neal Salisbury, *A Companion to American Indian History* (Malden, MA: Blackwell Publishing, 2004). Organized by first contacts, Native practice and belief, then language, identity, expression, then exchange and social relations, and finally governmental relations, this anthology incorporates major historians in the field of American Indian studies, many of which have tribal affiliations. Native perspectives provide non-Indian scholars and readers the most important view into traditional life, and numerous notable anthropologists and Native scholars have collected oral histories that give readers a window that otherwise would be closed. As Philip Deloria described, "Arthur C. Parker, Edward Dozier, J.N.B. Hewitt, and D'Arcy McNickle," as well as "writers Zitkala Sä, Pauline Johnson, Charles Eastman, and John Joseph Mathews," all with tribal affiliations, provide readers of Indian history from a Native perspective (Deloria and Salisbury, *Companion,* 17). Finally, one would be remiss to not include the fascinating and important perspective of Vine Deloria, Jr., especially his *Custer Died for Your Sins: An Indian Manifesto* (Norman: University of Oklahoma, 1988), an excellent and delightfully critical Indian perspective on Indian and U.S. history.

But in the end, one must ask the question: who can write American Indian history? Does anyone actually *own* the right to write history? Certainly historians without American Indian cultural knowledge from the inside (those who come from traditional cultural affiliations, life experience, and traditional knowledge, for example) will never truly understand how to describe accurately what the experiences must have been like for an American Indian who lived through the events within the scope of history, but does that preclude non-Indians from researching and writing about American Indians? Or does it mean that one should only assign or read American Indian history written from a Native perspective? Certainly our understanding of their experiences would be far richer, but meticulous readers or scholars should never relegate themselves to reading history through only one lens—even if it is a lens that has been left out until only recently. I believe the most important lessons that the late 20th century scholarship has illustrated to those who study the American

Klee Benally, a member of the Save the Peaks Coalition, bellows an American Indian Movement song during a press conference challenging a U.S. Forest Service decision to allow snowmaking at the Arizona Snowbowl at Flagstaff City Hall. (Jill Torrance/Arizona Daily Sun)

West, or American Indian history in particular, is that the public needs to be far better informed of the myths and realities of the American Indian experience and how it has been portrayed; to read widely but to *always* incorporate the Indian perspective as a key for a better understanding of their experiences; to be open to new interpretations of events that perhaps have always been portrayed from one lens; and to be considerate of traditional knowledge and respectful of the people about whom we seem to be fascinated as a country—but one that the U.S. government has long attempted to destroy: the American Indian.

CHRONOLOGY

50,000–   Pre–Projectile point era
25,000 BCE

25,000–   Paleo-Indian stage
8000 BCE

15,000–   Clovis point stage (first use of large spear points of the
11,000 BCE   Clovis type)

11,000–   Folsom point stage
8000 BCE

8000–1200   Archaic Age (development of cultural systems)
BCE

1200 BCE–   Distinct cultures develop (e.g., Eastern cultures include
1250 CE   Adena, Hopewell, and Mississippian; Western cultures in-
                     clude Mogollón, Hohokam, Anasazi, Patayán, Sinagua)

200 CE   Clay pots used by Southwestern peoples

500   Pottery is widespread

700–1100   Tallgrass prairies emerge; Plains people begin cultivating
                     corn and beans

800–1400   Hohokam build sophisticated irrigation systems

900–1300   Anasazi culture develops and reaches its height: domesti-
                     cated agriculture, used pottery and baskets, studied as-
                     tronomy, achieved architectural accomplishments

1064	Sunset Crater erupts near Flagstaff, Arizona
1100–1130	Drought causes realignment, shifting populations in the Southwest
1150–1300	The Great Migration of the Anasazi peoples
1250–1500	Evolution of language families
1492	Spanish make landfall in the Americas, downfall of Caribbean tribes begins (90 to 100 percent mortality as a result of warfare and disease)
1513	*Requerimiento* issued by the Spanish crown
1520–1530s	Álvar Núñez Cabeza de Vaca's expedition throughout the South; Spain realizes illegal Indian slave trade is taking place in Northwest New Spain
1532	Voyage of Jacques Cartier into Bay of Saint Lawrence; begins contact between French and Algonkin, Huron, Montagnais (and results in introduction of disease, fur trade, slow breakdown of cultures)
1539	Expedition by Fray Marcos de Niza and Estevan
1540	Two major expeditions by Spain: Juan Rodríguez Cabrillo and Francisco Vásquez de Coronado
1541	Cartier reaches Stadacona
1550	*Encomienda* officially ends; *repartimiento* replaces it
1598	Establishment of permanent Spanish colony in New Mexico
1608	Quebec established
1610s	Dutch arrive south of the Saint Lawrence River along Hudson River
1630s	The Huron, having trapped out their homelands, are encouraged by the French to move westward; the French first encounter the Ho-Chunk

1634	Three Rivers community established on the Saint Lawrence River
1639–1640	Smallpox hits Huronia
1660s	French population in New France is only 3,200; mostly at Three Rivers, Quebec, and Montreal
1670	The Hudson Bay Company is established by British royal charter
1673	Louis Joliet and Jacques Marquette reach Green Bay and explore the upper Mississippi River
1680	Pueblo Revolt led by Popé
1682	Robert de La Salle follows Mississippi River to mouth and will claim all for the French king, Louis XIV
1690s	Settlement of Arizona under Father Francisco Eusebio Kino
1692	Permanent reoccupation of New Mexico by Spanish under Don Diego de Vargas
1700s	Settlement of Texas
1701	New France establishes peace with the Iroquois
1713	Treaty of Utrecht allows the English to have a foothold at Hudson Bay
1720	Villasur expedition
1730s	Fox Indian resistance to French expansion
	Lieutenant Pierre Gaultier de Varennes et de La Vérendrye plans expeditions to the west to reach western ocean via a northern route; reaches Rocky Mountains
1740s	Russians appear in Aleutian Chain; destruction of Aleut culture and livelihood begins

1745	Last battle between Ojibwa and Sioux fought on Strawberry Island, Lac du Flambeau Chippewa Reservation
1753	The French king, Louis XV, is shocked by cost of colonial upkeep
1754	The French and Indian War breaks out
1759	Quebec and Niagara fall to the English
1760s	Aleut uprising
	Opening of three major trails between Santa Fe and San Antonio with the newly acquired regions from the French
1763	French and Indian Wars end; France loses claims in North America but gives Spain everything west of the Mississippi
1769	Settlement of California and the beginning of Missionary Era
1776	Spanish expedition into the Four Corners region
1783	Peace treaty with Great Britain establishes U.S. sovereignty
	Grigorii Shelikhov begins expedition to Alaska
1786	The Comanche Peace
1790	Aleksandr Baranov becomes director of Russian Alaska enterprise
1794	First Russian Orthodox mission is established in Alaska
1795	Baranov is named first Russian governor of Alaska; he establishes the Russian post known as Old Sitka
1799	Russian American Company is formally established
1800	Russians establish post at Alexander Archipelago
1802–1860s	Tlingit insurgence is ongoing against the Russians

1802	Tlingit Indians kill 20 Russians and more than 125 Aleut workers at Sitka
1803	The United States acquires the Louisiana Purchase from France; Lewis and Clark's expedition begins to form
1804	Russians reoccupy Sitka
1806	Zebulon Montgomery Pike launches expedition to the Southwest
	Tlingit destroy Russian settlement at Yakutat
1808	Russian capital moves to New Archangel
1812	First Russian Orthodox mission is established in Southwest Alaska
1818	Alexandrovskii Redoubt is ordered for Nushagak River
1821	Mexico gains independence from Spain
	Russian navy forbids all foreign ships from entering Alaskan waters
1824	Russians begin exploring the Nushagak, Kuskokwim, Yukon, and Koyuk rivers and the interior of Alaska
1834	Father Ivan Veniaminov moves to Sitka
1840	Veniaminov is consecrated Bishop Innokenty
	Native languages can be used officially in the Russian Orthodox liturgy
1847	Fort Yukon is established
1848	Treaty of Guadalupe Hidalgo: the United States takes northern portion of Mexico after Mexican War
	Whalers from northeastern United States begin commercial whaling in Alaskan waters
1867	The United States acquires Alaska from Russia

GLOSSARY

animism A belief that all things existing in nature, both animate and inanimate, have a spirit. Common to many indigenous belief systems.

atlatl Spear thrower; either a stone, wood, or leather thong that launches a spear accurately up to three times farther than without using *atlatl.*

BCE Before the Common Era.

Beringia 800-mile-wide land "bridge" that allowed Siberian hunters to cross into the Americas approximately 25,000–12,000 BCE.

Black Legend Started when Bartolomé de las Casas's book, *Destruction of the Indies,* was translated into many languages. The English used the book to decry the Spanish as being uniquely cruel in their conquest of the New World and to discredit them internationally. The Black Legend continues to lead to misperceptions of people of Spanish descent.

Black Robe Refers to the "uniform" of the Jesuit fathers in the Americas; the Indian people often referred to the Jesuits as "Black Robe."

cacique Spanish term for tribal leader.

carrying capacity Ability of the land to produce enough calories to sustain an individual.

clan Blood relative–based grouping, often represented by an item from natural world (e.g., bear, corn, deer, turtle). Clan members were not to marry within their own clan.

Clovis point   Fluted spearpoint used by Paleo-Indians, sometimes used with an atlatl to hunt large game.

coureur de bois   Term for a French fur trader who moves into the "wilderness" to live and trade among the native peoples. Periodically, these men married into tribes to gain a trading advantage.

empresario   A grant to a U.S. citizen to bring a group of settlers to Texas during the Mexican period to establish ranches or farms. These immigrants purportedly would have to obey Mexican law, learn Spanish, and become Catholic.

encomienda   A Spanish grant of tribute given by a licensed governor of a province to a colonist. The encomendero collected tribute from a designated number of heads of households within Indian villages. Encomenderos lived near Indian villages, protecting them from enemies and converting them to Christianity and Spanish civilization. Some Spanish women held encomiendas. Encomenderos often abused their authority, even though Indians had a right to bring charges against them for abuse of their "statutory rights." The encomienda was phased out by the Spanish authorities after the 1550s due to abuse of the institution.

friars   Members of religious orders (including Jesuits, Dominicans, Franciscans) who came to the Americas to convert Indian people to Catholicism. Later, the missions they established would become secularized, that is, turned over to the priests of the "regular" orders, so they could be turned into parishes charged with maintaining the faith.

índio ladino   Indian living in the Spanish empire who had culturally adapted to Spanish civilization.

jacal   Type of construction that involving planting 4- to 8-foot-long wooden branches in the ground, bound to each other, for either fences, house walls, or ceilings.

jump kill   A method of hunting in which Paleo-Indians surrounded and startled larger game animals and directed them toward a cliff edge, where they would plunge to their death. The hunters then slaughtered and skinned the animals, collecting their bones and other items to make food, shelter, tools, and clothing.

kiva   Ceremonial chamber, partially subterranean, used by Pueblo Indians of the Southwest.

moeity   A subdivision of a tribe; more populous tribes consisted of two moeities, made up of numerous clans. On some occasions, a tribe might have three moeities (Choctaw, for example). Moeities had essential obligations within the tribe.

order   A religious group; regular orders include monastic groups such as the Franciscans, Dominicans, and Jesuits, for example, and are charged with converting non-Christians. The missions they ran were supported by the religious authorities (or in the case of Spain, the Spanish crown). The secular branch of the Catholic Church consisted of parish priests who oversaw self-supporting parishes.

Paleo-Indian   Stone Age ancestors to today's American Indians

pit house   Early structure used particularly by Southwestern tribes; consisted of approximately two to three feet of subterranean flooring, with jacal structures supporting roof.

potlatch   Ceremony held in the Pacific Northwest region in which a tribal member hosted a gathering and celebration and gave away all or most of his possessions to other members of the tribe. Considered honorable and status was gained in tribe for this act of generosity.

promyshleniki   Fur hunters from Siberia who, independently and through contracts, operated in the Aleutian Chain and Alaska until approximately 1799.

repartimiento   System of organized labor whereby Indian workers would work in mines or for plantation owners; in return, the recipient of the labor paid labor taxes and Christianized the Indian laborers. The system was abused more often than not.

Requerimiento   Issued by order of the Spanish king by theologians who had carefully studied Catholic law, this decree required Indian people to recognize that the Christian God was the only God and supreme ruler of the world and to recognize the authority of the pope. If they agreed to these terms, the Spanish would receive them "in all love and charity" and would not enslave them. If they refused, a just war could be declared according to Christian doctrine, and the Spanish would make war, take away their goods, and force them into slavery, and it would all be their fault for not having acquiesced.

reservation   land set aside for exclusive use of the Indians; reservations were originally set up by the British government to separate the Indians from colonists. The idea of reservations was adopted by the United States, and eventually they served as a "holding" facility to keep the Indians away from the overland trail migrants.

shaman   Term traditionally accepted by historians to refer to a medicine man, or healer; this term has come under fire lately by Indian historians as inaccurate.

syncretism   Mixing of religious traditions, in this case, traditional Indian sacred beliefs and Catholicism or other forms of Christianity.

toion   Leader of Northwest Coastal tribe, such as the Tlingit and Haida. Sometimes they were appointed by the Russians in the later colonial period among other tribes as well.

viceroy   Spanish king's representative in the New World who has the authority to make and enforce laws. The West used to be located in the northern reaches of the viceroyalty of Nueva España.

SELECT BIBLIOGRAPHY

Adams, Eleanor B., and Fray Angélico Chávez, trans. and eds. *The Missions of New Mexico, 1776: A Description by Fray Francisco Atanasio Domínguez with Other Contemporary Documents.* Albuquerque: University of New Mexico Press, 1956.

Adams, Richard E. W., and Murdo J. MacLeod, eds. *The Cambridge History of the Native Peoples of the Americas.* Cambridge, UK: Cambridge University Press, 2000.

Adorno, Rolena, and Patrick Charles Pautz. *Álvar Núñez Cabeza de Vaca: His Account, His Life, and the Expedition of Pánfilo de Narváez.* 3 vols. Lincoln: University of Nebraska Press, 1999.

Alekseev, A. I. *The Destiny of Russian America, 1741–1867.* Edited by Richard A. Pierce. Translated by Marina Ramsay. Kingston, Ontario: Limestone Press, 1991.

Ames, Kenneth M., and Herbert D. G. Maschner. *Peoples of the Northwest Coast: Their Archaeology and Prehistory.* London: Thames and Hudson, 1999.

Andreyev, Aleksandr I. *The Destiny of Russian America, 1741–1867.* Kingston, Ontario: Limestone Press, 1991.

Andreyev, Aleksandr I. *Russian Discoveries in the Pacific and North America in the Eighteenth and Nineteenth Centuries.* Translated by Carl Ginsburg. Ann Arbor: University of Michigan Press, 1952.

Bandelier, Adolph Francis Alphonse. *The Delight Makers: A Novel of Prehistoric Pueblo Peoples.* 1890. Reprint, New York: Harvest/HBJ Books, 1971.

Barton, Bruce Walter. *The Tree at the Center of the World: A Story of the California Missions.* Santa Barbara, CA: Ross-Erikson Publishers, 1980.

Basso, Keith H. *Wisdom Sits in Places: Landscape and Language among the Western Apache.* Albuquerque: University of New Mexico Press, 1996.

Beckham, Stephen Dow. *The Indians of Western Oregon: This Land Was Theirs.* Coos Bay, OR: Arago Books, 1977.

Benavides, Fray Alonso de. *The Memorial of Fray Alonso de Benavides, 1630.* Albuquerque: Horn and Wallace, 1965.

Berkh, Vasilii Nikolaevich. *The Chronological History of the Discovery of the Aleutian Islands; or, The Exploits of the Russian Merchants: With the Supplement of Historical Data on Fur Trade.* Translated by Dmitri Krenov and Richard A. Pierce. Kingston, Ontario: Limestone Press, 1974.

Black, L. T. *Russians in Alaska, 1732–1867.* Fairbanks: University of Alaska Press, 2004.

Bolton, Herbert Eugene. *Anza's California Expeditions.* 5 vols. Berkeley: University of California Press, 1930.

Bolton, Herbert Eugene. *Coronado, Knight of Pueblos and Plains.* Introduction by John L. Kessell. Albuquerque: University of New Mexico Press, 1990.

Bolton, Herbert Eugene. *The Hasinais, Southern Caddoans as Seen by the Earliest Europeans.* Edited by Russell M. Magnaghi. Norman: University of Oklahoma Press, 1987.

Bolton, Herbert Eugene. *The Padre on Horseback: A Sketch of Eusebio Francisco Kino, S.J., Apostle to the Pimas.* San Francisco: Sonora Press, 1932.

Bolton, Herbert Eugene, ed. *Kino's Historical Memoir of Pimería Alta; A Contemporary Account of the Beginnings of California, Sonora, and Arizona, by Father Eusebio Francisco Kino, S. J., Pioneer Missionary Explorer, Cartographer, and Ranchman, 1683–1711.* Cleveland: Arthur H. Clark Company, 1919.

Bolton, Herbert Eugene, trans. and ed. *Pageant in the Wilderness: The Story of the Escalante Expedition to the Interior Basin, 1776, Including the Diary and Itinerary of Father Escalante.* Salt Lake City: Utah State Historical Society, 1950.

Bonnichsen, Robson. *Method and Theory for Investigating the Peopling of the Americas.* College Station, TX: Center for the Study of the First Americans, 1994.

Bouvier, Virginia Marie. *Women and the Conquest of California, 1542–1840: Codes of Silence.* Tucson: University of Arizona Press, 2001.

Bowers, Alfred W. *Hidatsa Social and Ceremonial Organization.* Washington, DC: Smithsonian Institution, 1963.

Bowers, Alfred W. *Mandan Social and Ceremonial Organization.* Lincoln, NE: Bison Books, 2004.

Brooks, James L. *Captives and Cousins: Slavery, Kinship, and Community in the Southwest Borderlands.* Chapel Hill: University of North Carolina Press, 2002.

Brown, Jennifer S. H. *Strangers in Blood: Fur Trade Company Families in Indian Country.* Norman: University of Oklahoma, 1999.

Bruhns, Karen Olsen, and Karen E. Stothert. *Women in Ancient America.* Norman: University of Oklahoma Press, 1999.

Burch, Ernest S., Jr. *The Iñupiaq Eskimo Nations of Northwest Alaska.* Fairbanks: University of Alaska Press, 1998.

Calloway, Colin G. *First Peoples: A Documentary Survey of American Indian History.* Boston: Bedford/St.Martin's, 1999.

Calloway, Colin G. *New Worlds for All: Indians, Europeans, and the Remaking of America.* Baltimore: Johns Hopkins University Press, 1997.

Calloway, Colin G. *One Vast Winter Count: The Native American West before Lewis and Clark.* Lincoln: University of Nebraska Press, 2003.

Chevigny, Hector. *Lord of Alaska: Baranov and the Russian Adventure.* New York: Robert Hale Limited, 1942.

Chevigny, Hector. *Russian America: The Great Alaskan Adventure, 1741–1867.* New York: Ballantine Books, 1965.

Chipman, Donald E. *Spanish Texas, 1519–1821.* Austin: University of Texas Press, 1992.

Chipman, Donald E., and Harriett Denise Joseph. *Notable Men and Women of Spanish Texas.* Austin: University of Texas Press, 1999.

Cook, Warren L. *Flood Tide of Empire: Spain and the Pacific Northwest, 1543–1819.* New Haven, CT: Yale University Press, 1973.

Cordell, Linda S., and George J. Gumerman. *Dynamics of Southwestern Prehistory.* Washington, DC: School of American Research, 1989.

Crosby, Harry W. *Antigua California: Mission and Colony on the Peninsular Frontier, 1697–1768.* Albuquerque: University of New Mexico Press, 1994.

Crown, Patricia L., and W. James Judge, eds. *Chaco and Hohokam: Prehistoric Regional Systems in the American Southwest.* Santa Fe, NM: School of American Research Press, 1991.

Cuch, Forrest S. ed. *A History of Utah's American Indians.* Salt Lake City: Utah State Division of Indian Affairs, Utah State Division of History, 2000.

Curtis, Edward S. *The North American Indian.* 20 vols. Cambridge: Cambridge University Press, 1907.

Cutter, Charles R. *The Legal Culture of Northern New Spain, 1700–1810.* Albuquerque: University of New Mexico Press, 1995.

Cutter, Charles R. *The Protector de Indios in Colonial New Mexico, 1659–1821.* Albuquerque: University of New Mexico Press, 1986.

Dalrymple, Larry. *Indian Basketmakers of California and the Great Basin and Indian Basketmakers of the Southwest.* Santa Fe: Museum of New Mexico Press, 2000.

de la Teja, Jesús Frank. *San Antonio de Béxar, A Community on New Spain's Northern Frontier.* Albuquerque: University of New Mexico Press, 1995.

Debo, Angie. *A History of Indians of the United States.* Norman: University of Oklahoma Press, 1970.

Delanglez, Jean. *Frontenac and the Jesuits.* Chicago: Institute of Jesuit History, Loyola University, 1939.

Denetdale, Jennifer Nez. *The Navajos.* New York: Chelsea House Publications, 2005.

Dietrich, William. *Northwest Passage: The Great Columbia River.* Seattle: University of Washington Press, 1995.

Dillehay, Thomas D. *The Settlement of the Americas: A New Prehistory.* New York: Basic Books, 2000.

Divin, Vasilii Afanasevich. *The Great Russian Navigator, A.I. Chirikov.* Translated by Raymond Henry Fisher. Fairbanks: University of Alaska Press, 1993.

Dozier, Edward P. *Pueblo Indians of North America.* Prospect Heights, IL: Waveland Press, 1983.

Driver, Harold E. *Indians of North America.* Chicago: University of Chicago Press, 1961.

Dunne, Peter M. *Pioneer Black Robes on the West Coast.* Berkeley: University of California Press, 1940.

Earle, Timothy K., and Jonathon E. Ericson. *Exchange Systems in Prehistory.* New York: Academic Press, 1977.

Eccles, W. J. *The Canadian Frontier, 1545–1760.* Albuquerque: University of New Mexico Press, 1969

Eccles, W. J. *Essays on New France.* Oxford: Oxford University Press, 1987.

Eccles, W. J. *The French in North America, 1500–1783.* Markham, Ontario: Fitzhenry and Whiteside, 1998.

Eccles, W. J. *Frontenac: The Courtier Governor.* Lincoln: University of Nebraska Press, 2003.

Eccles, W. J. *The People of New France.* Toronto: University of Toronto Press, 1997.

Edmunds, R. David, and Joseph L. Peyser. *The Fox Wars: The Mesquakie Challenge to New France.* Norman: University of Oklahoma Press, 1993.

Engstrand, Iris H. W., and Donald C. Cutter. *Spanish Settlement in the Far Southwest: Arizona, California, and New Mexico, 1530–1821.* Golden, CO: Fulcrum Publishing, 1996.

Ericson, Jonathon, and Timothy G. Baugh. *The American Southwest and Mesoamerica: Systems of Prehistoric Exchange.* New York: Plenum Press, 1993.

Fletcher, Alice C., and Francis La Flesche. *The Omaha Tribe.* 2 vols. Lincoln, NE: Bison Books, 1972.

Forbes, Jack D. *Apache, Navaho, and Spaniard.* 2nd ed. Norman: University of Oklahoma Press, 1994.

Ford, Corey. *Where the Sea Breaks Its Back: The Epic Story of Early Naturalist Georg Steller and the Russian Exploration of Alaska.* Anchorage: Alaska Northwest Books, 1966.

Foster, William C. *Spanish Expeditions into Texas, 1689–1768.* Austin: University of Texas Press, 1995.

Frison, George C. *Prehistoric Hunters of the High Plains,* 2nd ed. San Diego: Academic Press, 1991.

Frank, Ross. *From Settler to Citizen: New Mexican Economic Development and the Creation of Vecino Society, 1750–1820.* Berkeley: University of California Press, 2000.

Geiger, Maynard. *Franciscan Missionaries in Hispanic California, 1769–1848: A Biographical Dictionary.* San Marino, CA: Huntington Library, 1969.

Geiger, Maynard. *The Life and Times of Fray Junípero Serra, O.F.M.* 2 vols. Washington, DC: Academy of American Franciscan History, 1959.

Gerhard, Peter. *The North Frontier of New Spain.* Rev. ed. Norman: University of Oklahoma, 1993.

Gerhard, Peter. *Pirates of the Pacific, 1575–1742.* Lincoln: University of Nebraska Press, 1990.

Gibson, Arrell Morgan. *The American Indian: Past and Present.* Lexington, MA: D.C. Heath and Company, 1980.

Gibson, James R. *Feeding the Russian Fur Trade: Provisionment of the Okhotsk Seaboard and the Kamchatka Peninsula, 1639–1856.* Madison: University of Wisconsin Press, 1969.

Gibson, James R. *Imperial Russia in Frontier America.* New York: Oxford University Press, 1976.

Golder, Frank A. *Bering's Voyages,* 2 vols. New York: National Geographic Society, 1925.

Golder, Frank A. *Russian Expansion in the Pacific.* Cleveland: Arthur Clark Company, 1914.

Golder, Frank A., ed. *Bering's Voyages: An Account of the Efforts of the Russians to Determine the Relation of Asia and America.* American Geographical Society, Research Series, nos. 1–2 (New York: American Geographical Society, 1922–1925.

Grayson, Donald K. *The Desert's Past: A Natural Prehistory of the Great Basin.* Washington, DC: Smithsonian Institution Press, 1993.

Greer, Allan, ed. *The Jesuit Relations: Natives and Missionaries in Seventeenth-Century North America.* Boston: Bedford/St. Martin's Press, 2000.

Grinev, Andrei Val'terovich. *The Tlingit Indians in Russian America, 1741–1867.* Translated by Richard L. Bland and Katerina G. Solovjova. Lincoln: University of Nebraska Press, 2005.

Habig, Marion A. *Spanish Texas Pilgrimage: The Old Franciscan Missions and Other Spanish Settlements of Texas, 1632–1821.* Chicago: Franciscan Herald Press, 1990.

Haley, James L. *Apaches: A History and Culture Portrait.* Norman: University of Oklahoma Press, 1997.

Halliday, Jan. *Native Peoples of Alaska.* Seattle: Sasquatch Books, 1998.

Hammond, George P., and Agapito Rey, eds. *Don Juan de Oñate: Colonizer of New Mexico, 1595–1628.* 2 vols. Albuquerque: University of New Mexico Press, 1953.

Hammond, George P., and Agapito Rey, eds. *Narrative of the Coronado Expedition 1540–1542.* Albuquerque: University of New Mexico Press, 1940.

Harris, R. Cole. *Canada before Confederation.* Montreal: McGill-Queens University Press, 1991.

Harris, R. Cole, ed., and Geoffrey J. Matthews, cartographer. *Historical Atlas of Canada.* Toronto: University of Toronto Press, 1988.

Heizer, Robert Fleming, and Albert B. Elsasser. *The Natural World of the California Indians.* Berkeley: University of California Press, 1980.

Henry, Alexander. *Travels and Adventures in Canada and the Indian Territories, 1760–1776.* Edited by James Bain. Boston: Little, Brown & Company, 1901.

Hickerson, Nancy P. *The Jumanos: Hunters and Traders of the Southern Plains.* Austin: University of Texas Press, 1994.

Himmel, Kelly F. *The Conquest of the Karankawas and the Tonkawas, 1821–1859.* Elma Dill Russell Spencer Series in the West and Southwest. College Station: Texas A&M Press, 1999.

Hines, Donald M. *Ghost Voices: Yakima Indian Myths, Legends, Humor and Hunting Stories.* Issaqua, WA: Great Eagle Publishing, 1992.

Hungry Wolf, Adolf. *The Good Medicine Book.* New York: Warner Paperback Library Edition, 1973.

Hunt, William R. *Arctic Passage: The Turbulent History of the Land and People of the Bering Sea, 1697–1975.* New York: Scribners, 1975.

Hurtado, Albert L. *Indian Survival on the California Frontier.* New Haven, CT: Yale University Press, 1988.

Hyde, George E. *The Pawnee Indians.* Norman: University of Oklahoma Press, 1974.

Innis, Harold A. *The Fur Trade in Canada: An Introduction to Canadian Economic History.* Toronto: University of Toronto Press, 1999.

Iverson, Peter J. *Dine: A History of the Navajos.* Foreword by Ada E. Deer. Albuquerque: University of New Mexico Press, 2002.

Jennings, Francis. *The Invasion of America: Indians, Colonialism and the Cant of Conquest.* Chapel Hill: University of North Carolina Press, 1975.

Jennings, Jesse David. *Prehistory of North America.* 3rd ed. Mountain View, CA: Mayfield Publishers, 1989.

John, Elizabeth A. H. *Storms Brewed in Other Men's Worlds: The Confrontation of Indians, Spanish, and French in the Southwest, 1540–1795.* Lincoln: University of Nebraska Press, 1975.

Jones, Oakah L., Jr. *Los Paisanos: Spanish Settlers on the Northern Frontier of New Spain.* Norman: University of Oklahoma Press, 1996.

Jones, Oakah L., Jr. *Pueblo Warriors & Spanish Conquest.* Norman: University of Oklahoma Press, 1966.

Josephy, Alvin M., Jr. *500 Nations: An Illustrated History of North American Indians.* New York: Gramercy, 2002.

Josephy, Alvin M., Jr. *The Indian Heritage of America.* New York: Alfred A. Knopf, 1968.

Josephy, Alvin M., Jr. *The Nez Perce Indians and the Opening of the Northwest.* New Haven, CT: Yale University Press, 1965.

Kamp, Kathryn. *Life in the Pueblo: Understanding the Past through Archaeology.* Prospect Heights, IL: Waveland Press, 1997.

Kavanagh, Thomas W. *Comanche Political History: An Ethnohistorical Perspective, 1706–1875.* Lincoln: University of Nebraska Press, 1995.

Kavanagh, Thomas W. *The Comanches: A History, 1706–1875.* Lincoln: University of Nebraska Press, 1996.

Keegan, Marcia. *Mother Earth, Father Sky: Pueblo and Navajo Indians of the Southwest.* Santa Fe, NM: Clear Light Books, 1989.

Kessell, John L. *Mission of Sorrows: Jesuit Guevavi and the Pimas, 1691–1767.* Tucson: University of Arizona Press, 1970.

Kessell, John L. *Spain in the Southwest: A Narrative History of Colonial New Mexico, Arizona, Texas, and California.* Norman: University of Oklahoma Press, 2002.

Khlebnikov, Kiril Timofeevich. *Baranov, Chief Manager of the Russian Colonies in America.* Kingston, Ontario: Limestone Press, 1973.

Khlebnikov, Kiril Timofeevich. *Notes on Russian America, Part I: Novo-Arkhangel'sk*. Fairbanks: University of Alaska Press, 1995.

Khlebnikov, Kiril Timofeevich. *Notes on Russian America, Parts II–V: Kad'Iak, Unalashka,Atkha, the Pribylovs*. Kingston, Ontario: Limestone Press, 1995.

Knaut, Andrew. *The Pueblo Revolt: Conquest and Resistance in Seventeenth-Century New Mexico*. Norman: University of Oklahoma Press, 1997.

Krech, Shepard. *The Ecological Indian: Myth and History*. New York: W. W. Norton, 1999.

Kroeber, A. L. *Handbook of the Indians of California*. New York: Dover, 1976.

Lamar, Howard R. *The New Encyclopedia of the American West*. New Haven, CT: Yale University Press, 1998.

Landis, Ruth. *The Ojibwa Woman*. Lincoln: University of Nebraska Press, 2006.

Langdon, Steven J. *The Native People of Alaska*. 3rd ed. Anchorage: Greatland Graphics, 1998.

Lantzeff, George V. *Eastward to Empire: Exploration and Conquest on the Russian Open Frontier to 1750*. Montreal: McGill-Queen's University Press, 1973.

las Casas, Bartolomé de. *Short Account of the Destruction of the Indies*. New York: Penguin Classics, 1999.

Lewis, Oscar. *The Effects of White Contact upon Blackfoot Culture with Special Reference to the Role of the Fur Trade*. Seattle: University of Washington Press, 1966.

Lister, Robert H. *Those Who Came Before: Southwestern Archaeology in the National Park System*. 2nd rev. ed. Tucson, AZ: Southwest Parks & Monuments Association, 1993.

Lowie, Robert H. *The Crow Indians*. Lincoln, NE: Bison Books, 1983.

Lowie, Robert H. *Indians of the Plains*. Lincoln: University of Nebraska Press, 1982.

MacLeod, William Christie. *The American Indian Frontier*. New York: Routledge, 1996.

Makarova, Raisa V., Richard A. Pierce, and A. S. Donelly, eds. and trans., *Russians on the Pacific, 1743–1799*. Kingston, Ontario: Limestone Press, 1975.

Mangusso, Mary Childers, and Stephen W. Haycox, eds., *Interpreting Alaska's History: An Anthology.* Seattle: University of Washington Press, 1995.

Martin, Joel W. *The Land Looks After Us: A History of Native American Religion.* New York: Oxford University Press, 2001.

Mathes, Michael W. *Vizcaíno and Spanish Expansion in the Pacific Ocean, 1580–1630.* San Francisco: California Historical Society, 1968.

Mathews, John J. *The Osages: Children of the Middle Waters.* Norman: University of Oklahoma Press, 1961.

McCarty, Kieran, ed. *Desert Documentary: The Spanish Years, 1767–1821.* Tucson: Arizona Historical Society, 1976.

McNitt, Frank. *The Indian Traders.* Norman: University of Oklahoma Press, 1962.

Meyer, Roy Willard. *History of the Santee Sioux: United States Indian Policy on Trial.* Lincoln: University of Nebraska Press, 1993.

Meyer, Roy Willard. *The Village Indians of the Upper Missouri.* Lincoln: University of Nebraska Press, 1977.

Milloy, John S. *The Plains Cree: Trade, Diplomacy and War, 1790 to 1870.* Winnipeg: University of Manitoba Press, 1988.

Mims, Stewart L. *Colbert's West Indian Policy.* New Haven, CT: Yale University Press, 1912.

Moore, John H. *The Cheyenne.* Cambridge, MA: Basil Blackwell, 1996.

Moore, John H. *The Cheyenne Nation: A Social and Demographic History.* Lincoln: University of Nebraska Press, 1987.

Morice, Adrien Gabriel. *The History of the Northern Interior of British Columbia.* 1906. Reprint, Fairfield, WA: 1971.

Morton, A. S. *A History of the Canadian West to 1870–71: Being a History of Rupert's Land (The Hudson's Bay Company's Territory) and of the North-West Territory (including the Pacific Slope).* 2nd ed. Toronto: University of Saskatchewan by University of Toronto Press, 1973.

Murphy, Yoland. *Women of the Forest.* New York: Columbia University Press, 1985.

Naske, Claus-M., and Herman E. Slotnick. *Alaska: A History of the 49th State.* Norman: University of Oklahoma Press, 1979.

Nelson, Byron, Jr. *Our Home Forever: The Hupa Indians of Northern California.* Edited by Laura Bayer. Salt Lake City: Howe Bros., 1988.

Newkumet, Vynola Beaver, and Howard L. Meredith. *Hasinai: A Traditional History of the Caddo Confederacy.* College Station: Texas A&M University Press, 1988.

Nichols, Roger L. *American Indians in U.S. History.* Norman: University of Oklahoma, 2004.

Okum, Semen Bentsionovich. *The Russian-American Company.* Cambridge, MA: Harvard University Press, 1951.

O'Meara, Walter. *Daughters of the Country: The Women of the Fur Traders and Mountain Men.* New York: Harcourt, Brace & World, Inc., 1968.

Ortiz, Alfonso. *The Tewa World: Space, Time, Being, and Becoming in a Pueblo Society.* Chicago: University of Chicago Press, 1972.

Oswalt, Wendell H. *Bashful No Longer: An Alaskan Eskimo Ethnohistory, 1778–1988.* Norman: University of Oklahoma Press, 1990.

Oswalt, Wendell H. *This Land Was Theirs: A Study of North American Indians.* 5th ed. Mountain View, CA: Mayfield Publishing Company, 1995.

Parsons, Elsie Clews M. *Pueblo Indian Religion.* 2 vols. Lincoln: University of Nebraska Press, 1996.

Perttula, Timothy K. *The Caddo Nation: Archaeological and Ethnohistoric Perspective.* Austin: University of Texas Press, 1992.

Peters, Virginia Bergman. *Women of the Earth Lodges: Tribal Life on the Plains.* Norman: University of Oklahoma Press, 2000.

Phillips, George Harwood. *Indians and Intruders in Central California, 1769–1849.* Norman: University of Oklahoma Press, 1993.

Pierce, Richard A. *Russian America: A Biographical Dictionary.* Kingston, Ontario: Limestone Press, 1990

Pierce, Richard A., ed. *Russia in North America.* Kingston, Ontario: Limestone Press, 1990.

Pierce, Richard A., ed. *Russia's Hawaiian Adventure, 1815–1817.* Kingston, Ontario: Limestone Press, 1976.

Pierce, Richard A., ed. and trans. *The Russian-American Company: Correspondence of the Governors, Communications Sent, 1818.* Kingston, Ontario: Limestone Press, 1984.

Powell, Phillip Wayne. *Soldiers, Indians, and Silver: The Northward Advance of New Spain, 1550–1600.* Berkeley: University of California Press, 1952.

Pritzker, Barry M. *A Native American Encyclopedia: History, Culture, and Peoples.* New York: Oxford University Press, 2000.

Radding, Cynthia. *Wandering Peoples: Colonialism, Ethnic Spaces, and Ecological Frontiers in Northwestern Mexico, 1700–1850.* Durham, NC: Duke University Press, 1997.

Ray, Arthur J. *Indians in the Fur Trade: Their Roles as Trappers, Hunters, and Middlemen in the Lands Southwest of Hudson Bay, 1660–1870.* Toronto: University of Toronto Press, 1974.

Richman, Irving Berdine. *California under Spain and Mexico, 1535–1847; A Contribution toward the History of the Pacific Coast of the United States, Based on Original Sources, Chiefly Manuscript, in the Spanish and Mexican Archives and Other Repositories.* Reprint, 1911. New York: Cooper Square Publishers, 1965.

Ritter, Harry *Alaska's History: The People, Land, and Events of the North Country.* Anchorage: Alaska Northwest Books, 1993.

Ruby, Robert H., and John A. Brown. *The Cayuse Indians.* Norman: University of Oklahoma Press, 1972.

Ruby, Robert H., and John A. Brown. *The Chinook Indians: Traders of the Lower Columbia River.* Norman: University of Oklahoma Press, 1976.

Ruby, Robert H., and John A. Brown. *Indian Slavery in the Pacific Northwest.* Spokane, WA: Arthur H. Clark, 1993.

Ruby, Robert H., and John A. Brown. *Indians of the Pacific Northwest.* Norman: University of Oklahoma Press, 1981.

Sánchez, Joseph P. *Explorers, Traders, and Slavers: Forging the Old Spanish Trail, 1678–1850.* Salt Lake City: University of Utah Press, 1997.

Sando, Joe S. *Nee Hemish: A History of Jemez Pueblo.* Albuquerque: University of New Mexico Press, 1982.

Sando, Joe S. *Pueblo Nations: Eight Centuries of Pueblo Indian History.* Santa Fe, NM: Clear Light Books, 1992.

Sando, Joe S., and Herman Agoyo, eds. *Po'pay: Leader of the First American Revolution.* Santa Fe, NM: Clear Light Publishers, 2005.

Sandos, James A. *Converting California: Indians and Franciscans in the Missions.* New Haven, CT: Yale University Press, 2004.

Saum, Lewis O. *The Fur Trader and the Indian.* Seattle: University of Washington Press, 1966.

Schlesier, Karl H., ed. *Plains Indians, CE 500–1500: The Archaeological Past of Historical Groups.* Norman: University of Oklahoma Press, 1994.

Shelikhov, Grigorii I. *A Voyage to America, 1783–1786.* Kingston, Ontario: Limestone Press, 1981.

Sheridan, Thomas E., and Nancy J. Parezo. *Paths of Life: American Indians of the Southwest and Northern Mexico.* Tucson: University of Arizona Press, 1996.

Simmons, Virginia McConnell. *The Ute Indians of Utah, Colorado, and New Mexico.* Niwot: University Press of Colorado, 2001.

Sleeper-Smith, Susan. *Indian Women and French Men: Rethinking Cultural Encounter in the Western Great Lakes.* Native Americans of the Northeast. Amherst: University of Massachusetts Press, 2001.

Smith, Courtland. *Salmon Fishers of the Columbia.* Corvallis: Oregon State University Press, 1979.

Smith, F. Todd. *The Caddo Indians: Tribes at the Convergence of Empires, 1542–1854.* College Station: Texas A&M University Press, 1996.

Snow, Dean R. *The Archaeology of North America.* New York: Chelsea House, 1989.

Spicer, Edward H. *Cycles of Conquest: The Impact of Spain, Mexico, and the United States on the Indians of the Southwest, 1533–1960.* Tucson: University of Arizona Press, 1976.

Stands in Timber, John, and Margot Liberty. *Cheyenne Memories.* Lincoln: University of Nebraska Press, 1972.

Steward, Julian H., and Erminie Wheeler-Voegelin. *The Northern Paiute Indians.* New York: Garland Publishing, 1974.

Stewart, Omer C. *The Northern Paiute Bands.* Berkeley: University of California Press, 1939.

Stockel, H. Henrietta. *Chiricahua Apache Women and Children: Safekeepers of the Heritage.* Elma Dill Russell Spencer Series in the West and Southwest 21. College Station: Texas A&M University Press, 2000.

Stockel, H. Henrietta. *The Lightning Stick: Arrows, Wounds, and Indian Legends.* Las Vegas: University of Nevada Press, 1995.

Stockel, H. Henrietta. *On the Bloody Road to Jesus: Christianity and the Chiricahua Apaches.* Albuquerque: University of New Mexico Press, 2004.

Strong, Emory. *Stone Age on the Columbia River.* Portland, OR: Binfords and Mort, 1959.

Stubbs, Roy St. George. *Four Recorders of Rupert's Land: A Brief Survey of the Hudson's Bay Company Courts of Rupert's Land.* Winnipeg, Manitoba: Peguis Publishers 1967.

Sturtevant, William, general editor. *Handbook of North American Indians.* Washington, DC: Smithsonian Institution. David Damas, ed., *Arctic,* vol. 5 (1984). June Helm, ed., *Subarctic,* vol. 6 (1981). Wayne Suttles, ed., *Northwest Coast,* vol. 7 (1990). Robert F. Heizer, ed., *California,* vol. 8 (1978). Alfonzo Ortiz, ed., *Southwest,* vol. 9 and vol. 10 (1979). Warren L. D'Azevedo, ed., *Great Basin,* vol. 11 (1986). DeWard E. Walker, ed., *Plateau,* vol. 12 (1998). Raymond J. DeMallie, ed., *Plains,* vol. 13, parts 1 and 2 (2001). Bruce G. Trigger, ed., *Northeast* vol. 15 (1978).

Tanner, Helen Hornbeck. *Atlas of Great Lakes Indian History.* Norman: University of Oklahoma Press, 1984.

Thomas, Alfred Barnaby, ed. *The Plains Indians of New Mexico, 1751–1778.* Albuquerque: University of New Mexico Press, 1940.

Thompson, David, John Macdonell, Charles W. McKenzie, Francois-Antoine Larocque, W. Raymond Wood, and Thomas D. Thiessen, eds. *Early Fur Trade on the Northern Plains: Canadian Traders among the Mandan and Hidatsa Indians, 1738–1818.* Norman: University of Oklahoma Press, 1999.

Thwaites, Reuben G., ed. *The Jesuit Relations and Allied Documents: Travels and Explorations of the Jesuit Missionaries in New France 1610–1791.* 73 vols. Cleveland: Burrows Brothers, 1896–1901.

Tikhmenev, P. A. *A History of the Russian-American Company.* Seattle: University of Washington Press, 1978.

Trenholm, Virginia Cole. *The Arapahoes, Our People.* Norman: University of Oklahoma Press, 1986.

Trimble, Stephen. *The People: Indians of the American Southwest.* Santa Fe, NM: School of American Research, 1995.

Trudel, Marcel. *Introduction to the History of New France.* Toronto: Holt, Rinehart and Winston of Canada, 1968.

Twitchell, Ralph Emerson. *Spanish Archives of New Mexico: Compiled and Chronologically Arranged with Historical, Biographical and Genealogical Annotations and Translations.* 2 vols. Albuquerque: Horn and Wallace, 1965.

Underhill, Ruth Murray. *The Northern Paiute Indians of California and Nevada.* Edited by William W. Beatty. Washington, DC: Education Division, U.S. Office of Indian Affairs, 1941.

Unrau, William E. *The Kansa Indians: A History of the Wind People, 1673–1873.* Norman: University of Oklahoma Press, 1998.

Van Kirk, Sylvia. *Many Tender Ties: Women in Fur-Trade Society, 1670–1870.* Norman: University of Oklahoma Press, 1983.

VanStone, James W. *Eskimos of the Nushagak River: An Ethnographic History.* Seattle: University of Washington Press, 1967.

VanStone, James W., ed. *Russian Exploration in Southwest Alaska: The Travel Journals of Ptr Korsakovskiy (1818) and Ivan Ya. Vasilev (1829).* Translated by David H. Kraus. Fairbanks: University of Alaska Press, 1988.

Vaughan, Richard. *The Arctic: A History.* Dover, NH: Alan Sutton Publishing Inc., 1994.

Veniaminov, Ivan E. *Notes on the Islands of the Unalashka District.* Translated by L. T. Black and R. H. Geoghegan. Edited by Richard. A. Pierce. Kingston, Ontario: Limestone Press, 1984.

Wagner, Henry R. *The Spanish Southwest, 1542–1794.* 2 parts. Albuquerque: Quivira Society, 1937.

Wagoner, Jay J. *Early Arizona, Prehistory to Civil War.* Tucson: University of Arizona Press, 1975.

Wallace, W. S. *The Pedlars from Quebec and other Papers on the Nor'Westers.* Toronto: Ryerson Press, 1954.

Wallis, Velma. *Bird Girl and the Man Who Followed the Sun: An Athabaskan Indian Legend from Alaska.* New York: Harper Perennial, 1997.

Wallis, Velma. *Two Old Women: An Alaskan Legend of Betrayal, Courage and Survival.* New York: Perennial, 1993.

Warner, Ted J., ed. *The Domínguez-Escalante Journal: Their Expedition through Colorado, Utah, Arizona, and New Mexico in 1776.* Translated by Fray Angélico Chávez. Salt Lake City: University of Utah Press, 1995.

Waters, Frank. *The Book of the Hopi.* New York: Penguin, 1977.

Weber, David J. *Índios Bárbaros: Spaniards and Their Savages in the Age of Enlightenment.* New Haven, CT: Yale University Press, 2005.

Weber, David J. *The Spanish Frontier in North America.* New Haven, CT: Yale University Press, 1994.

Weddle, Robert S. *The French Thorn: Rival Explorers in the Spanish Sea, 1682–1762.* College Station: Texas A&M University Press, 1991.

Weddle, Robert S. *San Juan Bautista: Gateway to Spanish Texas.* Austin: University of Texas Press, 1968.

Weddle, Robert S. *The San Sabá Mission, Spanish Pivot in Texas.* Austin: University of Texas Press, 1964.

Weddle, Robert S. *Spanish Sea: The Gulf of Mexico in North American Discovery, 1500–1685.* College Station: Texas A&M University Press, 1985.

Weddle, Robert S. *Wilderness Manhunt: The Spanish Search for La Salle.* Austin: University of Texas Press, 1973.

White, Richard. *The Middle Ground: Indians, Empires, and Republics in the Great Lakes Region, 1650–1815.* Studies in North American Indian History. Cambridge, UK: Cambridge University Press, 1991.

Will, George F., and George E. Hyde. *Corn among the Indians of the Upper Missouri.* Lincoln: University of Nebraska Press, 1964.

Wishart, David J., ed. *Encyclopedia of the Great Plains Indians.* Lincoln, NE: Bison Books, 2007.

Wood, Raymond W. *Archaeology on the Great Plains.* Lawrence: University Press of Kansas, 1998.

Wood, Raymond W., and Thomas D. Thiessen, eds. *Early Fur Trade on the Northern Plains: Canadian Traders among the Mandan and Hidatsa Indians, 1738–1818.* Norman: University of Oklahoma Press, 1985.

Zolbrod, Paul G., trans. *Diné Bahané: The Navajo Creation Story.* Albuquerque: University of New Mexico Press, 1988.

Zoltvany, Yves F. *The Government of New France: Royal, Clerical, or Class Rule?* Toronto: Prentice-Hall of Canada, 1971.

INDEX

Note: italic page numbers indicate images.

ABOUT THE AUTHOR

Sandra K. Mathews was born in Evanston, Illinois, and graduated from Nebraska Wesleyan University (NWU) in 1986 with BA degrees in History and Spanish. She moved to Albuquerque to attend the University of New Mexico (UNM) where she completed her MA in Latin American history, with specialties in History and Political Science. After a stint as office manager for a general contractor, she re-enrolled at UNM to complete her PhD in History of the American West, with a second major and minor in Modern and Colonial Latin America. With both degrees, she did most of her research in the fields of water rights, land grants, social revolutions, and indigenous communities.

Mathews began teaching history at her alma mater in 1996, earning her PhD in 1998. During her first 11 years at NWU, she taught a variety of courses, including American Indian History, American Indian Biography, American Indians and U.S. Indian Policy (with a variety of titles), Western History, Western Women's History, and Environmental History. Her other publications include *Between Breaths: A Teacher in the Alaskan Bush* (University of New Mexico Press, 2006), the upcoming textbook *New Mexico!* (University of New Mexico Press, expected 2008), *Women's Experiences on the North American Plains* (Plains History Series, Texas Tech University Press, expected 2008), and other chapters on Pueblo Indian land grants and Hispanic water rights in early New Mexico.